Information Systems in Construction Management

Principles and Applications

edited by Paul Barton
BSc (Hons) MSc MCIOB

Principal Lecturer in Construction Management, Sheffield City Polytechnic

Batsford Academic and Educational London

To Julie, David, Naomi, Michael and Peter, with love

© Paul Barton 1985

First published 1985

All rights reserved. No part of this publication
may be reproduced, in any form or by any means,
without permission from the Publisher

Phototypeset in Linotron Baskerville
by Input Typesetting Ltd, London SW19 8DR
and printed in Great Britain by
Anchor Brendon Ltd, Tiptree, Essex

Published by Batsford Academic and Educational
an Imprint of B. T. Batsford Ltd
4 Fitzhardinge Street, London W1H 0AH

British Library Cataloguing in Publication Data

Information systems in construction management :
   principles and applications.—(Mitchell's
   professional library)
   1. Construction industry—Management—Data processing
   I. Barton, Paul K.
   624′.068   HD9715.A2

ISBN 0-7134-4790-7
ISBN 0-7134-4791-5 Pbk

CONTENTS

LIST OF CONTRIBUTORS

B. Atkin BSc MPhil ARICS
Department of Construction Management, University of Reading

N. Ewin BSc(Hons)
Department of Building, Sheffield City Polytechnic

G. N. Fisher MSc PG DipIndMan MCIOB MBIM
Department of Construction Management, University of Reading

P. Harding MSc DMS FCIOB MBIM
Department of Building, Sheffield City Polytechnic

D. J. Heath BSc(Hons)
School of Constructional Studies, Leeds Polytechnic

M. Jackson MEng CEng MICE
Department of Civil Engineering, University of Newcastle upon Tyne

R. H. Neale BSc(Eng) MSc MICE MCIOB
Department of Civil Engineering, Loughborough University

R. N. Ormerod BSc(Hons) MCIOB
Department of Construction Management, University of Reading

R. Oxley MSc MCIOB MBIM
Department of Building, Sheffield City Polytechnic

P. Stephenson MSc MCIOB
Department of Building, Sheffield City Polytechnic

B. Wroe BA MSc
Department of Mathematics and Computing, Leicester Polytechnic

PREFACE

In recent years the construction industry has started to take advantage of new developments in information technology, particularly in the field of construction management. These developments have been assisted by an upsurge of research interest covering a wide range of application areas, carried out by researchers from a wide range of specialisms. As a result, there now exists an established body of expertise in the field of information systems relating to construction management.

This book draws on this body of expertise to produce a review of current and future developments in the application of information technology in construction management and, as such, should be of use to students and practitioners in this field.

The scope of the subject is so broad and developments in information technology so rapid that it would be very difficult to produce a comprehensive book on the subject that would stand the test of time. Instead, this book consists of a number of contributions from various experts in the field. The chapters have been planned to indicate a range of possibilities which, apart from illustrating the current state of the art, should also stimulate readers into thinking of new possibilities.

The book is not a book on computing, although computers will be mentioned many times. Instead, the emphasis is on the analysis and design of information systems that will enable the reader to take advantage of the whole range of information technology, of which computers are but a part.

Readers should, therefore, be able to appreciate what is involved in the design and implementation of such systems should they become concerned with such matters at any time during their careers.

Part I explains some of the basic concepts of Information Systems and should be of use to those new to the field. The first chapter outlines the basic principles of information systems and their potential weaknesses. It also describes the interrelationship between the information system and the computer and the basic procedure that should be adopted when designing such systems. The majority of computerised information systems in construction management involve the use of small computers and so in Chapter 2 the basic principles of these systems and their typical uses are discussed. However, the main thrust of the book is in the analysis and design of the information systems themselves, which are a necessary pre-requisite of any computer application. Consequently, Chapter 3 illustrates how such analysis and design can be undertaken using the technique of structured systems analysis. This theme is continued in Chapter 4 in which the main requirements of a management information system to assist the planning and control of construction projects are discussed.

Part II provides a range of more detailed perspectives on the theme of construction management information systems. The chapters have been selected to provide a balance between current and future practice whilst at the same time indicating the range of applications that are possible.

Chapters 5, 6 and 7 cover more immediate small scale applications. Chapter 5 illustrates the use of database management theory in devising a financial accounting system for a small building firm. Chapter 6 applies structured systems analysis to a medium sized building firm in order to produce a plant management system, whilst Chapter 7 provides a commentary on the implementation of integrated cost control systems in construction. The next two chapters look at developments in project planning systems. Chapter 8 indicates how interactive graphics can be used to produce a more flexible planning system and Chapter 9 describes a form of expert system that evaluates risks on building projects.

The remaining chapters in this section continue to look at future developments in both hardware and software and their relevance to the construction industry. Chapter 10 explains how computer graphics can improve communications on construction projects. Similarly, Chapter 11 describes how current and future developments in information technology (i.e. the hardware) can produce more effective management information systems. The last chapter looks at a new development in software, namely fourth generation software, and describes how it can be used to produce an estimating system for a housebuilding firm.

No book on information systems would be complete without reference to the behavioural issues involved in their use. These are contained in Part III, which includes a chapter on the interrelationship between information systems and the manager, and a chapter on problems faced by organisations when implementing information systems.

It should be noted that the chapters in Part II very rarely refer to commercially available systems. This is because the range and availability of these systems is constantly changing. Information about them is more suited to periodicals than books. At present, the *Construction Computing* magazine published by the Chartered Institute of Building and the newsletter of the Construction Industry Computing Association are the two best references in this area.

Finally, I would like to thank all the contributors for making time to produce their particular chapters. I would also like to thank Ray Oxley for his helpful comments on Chapter 2 and Barry Fryer for his advice in preparing Chapter 13.

Paul Barton
Sheffield, June 1985

I Basic Concepts
1 Information Systems – An Overview
Paul Barton

WHAT IS INFORMATION?

The concept of information is related to facts, data and knowledge. A fact is something that has happened in the real world and that can be verified. Data are facts obtained through empirical research or observation. Knowledge represents facts or data gathered in any way and stored for future reference. It may be thought of as a body of well-confirmed, law-like generalisations which relate data to their environment.

Information represents data or knowledge evaluated for specific use. Consequently, facts or data are processed to provide meaningful information.

COMMUNICATION

Information is transmitted by the process of communication. It is, therefore, important to understand the process of communication and its relationship to organisation and management.

Communication involves the interchange of thoughts or opinions by words, letters or similar means. It also involves the concept of

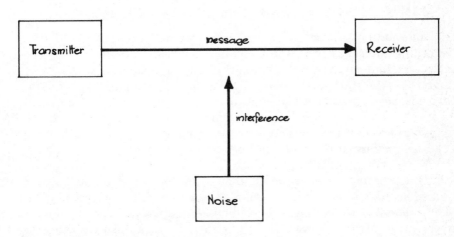

1.1 *A general model of the communication process*

communication systems, e.g. telephone, television. Irrespective of the sophistication of the transmission however, a basic process is involved.

In all cases, there is an information source which provides the raw material for a message which is to be transmitted to a destination. Consequently a general model would include a transmitter and a receiver. Also involved is the concept of a noise source which theoretically interferes with information flow between the transmitter and the receiver.

The general model including these concepts is illustrated in Fig. 1.1.

INFORMATION FLOW AND ORGANISATION

For many organisations, communication systems have been designed to follow organisational lines without recognition of the fact that this may not provide for optimal flows of information for decision making. Some of the problems in communication systems for decision making have resulted from changes in organisational relationships in recent years. Firms have been faced with dynamic situations, rapidly changing technology, changing markets etc. which have required adaptation on their part. Adjustments have been made, but without recognition, in many cases, of the impact of the organisational changes on their communication systems. Thus much information that was appropriate under older arrangements has now become obsolete. Furthermore, additional types of information are needed to plan and control current operations.

When such changes are required, problems can be minimised by focusing attention on decision-making needs of the new system. Information flow should be related to decision making and the resultant communication system should be an indicator of the way the organisation actually functions.

A MANAGEMENT INFORMATION SYSTEM DEFINED

An information system is an organised way of sending, receiving and recording messages. Examples include the firm's accounting process, messages sent informally 'by the grapevine' and memos sent between managers. A firm's total information system is, therefore, all the ways it sends, receives and records information.

Ideally, the total information system should contain no overlaps, no gaps and no contradictions. Information should be accurate and timely. The same information should not be collected by more than one department. Once it is collected, the data should be available to anyone who needs it. Redundant information should not be recorded and kept.

Unfortunately, most firms do not have a unified information system. There are many overlaps, contradictions, gaps and delays. Some of these problems may never be fully solved. For example, the employee who spreads false rumours may distort management's messages and cause morale to suffer. The weaknesses of formal information systems can be remedied more easily.

WEAKNESSES OF FORMAL INFORMATION SYSTEMS

Although organisations have always had many means of collecting, recording and using data, these techniques have often contained a number of weaknesses.

1 Slowness
To be of value, information must reach management in time to affect decisions. Otherwise it is historical data. Accounting data is often criticised for these reasons since it tells managers only where they have been, and not where they are going.

2 Information gaps
In addition to the lack of speed, information has been incomplete. While the monthly cost sheets will tell a manager something about costs incurred, they will not tell him about other things he may need to know. Is there a cheaper excavator available? How many bricks are on Site A? These are typical of the many questions that a manager may want his information system to answer.

3 Costs
Information must be worth its cost. Often information that would improve decision making has not been collected and processed because of the costs involved. The expense involved has been considered greater than the improvement the information would make to the decision.

4 Duplication of information
The same information has often been collected separately by two or more departments in the same firm. While different departments may have different uses for the data, it needs to be collected only once. For instance, the hours worked by employees and the work done on site are data required by wage clerks, bonus surveyors and surveyors involved in calculating interim valuations.

COMPUTERS AND INFORMATION SYSTEMS

Computers have become closely related to information systems, initially because data processing can be carried out much more quickly. They have also allowed the same data to be presented in many different forms once they are collected. However, it should be noted that a computer does not guarantee a unified information system. It can only help in the following ways:

1 Rapid data processing
Computers can process data in a few minutes that would otherwise take days. This speed means that information delay is reduced and that

management has more information available in time to help with decisions. For example, the site manager can now have 'immediate information' on the state of progress on his contract, thus enabling him to take instant action. Before computers, this information would have taken days to prepare.

2 Accuracy

Given correct information, the computer can do many things with it and make no mistakes. Manual methods are more likely to result in errors when transferring information from one source to another and when making calculations. Of course, a computer will make errors if it is given the wrong data to process. GIGO (Garbage In/Garbage Out) is a well known principle of computing.

3 Avoiding duplication

A computer's storage devices can act as a common data base for the entire organisation. Once information is collected, it can be stored and then used by any department needing it. Whenever a user needs the information, the computer can be ordered to print it out or display it on a screen. The same information can be shown in different forms depending on the user's needs.

4 Forecasting outcomes

Using mathematical models, computers can sometimes tell management what the results of a decision will be before it is made. This technique is call *simulation*.

5 Making decisions for management

In some cases, management may use the computer to make decisions on routine problems where the procedure for solving the problem follows a series of logical steps. These systems are usually called 'expert systems'.

6 Real-time information systems

Fast information is often needed to make decisions. How fast one needs information depends on the type of decision being made. Where instant information is critical to the decision, a real-time or interactive system is needed. The needs of the site manager mentioned previously are a perfect example of such a situation.

The opposite of a real-time system is batch processing. Here, information is collected for a period of time such as a day or a week and then put into the computer all at once. The information system is thus not up-to-date all the time. Payroll calculations are normally carried out in this way.

DESIGNING INFORMATION SYSTEMS

A computer is not an information system – it is a tool for developing a more effective system. Computers, like any tool, can be used ineffectively. Some managements have purchased them with the vague hope that they would somehow improve the firm's decision making. But with a badly designed system, the computer may only process redundant information faster.

If this is to be prevented, the following steps should be followed:

1 Determine information needs
The first step in system design is the most basic and the most important. Each manager must decide what information he needs to carry out his managerial tasks. This can be very difficult since many managers will not have thought out their information needs carefully.

2 Integrate information needs
The same information will often be wanted by more than one manager. When this is so, it should be collected only once. Enough information should be gathered to meet the needs of management. Data need not be collected if they meet no management needs.

3 Produce the specification
On the basis of the previous analysis it is then possible to specify the system appropriate to the particular situation.

4 Obtain the relevant software
The computer requires software to meet the specified needs. This may already be available in the form of *standard packages*, i.e. software produced to solve problems in industry and commerce, or may have to be produced specifically for the particular system.

5 Select the appropriate hardware
Once this has been done, it should then be possible to select the appropriate hardware or combination of computing equipment that will suit the software.

Finally, it should be remembered that information systems are not an end in themselves. Construction management is concerned with providing acceptable quality buildings, on time, at the right price. If information systems can help achieve these objectives then they are of use. If not, they can be an expensive luxury.

2 Small Computers in Construction Management
Paul Barton

INTRODUCTION

For many years the use of computers in construction management has been limited to the use of mainframe and minicomputers for financial accounting procedures and some critical path planning on large projects. Furthermore, their use has mainly been limited to the larger firms.

Experiences were, in the main, poor, and these could be attributed to two major causes. Firstly, at that time, both mainframe and minicomputers were essentially operated on a batch basis, with the result that data was difficult and time-consuming to enter and the resultant reports often too late to take action on, particularly in an industry where a large proportion of managerial decisions are short term and require 'instant' information. Secondly, these types of computers tended to be the province of specialists who had little knowledge of the construction industry, with the result that the software they produced did not always meet the needs of the users.

More recently, the emergence of the microcomputer has altered things quite dramatically. The reason for this is that these types of computer are:
1 cheap
2 portable
3 capable of operating in most working environments
4 interactive
5 capable of providing relatively inexpensive graphics facilities.

Because of this, computing power is now within the price range of a greater number of construction firms, the computers can be moved around between site and office, the results can be obtained on request and the method of communication can be in a manner which is second nature to most construction personnel, i.e. charts and diagrams.

The remainder of this chapter describes the basic components of these smaller computer systems and how they are currently being used in the construction industry. In doing so it assumes minimal knowledge of computer technology.

COMPONENTS OF SMALL COMPUTER SYSTEMS

The two main components of any computer system are *hardware* and *software*. Hardware is the equipment itself, things that can be seen and touched. By itself, however, hardware can do nothing. It requires something else to make it work for us, and this is known as software: instructions, in the form of programs, that activate the various pieces of equipment and make them do meaningful things.

Hardware
The basic configuration of a small computer system consists of:
1 a *central processing unit*
2 a *memory*
3 a *visual display unit*
4 a *keyboard*
5 *mass storage*
6 a *printer*
This is represented diagrammatically in Fig. 2.1.

1 Central processing unit
The central processing unit (CPU) is the master of ceremonies, linking all the other parts of the system together.

2 Memory
The memory is that part of the system in which data and programs can be stored and manipulated. There are two types of memory – *read only memory* (ROM) and *random access memory* (RAM). ROM is permanent – that is to say any programs or data stored in this part of the memory remain there when the computer is switched off. RAM, however, is volatile and only operates whilst the computer is switched on. Conse-

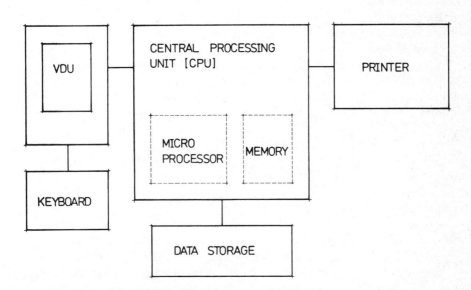

2.1 *Essential parts of a small computer system*

quently, any programs or data in this part of the memory will be lost when the computer is switched off.

3 Visual display unit

The visual display unit (VDU), as the name suggests, is a screen which displays information to the user and provides the interactive nature of the small computer.

4 Keyboard

The keyboard is the most common way of entering information into the computer. It works in conjunction with the VDU in that the VDU displays information as it is entered via the keyboard, thus acting as a check on data entry. Consequently, input errors can be rectified immediately.

5 Mass storage

Mass storage is the way of overcoming the problems associated with RAM described earlier. Mass storage devices in the form of *cassettes*, *floppy disks* or *hard disks* provide a permanent storage medium for the programs and data used in RAM. These programs or data are loaded into the computer from the storage device when required for use, and any subsequent modifications or additions saved back on to the storage device before the computer is switched off. At present, the majority of commercial applications use the floppy disk as a mass storage device. This is a disk 5¼in in diameter which is placed in a *disk drive*, thus enabling the transfer of data between the disk and the computer. More recently, the use of a hard disk has become more popular. This does not require to be placed in and removed from a separate disk drive. Instead, it is a complete sealed unit in itself which is sometimes an integral part of the computer.

6 Printers

The majority of applications on computers require some form of printed or *hard copy* output, and this is provided by a printer. There are many types of printer but the two most commonly used are the *dot matrix* type and the *daisy wheel*. Basically speaking, the dot matrix quickly provides an acceptable quality typeface and is therefore useful for producing information for internal use, whilst the daisy wheel type provides a letter quality typeface, albeit rather more slowly, which can be used for producing information for external use.

The way in which these pieces are physically combined varies. Sometimes the CPU, the VDU and keyboard are combined and the disk drives and printer are separate. Sometimes everything is in one integral unit apart from the printer.

In addition to these basic pieces of equipment, there are other pieces that can be added on to the system. The most common of these are the *digitising tablet*, the *lightpen*, the *mouse* and the *plotter*.

The digitising tablet is an electronic sketchpad consisting of an electronically sensitive surface upon which a stylus can be pointed or traced. This produces electronic impulses that can be recognised by the computer as meaningful data which it can manipulate accordingly. It is not difficult to appreciate how useful this can be in entering data from drawings.

The lightpen, as its name suggests, is a pen with an electronically sensitive nib which can be used to point at the screen of the computer. It is limited in its use in that it cannot actually draw things on the screen, but can simply identify characters or symbols already shown.

The mouse is a relatively new device which performs a similar function to the lightpen, although it is slightly more flexible in its use. It consists of a small box, about the size of a matchbox, with a ball-bearing type attachment underneath which enables it to be moved around the desk top. This movement, in turn, moves a cursor around the screen to point at characters and symbols or move them to other positions. In many instances the use of this device, in conjunction with carefully designed screens, has greatly reduced the use of the keyboard for operating the computer.

The plotter is an output device which can replace a printer and produce graphical information quickly and accurately. It is particularly useful in design applications.

A distinct trend of late has been for computers to get smaller and this has resulted in a wide range of portable computers. The range varies from *pocket computers*, which are extremely useful for applications involving repetitive calculations, e.g. surveying, through *lap computers*, which are small enough to fit into a briefcase and act as a portable diary/memo pad/calculator, to *transportable computers*, which are compact versions of the basic configuration outlined previously and can be used for most of the applications relevant to such computers.

Software

As previously stated, software consists of instructions, in the form of computer programs, that activate the hardware. There are various types of software. At the lowest level is *machine code*. This is the province of specialists, who use this form of instruction to produce a type of software called *system software*, or the operating system of the computer.

System software

This type of software instructs the computer to do the basic everyday things necessary for most applications. Such things as making a character appear on the screen when a key is pressed on the keyboard, or transferring information from the computer to the printer, are typical of facilities that system software provides. The most commonly known operating systems are CP/M, MSDOS and UNIX, which are used for a large number of computers, although some computers, notably Apple and Commodore, have their own operating system.

Application software

None of the software mentioned to date enables the computer to solve real world problems. In order to do this, application software is required and this is normally produced using a high-level language such as BASIC, COBOL or FORTRAN. These languages are sets of rules which, if followed, can instruct the computer to perform calculations, manipulate text, and store and retrieve information.

Software packages

It should not be difficult to appreciate that many problems in industry and commerce are common to many areas. In order to avoid duplication of effort, by people attempting to write their own program for an application similar to that required by others, another type of software is available. This is called *packaged software.*

A large number of these problems involve performing calculations on rows and columns of data, storing and retrieving data or manipulating and producing text. In order to enable computer users to solve such problems more easily, several types of standard packages have been produced.

1 *Spreadsheet packages*

The spreadsheet package enables the first type of problem to be solved. This package consists of a matrix of cells into which the user can put data or text. Additionally, any arithmetical relationship that exists between the cells can also be entered and stored in the computer's memory. As a result of this, if the value of any data in any cell is altered, the computer automatically recalculates the remainder of the matrix in a matter of seconds.

2 *Database packages*

Problems relating to information retrieval can be solved by database packages. These packages consist of a set of rules by which information can be stored, in order that it can be retrieved in a variety of ways by different users.

3 *Word processing packages*

The manipulation of text is carried out by word processing packages. These enable the user to enter text into the computer, correct mistakes in it, 'cut and paste' it and save it for future use. The use of such packages in producing reports and standard letters can save a tremendous amount of time.

4 *Construction packages*

Finally, there is a type of packaged software designed to solve industry-specific problems. In the construction industry, processes such as planning and estimating are done within the framework of certain accepted practices; accordingly, standard packages based on these practices have been produced. These will be discussed in more detail later in the chapter.

CURRENT USES OF SMALL COMPUTERS IN CONSTRUCTION MANAGEMENT

Because of the aforementioned advantages, the use of small computers in construction management has been increasing rapidly in the past few years, and this increase appears to be continuing. Current uses can be classified into several main areas in which standard packages have been produced.

Financial accounting/Job costing

The area of accounts, payroll and job costs is an obvious area for computer application, and a wide range of standard packages are available for use in this field. Although they vary in detail, they all follow the same pattern. Most importantly, they all cater for the peculiarities of the industry, such as sub-contractor's certificates, retention monies, pay scales, holidays with pay etc. The majority of general financial accounting packages do not allow for such things and care should be taken when selecting such a package for this type of application. Their operation is on a modular basis around the standard practice of using a nominal ledger, a payroll system, a sales ledger, a sub-contractor's account and a job costing ledger. The advantage offered by these packages is that information need be entered only once. For instance, pay details will be entered into the payroll system and wages automatically calculated. The computer will then transfer this information to the job costing module and distribute it, if necessary, between relevant jobs. A similar procedure is used with materials; consequently it is possible to have an up-to-date report of job costs at any time. This *single entry principle*, as it is often called, means that the whole accounting process can be speeded up, and inaccuracies (sometimes caused in the course of entering the same information into several ledgers) can be reduced.

Estimating

Estimating involves the calculation of a large number of unit rates to produce a priced bill of quantities, and so is ideal for computer application. However, the potential of computers in estimating is far greater than this. Computer systems are now available that can store a library of unit rates which can be accessed during the pricing of a bill and, in addition to producing the priced bill, produce various reports such as bills of materials for purchasing and details of labour and plant hours for planning. They can also provide the basis of a compatible valuation system and produce information for comparison with the above-mentioned job costing systems. In fact, these estimating packages are a good example of how computers can be used to do more than speed up an existing procedure – how they can actually provide more information than is currently provided by manual systems.

Planning

The idea of using a computer on a building site has long been regarded as impracticable by people both outside and inside the industry. It was not until the emergence of the microcomputer that this attitude was questioned by a few, and in recent times computers on site have become more common. Their main use has been for planning, using any of a number of project planning packages currently available. These packages are based on the critical path planning technique and can provide site managers with an up-to-date picture of progress on their site on request. The computer speeds up the updating process, which can be very time-consuming if done manually and was one of the reasons for the demise of critical path as a planning tool in the construction industry several years ago. However, these packages go further than merely speeding up calculations, in that the reports are produced in bar chart form, which is more acceptable to construction personnel and much easier to understand than the network diagram. Moreover, it is possible to obtain selective reports for a particular sub-contractor or a certain part of a contract, say, with the result that reports can also be provided for foremen and chargehands so that they can supervise their particular sections of work from a single update. In nearly every situation where a small computer has been used on site for these purposes the ultimate reaction has been 'how did we ever manage without one?'

Management accounting

The use of small computers for producing budgets, cash flow statements and similar types of information for many senior management decisions is now becoming very popular. Such information is provided using the spreadsheet package mentioned previously. This speeds up the calculations so much that not only is it possible to see how actual budgets and cash flows are being achieved, but predictions can be made on a variety of situations by trying out various 'what if?' questions.

In addition, it is now possible to represent this resultant information in graphical form, which can assist in its interpretation.

Administrative procedures

Many routine office procedures can be assisted by the use of computers. The two most common ways are through the use of data base packages and word processing packages.

Data base packages are useful for storing and retrieving information about personnel, suppliers, sub-contractors and clients, and so can be of use to wage clerks, buyers, surveyors and marketing directors.

Word processing packages are useful for standard documents such as letters of enquiry, orders and site reports. They are also useful for producing documents which may require several stages of editing before they are approved. Site meeting minutes and technical reports are typical of the documents whose preparation would benefit in such cases.

FUTURE USES OF COMPUTERS IN CONSTRUCTION MANAGEMENT

Information technology is progressing at such a rapid rate that it is difficult to predict too far into the future. Indeed, some of the statements made in this chapter may well be 'dated' before it is published. It is not the intention here to be too specific about the future, as many of the chapters in the second part of the book will do this much more effectively. It is possible, however, to make a few general statements.

One can safely predict that the hardware itself is going to get even smaller and hence more portable. The implications of this for site management and travelling contracts managers are obvious.

Another current phenomenon is the energy being concentrated on making computers easier to use. The digitiser and mouse already mentioned are examples of this trend, which could result in the mystique of computers finally being eliminated and their use being widened to a larger number of people.

It could be, therefore, that computers will become more commonplace on site to assist site management and will be used by more people generally within the industry. There are, however, two important factors affecting these predictions. Firstly, the software itself. It was stated at the start of this chapter that hardware is of no use without software, and it will be the quality of the software that will dictate the rate of progress. Secondly, and probably more importantly, construction personnel, both collectively and individually, have to decide how quickly they want to adopt the new technology. The industry has a reputation for being conservative, which, combined with any bad experiences suffered from poor or inappropriate software, as mentioned above, could result in its lagging behind others in taking advantage of technology that could improve its efficiency.

3 Structured Systems Analysis Applied to the Construction Industry

P. Stephenson and R. Oxley

INTRODUCTION

The systems approach to analysis is well recognised and has been used in data processing circles for quite some time. The emergence of new tools, however, has slightly altered previous methodology and, whilst the basic principles remain the same, these tools allow a clearer picture to be drawn of a business environment which is more readily understood.

The techniques are used as part of a systems investigation in order to obtain a model of the current business system, which, in turn, also forms the basis of problem identification. Concentration can then be centred on developing a model of a future system which will form the basis for a system design and, ultimately, a working application.

SYSTEMS INVESTIGATION

When entering a company as a researcher or analyst, it is difficult to identify or pinpoint problems and required changes at the outset. Clearly there is a need to obtain information about the present situation and systems used, but first it is important to obtain a general understanding about the company as a whole. As an outsider to the company, information can sometimes be difficult to obtain. Some employees may welcome the investigation and be forthcoming with the information required, whilst others tend to be suspicious and are reluctant to give precise details.

A background analysis is therefore a useful starting point and allows one to get a general feel of the company before conducting a detailed structured analysis.[1]

Fact finding can often be an interesting exercise because it gives an insight into the company and the whole business environment. Information can be collected under various headings, so enabling a general picture to be drawn. Such information could be sectionalised as follows:

1 Origin and history of the company
2 Structure of ownership and control
3 Size of the company
4 Charter of the company
5 Technology
6 Location
7 Resources
8 Relevant environment

This information will form the basis for further analysis and may, in fact, identify business problems and areas requiring immediate attention.

FACT FINDING TECHNIQUES

Fact finding in order to obtain information can take a number of forms, and it is largely up to the analyst and the organisation to decide what form this will take. Various methods can be adopted including interviews, questionnaires, observations and reading.[2] Statistics may also be published and are obtainable from various sources.

From a personal point of view it was decided early in the research to adopt interviews as the method of obtaining information. Questionnaires, whilst being useful, are probably more suited to the general type of survey and can often be restrictive due to poor responses. Similarly, observations made at an early stage can often be counterproductive, since the researcher is unknown to employees, and observing procedures can create resentment and give the impression of 'a spy in the camp'. Observations are best left until the researcher has been accepted into the organisation and employees are aware of his function. Reading pamphlets on the organisation and other published material is often a useful starting point, and acquaints the researcher with the organisation. This advanced knowledge can also help provoke discussion during interviews.

SOME GENERAL COMMENTS ON INTERVIEWING TECHNIQUE

Although interviewing is a job on its own, and numerous books have been written on the topic, it is probably best learnt through experience. Successful interviewing is easily achieved by practice, although several points can be highlighted which make the task easier.[3,4] Preparatory work is probably the key to successful interviewing. Arrangements should be made beforehand so the interviewee has some advance warning of the interviewer's arrival, and may consciously prepare himself with answers. The temptation to call in unannounced on someone should be avoided, since unexpected arrivals can often lead to poor interviews and poor data collection.

Before the interview, it is advisable to prepare a number of questions covering the topics requiring answers. These can be listed on a card for use during the interview and ticked off as each one is covered. This also acts as a prompt in cases where interviews are interrupted. Ringing telephones and interruptions from staff are common occurrences, especially when interviewing senior staff, so keeping track of the questions enables the interview to be resumed without much wasted time.

When commencing the interview it is best to explain briefly what is being done, and ultimately what the end result is likely to be. Although the interviewee may well be aware of the facts, this approach helps to break the ice and forms a relaxed atmosphere for the start of the interview. It is probably advisable to start with relatively easy questions which the interviewee understands and has knowledge of. This helps to ease the situation and promote confidence.

A useful point to note here, is, when asking questions, do not attempt to answer them at the same time. It is the interviewee who should provide the answers and it is he who should do most of the talking. With unstructured interviews, the interviewer should only step in when prompting is required.

On the other hand, it is quite probable when an interviewee starts talking that he never stops, and this is something the interviewer should be conscious of. In many cases this can be a good thing, since the interview can automatically develop into a general discussion and the information divulged can often be more than was originally expected. However, there is a danger of the interview wandering off course and, when this occurs, the interviewer should politely step in, and, referring to his card, lead off with another question.

With regard to data collection, the interviewee should be made aware beforehand of confidentiality. Various forms of collecting data are available, but tape recorders should only be used if permission is granted. Quite often these can do more harm than good, since some people do not like speaking into a microphone and choose their words carefully, often restricting the information they are prepared to release. Note-taking is often the best method and jotting down an occasional point is not generally distractive.

On completion of the interview it is advisable to write up the points discussed and send a copy to the interviewee asking for confirmation of the contents. It is quite easy during the interview to write down something incorrectly or misunderstand what has been said, so this procedure will allow the correction of any errors.

With regard to the number of interviews to conduct, this will depend chiefly on the size of organisation and the type of information required. When planning interviews, a top-down approach should be adopted where directors and senior managers are interviewed first, then middle managers, followed by departmental staff. Much information required on the background of the company, together with aims and objectives, is usually best obtained from senior people, and more detailed information on company procedures and departmental activities can be obtained from other members of staff.

As a final point on interviewing, success depends largely on the interviewer. Probably the two most important points to bear in mind are preparation for the interview and conducting the interview in an efficient manner. The chances are that, if one is fortunate enough to be able to interview a senior executive, his time will be limited, since most are extremely busy people. At the outset, one can expect an interview to last for an hour or maybe two at the most. Careful preparation beforehand and conducting the interview efficiently are therefore essential requisites, since a second meeting may not be possible.

Having conducted the initial interviews, and obtained a general understanding of the company, a more detailed analysis can now take place. This can be described as the structured analysis.

STRUCTURED ANALYSIS

After the background information has been obtained, the next stage is to carry out a more in-depth analysis of the organisation. Various tools are available for this and include hierarchy *business models* showing functional decomposition, together with *personnel/functional* matrices.[5] *Data flow diagrams* and *data dictionaries* can also be used, together with *decision trees* and *decision tables*, combined with *structured English* to analyse process logic.[6,7]

These tools enable the building of a model of the current system which forms the basis for future development. Their main features are that they are mostly graphical, which allows for clarity and easy understanding. As mentioned previously, interviews are a useful method for collecting information on company functions and activities, and these can be conducted with middle management and departmental staff.

Fig. 3.1 illustrates an organisation structure. It has been drawn in the form of a hierarchy, but this is purely illustrative. Companies vary considerably from one to another; some may be line and staff orientated, project or team based, or possibly organismic. Needless to say it is not uncommon to find companies operating a combination of several types. Whatever type is adopted, the identification of the organisation structure helps promote an understanding of the company and may, in fact, help locate key people for future interviewing. Fig. 3.2 illustrates the global model of a company showing functional decomposition, whilst Fig. 3.3 shows a personnel/functional matrix indicating the relevant staff involvement.

The movement of data through the organisation is represented by the use of data flow diagrams. The important point here is that the diagram should be drawn to represent logic (i.e. what is done), and not physical characteristics (i.e. how it is done). Physical characteristics can be considered later along with determining man/machine boundaries.

The idea of drawing the diagram is to represent what processes are carried out and where the data comes from and goes to. In order to determine this accurately, walkthroughs have to be conducted with the

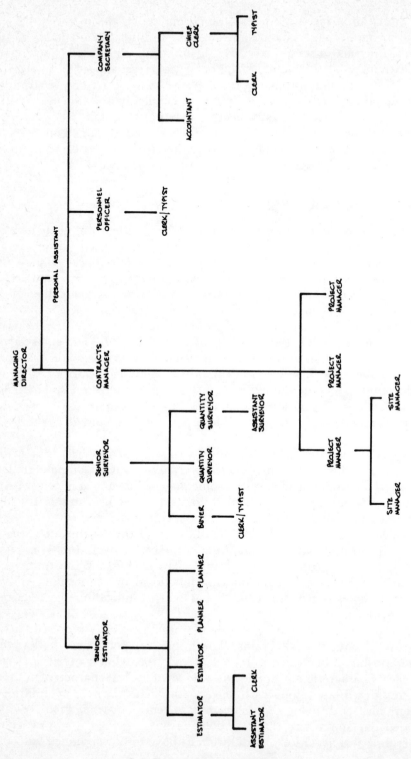

3.1 *Organisation structure*

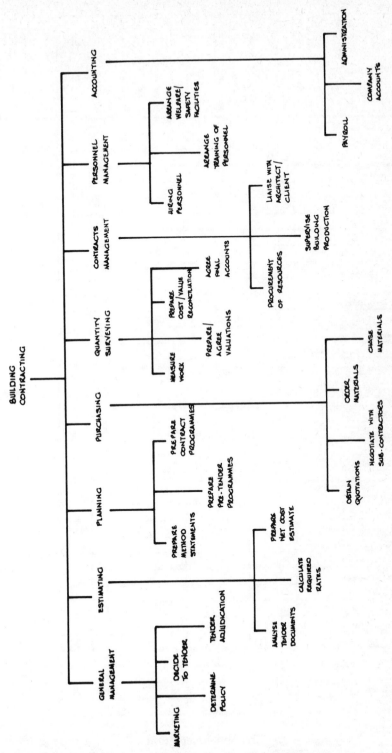

3.2 *Company model showing functional decomposition*

19

FUNCTION/ACTIVITY	Managing Director	Personal Assistant	Senior Estimator	Estimators	Assistant Estimator	Clerk	Planners	Senior Surveyor	Buyer	Clerk Typist	Quantity Surveyors	Assistant Surveyor	Contracts Manager	Project Managers	Site Managers	Personnel Officer	Clerk/Typist	Company Secretary	Accountant	Chief Clerk	Clerk	Typist
BUILDING CONTRACTING	●	●																				
GENERAL MANAGEMENT	●	●																				
MARKETING	●	●																				
DETERMINE POLICY	●																					
DECIDE TO TENDER	●		●																			
TENDER ADJUDICATION	●		●					●					●									
ESTIMATING			●																			
ANALYSE TENDER DOCUMENTS			●	●																		
CALCULATE REQUIRED RATES				●	●																	
PREPARE NET COST ESTIMATE				●	●																	
PLANNING							●															
PREPARE METHOD STATEMENTS							●															
PREPARE PRE-TENDER PROGRAMMES			●				●															
PREPARE CONTRACT PROGRAMMES							●						●									
PURCHASING									●													
OBTAIN QUOTATIONS									●	●												
NEGOTIATE WITH SUB-CONTRACTORS									●													
ORDER MATERIALS									●													
CHASE MATERIALS									●	●												
QUANTITY SURVEYING								●														
MEASURE WORK											●	●										
PREPARE/AGREE VALUATIONS											●	●										
PREPARE COST/VALUE RECONCILIATION											●	●										
AGREE FINAL ACCOUNTS								●			●	●										
CONTRACTS MANAGEMENT													●									
PROCUREMENT OF RESOURCES														●	●							
SUPERVISE BUILDING PRODUCTION													●	●	●							
LIAISE WITH ARCHITECT/CLIENT														●	●							
PERSONNEL MANAGEMENT																●						
HIRING PERSONNEL																●						
ARRANGE TRAINING OF PERSONNEL																●	●					
ARRANGE WELFARE/SAFETY FACILITIES																●	●					
ACCOUNTING																			●			
PAYROLL																				●	●	
COMPANY ACCOUNTS																			●	●	●	
ADMINISTRATION																				●	●	●

3.3 *Personnel/function matrix*

user to ensure that the representation is correct. The top-down approach is adopted initially where the domain of study is indicated by a context diagram. Each process can then be partitioned into its subsystems, thus producing a lower level of detail. This can be repeated to a number of levels until the required detail is reached. It is important, however, in the higher level diagrams, to try and avoid too much detail. The object of drawing diagrams is to present logic in a clear and precise manner which can be easily followed. Any error conditions that do exist can be highlighted at a lower level in more detail. Figs. 3.4 and 3.5 illustrate typical levelled data flow diagrams.

Having established the correctness of the diagram, other analysis tools can be brought in to add greater detail where required. At the lower level, diagram partitioning and levelling may have reached a limit, and therefore additional information about these primitives can be put into a data dictionary (see Fig. 3.6). Although the example shows the data from a data flow, this technique can be used to describe any part of the data flow diagram, including any data files and processes.

It should be noted, however, that data contained in a data dictionary should be written as simply as possible. The term used for this is *structured English*, the idea being to write in such a way that avoids all ambiguity and verbosity. The usage is particularly directed at declarative words and phrases in order to ensure clarity.

It may occur, in certain instances, that decisions affect the flow of data and thus present 'what-if' situations. When this occurs, additional tools such as decision trees and decision tables can be brought into play to describe process logic. This again shows precisely what the outcome is likely to be and adds more depth to the analysis.

Having reached this stage and verified correctness with the user, the various charts and diagrams represent the logical model of the current system. In arriving at this stage it may have been evident that certain inefficiencies exist in processes and data flows. Studying the model will therefore provide a charter for change and allow certain domains of change to be identified.

These domains can be dealt with separately and altered to suit company requirements. Once again, this can take the form of partitioning and top-down levelling incorporating data dictionaries and the use of other tools where required. On completion this will represent a model of a future system, albeit at a logic level. Physical characteristics can now be considered along with man/machine boundaries. Human aspects and organisational concepts will also have to be considered at this stage to see how the new system will fit in, and what organisational changes are necessary. Several options may have been uncovered during the analysis and these can be given further consideration and the most appropriate one chosen.

The collection of data, having considered all aspects, can now be represented as a structured specification which will provide a transition to the design stage.

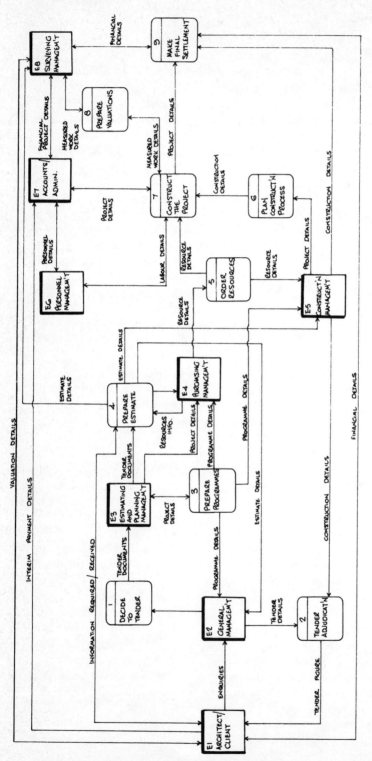

3.4 *Context data flow diagram*

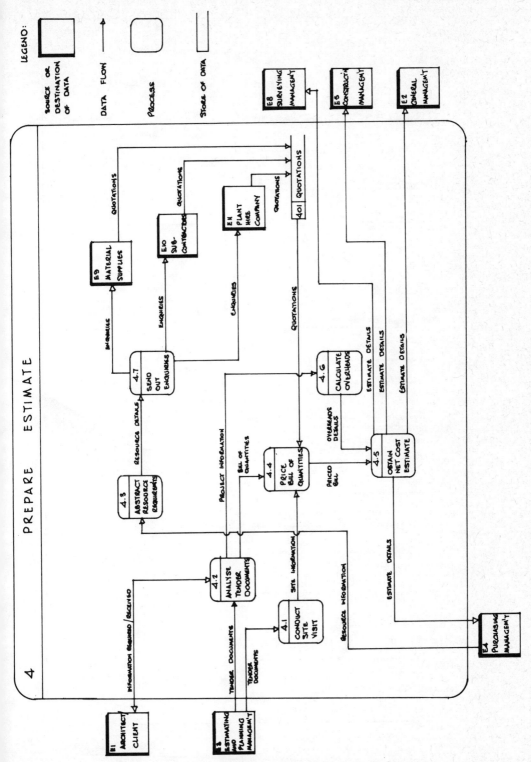

3.5 *Second level data flow diagram of 'prepare estimate' process*

Estimate Details   DATA FLOW

SOURCE REF: 4.5   DESCRIPTION: _Obtain Net Cost Estimate_

DEST'N REF: E2, E4, E5, E8   DESCRIPTION: _Gen Managem't, Purchasing, Surveying, Const'n Managem't_

EXPANDED DESCRIPTION: _Breakdown of cost elements comprising the estimate_

INCLUDED DATA STRUCTURES: OTHER INFORMATION:

Bill of Quantities Summary

Labour

Plant

Materials

Domestic Sub-Contractors

P.C. and Provisional Sums

Nominated Suppliers

Nominated Sub-Contractors

Provisional Sums

Contingencies

Overheads

Net Total

Initial data for tender adjudication. On award of contract data to be sent to Purchasing, Surveying and Construction Management for post contract purposes

3.6 _Data dictionary_

SUMMARY

The methodology described indicates briefly how the technique of structured systems analysis can be used to describe business systems and requirements. The use of the graphical language allows the analyst to prepare a model of the business which is clear and easily understood. The iterative process of establishing the models also allows greater communication and involvement between user and analyst, providing easy identification of current problem areas. Options can be considered in the analysis and followed through until the ideal system is attained. Collecting the information together allows the presentation of a structured specification for transition to the system design stage and, ultimately, a working application.

REFERENCES

1 HARDING, P., Unpublished Lecture Notes on Systems Analysis, Department of Building, Sheffield City Polytechnic, 1983
2 CLIFTON, H. D., *Business Data Systems – A Practical Guide to Systems Analysis and Data Processing*, Prentice-Hall International Inc., 1983
3 GORDEN, RAYMOND L., *Interviewing: Strategy, Techniques, and Tactics*, The Dorsey Press, 1975
4 BURCH Jr, JOHN G. and NATHAN HOD, *Information Systems: A Case-Workbook*, John Wiley & Sons Inc., 1975
5 MENDES, KATHLEEN S., 'Structured Systems Analysis: A Technique to Define Business Requirements', *Sloan Management Review* Summer 1980, pp. 51–63
6 DE MARCO, TOM, *Structured Analysis and System Specification*, Prentice-Hall Inc., 1979
7 GANE, CHRIS and TRISH SARSON, *Structured Systems Analysis: Tools and Techniques*, Prentice-Hall Inc., 1979

SELECTED BIBLIOGRAPHY

MOHR, WALTER, 'The Use of Systems in the Building Industry', *Chartered Builder*, 1978, 23, June/September, pp. 41–2, 45–7, 49, 51–2
ROSS, DOUGLAS T., 'Structured Analysis (SA): A Language for Communicating Ideas', *IEEE Transactions on Software Engineering*, Vol. SE-3, No. 1, January 1977, pp. 16–34
ROSS, DOUGLAS T. and KENNETH E. SCHOMAN Jr., 'Structured Analysis for Requirements Definition', *IEEE Transactions on Software Engineering*, Vol. SE-3, No. 1, January 1977, pp. 6–15
SOFER, CYRIL, *The Organization from Within*, Tavistock Publications, 1961

4 The Requirements of a Management Information System for the Planning and Control of Construction Projects
Paul Barton

The general objectives for an information system designed to aid management in the planning and control of construction projects may be stated as follows:

1 To provide an organised and efficient means of measuring, collecting, verifying and quantifying data reflecting the progress and status of operations on the project with respect to progress, cost, resources and quality.

2 To provide standards against which to measure or compare progress and costs. Examples of standards include CPM schedules, control budgets, materials schedules, quality control specifications and construction working drawings.

3 To provide an organised, accurate and efficient means of converting the data from the operations into information. The information system should be realistic and should recognise (a) the means of processing the information (e.g. manual versus computer), (b) the skills available, and (c) the value of the information compared with the cost of obtaining it.

4 To report the correct and necessary information in a form which can best be interpreted by management, and at a level of detail most appropriate for the individual managers or supervisors who will be using it.

In keeping with the principles of management by exception, the following two objectives should be added:

5 To identify and isolate the most important and critical information for a given situation, and to get it to the correct managers and supervisors, that is those in a position to make best use of it.

6 To deliver the information to them in time for consideration and decision making so that, if necessary, corrective action may be taken on those operations that generated the data in the first place.

PROJECT PLANNING AND CONTROL: A MODEL

The flowchart in the figure (4.1) models the operations, flow of information, and decision-making processes characteristic of a feedback control system appropriate for a medium to large sized construction

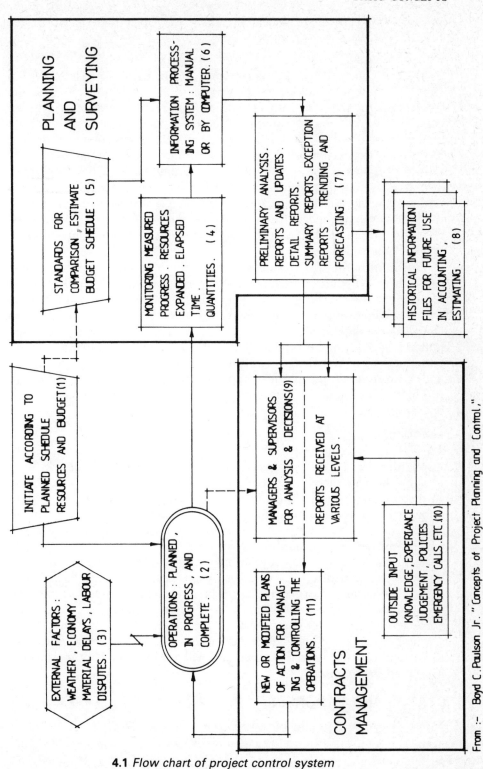

PLANNING AND SURVEYING

STANDARDS FOR COMPARISON, ESTIMATE, BUDGET SCHEDULE. (5)

INFORMATION PROCESSING SYSTEM : MANUAL OR BY COMPUTER. (6)

MONITORING MEASURED PROGRESS, RESOURCES EXPANDED, ELAPSED TIME, QUANTITIES. (4)

PRELIMINARY ANALYSIS. REPORTS AND UPDATES. DETAIL REPORTS. SUMMARY REPORTS, EXCEPTION REPORTS. TRENDING AND FORECASTING. (7)

HISTORICAL INFORMATION FILES FOR FUTURE USE IN ACCOUNTING, ESTIMATING. (8)

INITIATE ACCORDING TO PLANNED SCHEDULE RESOURCES AND BUDGET (1)

MANAGERS & SUPERVISORS FOR ANALYSIS & DECISIONS (9) REPORTS RECEIVED AT VARIOUS LEVELS.

EXTERNAL FACTORS : WEATHER, ECONOMY, MATERIAL DELAYS, LABOUR DISPUTES. (3)

OPERATIONS : PLANNED, IN PROGRESS, AND COMPLETE. (2)

OUTSIDE INPUT KNOWLEDGE, EXPERIENCE, JUDGEMENT, POLICIES, EMERGENCY CALLS. ETC. (10)

NEW OR MODIFIED PLANS OF ACTION FOR MANAGING & CONTROLLING THE OPERATIONS. (11)

CONTRACTS MANAGEMENT

From :- Boyd C. Paulson Jr. "Concepts of Project Planning and Control." Journal of the Construction Division, A.S.C.E. vol. 102.

4.1 *Flow chart of project control system*

project. It has been designed to reflect the objectives stated in the preceding section.)

Components

(In the flowchart, the project is initiated according to a predefined plan (box 1), and operations get underway (box 2). The plans also become reference standards for control purposes (box 5). As operations continue, external factors (box 3) such as recently imposed standards or newly available materials in design, or bad weather, strikes, material delays, foundation excavation problems or even unexpectedly good conditions on the site, may cause the course of operations to differ from the plan, or may provide opportunities for improving on the plan. The operations underway generate indicators of progress (quantities in place, elapsed time, money expended, or resources consumed) which may be measured (box 4) and fed as data into a system (box 6) to produce information for decision makers.

This information processing system refers to planned standards (box 5), such as schedules and budgets, to show deviations, variances, and trends. The information is analysed and made available through reports (box 7), which may be stored for future reference (box 8), or given to contracts managers and site agents for their further analysis and decision making (box 9), or both. They combine and compare this information with their own knowledge, experience, policies, and other qualitative and quantitative information and judgement (box 10) in order to produce new or modified plans for continuing and controlling the project operations (box 11).)

Feedback

This is a feedback control system, and it operates continuously throughout the life of a project. Associated with it is a feedback time. Ideally, the time through boxes 4, 6 and 7 should be as short as possible so that managers and supervisors can receive accurate and up-to-date information in time to make decisions and formulate plans of action, so as to have maximum impact in controlling those operations which are generating the information in the first place.

A major need in project planning and control is significantly to improve and expedite the operations represented by boxes 4, 5, 6 and 7 on the flowchart in order to help resolve these difficulties and improve the quality of information available to decision makers. This can be achieved by the use of computers.)

The following sections will focus on some of the key components of the system that has been described and will amplify some of the concepts presented in the model.

STATUS AND PROGRESS

Numerous measures can be taken to determine the progress or status of operations on a project. Quantities of work units can be physically surveyed and compared with those shown on the drawings. Elapsed time can be compared with the estimated activity or project durations. Money committed or expended can be compared with the estimated budget. Resource usage can be plotted versus expected requirements for labour, materials, and equipment. Finally, an experienced construction manager can simply apply his judgement to estimate the percentage completed on individual activities or on the project as a whole.

Each of these measures has its advantages and disadvantages. For example, field measurements may be more accurate than judgement estimates of percentage complete, but it is expensive to use a surveying crew to obtain these data. Judgement, in turn, can reflect qualitative factors, not evident in the quantities themselves. Just as pulse, temperature, blood tests and X-rays give several different readings on the condition of one's body, each of the aforementioned measures tells something different about the project. All of them are necessary to gain a full understanding of the status and progress of the operations.

Nonlinear relationships

In applying such measures, it is important to recognise nonlinear relationships among them. For example, there may be a nonlinear relationship between quantities in place and elapsed time. To illustrate, if the bulk of the work is scheduled to be completed earlier in the activity's scheduled duration, then when the time is 50 per cent elapsed, the work might actually and correctly be 60 per cent complete. Similar nonlinear relationships apply among the other measures. The time at which money is expended on materials, for example, might be only loosely related to the actual time those materials are used.

When comparing the expenditure of labour resources over time, one can also often recognise nonlinear *learning-curve* effects. Learning curves relate time, resources consumed, and quantities produced. Their basic principle is that skill and productivity in performing tasks improve with experience and practice. The nonlinear implications of learning curves are different for planning, or estimating, than they are for control.

Source of data

Data reflecting status and progress come from numerous sources. In the formal information system, sources include labour and plant time sheets, purchase orders, invoices, weekly and monthly measures, quality control reports, and so forth.

In addition to the formal sources, there are numerous other inputs to management, some of which short-circuit most of the regular steps.

Information processing

In concept, information processing systems take progress and status data, compare them against reference standards such as budgets or programmes, and convert the results to information needed by the managers and supervisors on the project. As stated in the objectives, the level of detail, the variety and the frequency of reports to be produced should be appropriate to the people who will use them; should be feasible for the means of processing the information (manual or computer); should recognise the skills available, and should realistically assess the value of the information compared with the cost of obtaining it. Finally, the system should be fast, efficient and accurate.

In practice, several related subsystems are needed fully to plan and control projects. Examples include activity and resource scheduling and control, cost control, materials ordering, scheduling and control, and quality control. Each of these systems is important, but if fully integrated into one system, the sheer volume of data would dominate and obscure the vital information that is needed for any one of them. An interrelated modular system is thus essential. That is, each subsystem should be largely self-sufficient, but it should be logically co-ordinated and compatible with the others.

Consider the whole process from the point of view of a network-based subsystem for activity and resource scheduling and control. Costs, materials, and quality functions can also be identified with activities, so it is possible to use the activities as a means to tie into other systems. In summary, an information processing system for project planning and control should recognise that there are many subsystems involved in the process, and it should further recognise the inter-relationships among those subsystems.

Reporting

Reporting can take many forms, ranging from conversations and telephone calls, through tabular presentations of cost information and graphical presentations on bar charts, cumulative progress ('S') curves and CPM diagrams, to up-to-the-minute reports from computers. Certain basic principles should guide each of these, however, if the reporting is to be effective for control purposes.

Content

Regardless of the form, in order to be effective for control purposes, a complete report should have five main components:

1 *Estimates*: either total, to date, or this period, that provide a reference standard against which to compare actual or forecast results.

2 *Actuals*: what has already happened, either this period or to date.

3 *Forecasts*: based on the best knowledge at hand, what is expected to happen to the project and its elements in the future.

4 *Variances*: how far actual and forecast results differ from those which were planned or estimated.

5 *Reasons*: anticipated or unexpected circumstances that account for the actual and forecast behaviour of the project and its operations, and especially that explain significant variances from the plans.

Selectivity and subreporting

One of the objectives stated previously was to report the correct and necessary information in a form which can best be interpreted by management, and at a level of detail most appropriate for the individual managers who will be using the information. Selectivity and subreporting are important here. Since time is among their scarcest resources, construction managers simply cannot afford to wade through piles of extraneous data to obtain the information they need.

Variances

Reports for control purposes should calculate variances to show which operations are relatively more in need of attention than others. *Variance* is used here to mean a deviation from a planned or budgeted item. The variances, in turn, should be expressible in both relative (percentage) and absolute (quantities, pounds, etc.) terms. For example, is it more important for a manager to focus attention on a £1,000,000 operation with an absolute variance of plus £2,000 (overrun) and a relative variance of plus 2 per cent, or on a £10,000 operation with a relative variance of plus 15 per cent and an absolute variance of £1,500? With both types of variance information, the manager can apply his judgement as he thinks best.

Management by exception

By showing only those operations with variances or other parameters exceeding certain predefined limits, exception reports focus management attention directly upon those operations most in need of control. The principle here is to identify and isolate the most important and critical information for a given situation, and to give it to the right person as quickly as possible for his consideration, decisions, and action.

Forecasting and trending

If management is to have clear vision ahead and be able to anticipate problems before they arise, reports must look to the future as well as document the past. Forecasting and trending are two means by which this is done.

Feedback time

In all the aforementioned cases, the information reported must be received in time so that, if necessary, corrective action may be taken on those operations that generated the information in the first place.

To summarise, any management information system designed to assist the planning and control of construction projects must fulfil these requirements, whether it be a manual system or one that utilises the latest developments in information technology.

II Applications
5 BIAS: A Database Approach to Contractor's Accounting
Brenda Wroe

The construction industry is a relatively new and reluctant user of computer systems and consequently has not as yet established any consistent, well-defined requirements to which the software industry can respond. Construction accounting software has developed slowly, even though there is a large market of small contractors and subcontractors.

This chapter illustrates the application of a contractor's accounting and costing system using a database with a commercial package called BIAS(TM). The benefits of a computer system design based on the logical structure of the data as opposed to the information required is contrasted with the more traditional approach.

TRADITIONAL DESIGN APPROACH

Microcomputers have provided many smaller companies with the opportunity to establish an information system to support the operations of their business. Such systems as there are for construction firms, have tended to reflect the existing practices of manual data processing with, for example, the organisation of the manual accounting ledgers being transferred to the computer with separate files, sometimes even separate disks for suppliers, clients, subcontractors and nominal accounts.

The eventual success or failure of any construction project depends upon the strengths and weaknesses of the initial analysis of requirements and design. This is no less so with a computer system, where the design of data files needs to be established at an early stage of any software package development. The initial design will govern how the programs can operate on the data stored in order to produce what the user is believed to require, in terms of management reports, the data input and the speed and flexibility needed.

Traditionally the facilities of computer systems are firmly fixed at this very early stage, when the designer defines the content and structure of the files. Unfortunately, many computer systems appear to meet the needs of the contractor but, when installed, the company feels restricted by its limitations and inflexibility.

The pitfalls of the traditional approach

The potential problems of a traditional approach can best be illustrated by the problems experienced by a typical small construction company. Company X decided relatively early that a microcomputer could assist them in the administrative tasks of handling the many small contracts which they undertook in their business as a subcontractor to other companies. Company X duly purchased the hardware and entered into an agreement with the supplier for accounting and payroll software. When the system was installed in the company, it was realised that some of the administrative peculiarities of the construction industry were not catered for with the packaged software, and the supplier agreed to make the necessary modifications.

With the progress of time, several related problems were experienced by Company X as a result of the system design:

1 The package proved to be rather inflexible when the more unusual situations arose, such as the need partially to pay supplier invoices in cases of dispute or to manipulate the cash flow.

2 A separate master (reference) file was created for retentions held by clients, which simply duplicated much of the data in the existing sales ledger master file and was a potential source of inconsistent details.

3 As the company grew the system developed rather haphazardly, and there was no co-ordinated view of the data as a whole. Several small related systems were developed independently and stood alone in the system with their own files.

4 Management, in fact, understood little of how the stored financial data was structured. They frequently required new reports but were frustrated by the time taken to get the programs written or the inability fully to exploit the data which they knew was available in the system.

5 Whenever seemingly small changes to the programs became necessary, such as those caused by tax rate changes, many programs had to be modified or rewritten resulting in the expense of unproductive maintenance.

6 Storage space on the system became critical as the files with redundant data grew, and the programs which searched for particular records were consequently slow.

A DATABASE APPROACH

More recently computer systems have been designed around a common database of information. Although the term 'database' is frequently used in the jargon of computer salesmen, the layman may not understand the implications. In computing terms, a database may be defined as a generalised integrated collection of data which is structured so that the data may be retrieved in any required order to fulfil the differing needs of many users.

Data is the raw elements of numbers and characters from which information is derived by assembling, analysing or summarising into a meaningful form. The data stored in a database reflects its logical structure rather than the particular physical structure as viewed from one particular application program. It can be manipulated and retrieved by many application programs (all of which may not be initially defined) and will ignore the separation of the data in existing clerical systems by presenting an integrated view to all the programs. Thus any new application programs can be designed at a later stage and will view the same database, but with its own window.

The benefits of a database approach

The problems experienced by Company X described above can be avoided or minimised by taking a fresh approach to the system with a common database.

1 Sharing the data between several systems can eliminate the duplication of data and thereby reduce the incidence of inconsistencies in detail. Hence much of the data (such as names and addresses) kept on Company X's sales ledger accounts of clients, and also kept on the retention accounts of the same clients, are in fact duplicated and therefore redundant. The speed of the system is also improved when less redundant data is stored.

2 The problem of non-productive maintenance is also resolved by isolating the data stored in files from the programs which manipulate it. File data rarely changes, once defined, but the operations of programs may change as users establish what they want to do with the data. In a database approach the task of maintaining program/data independence is undertaken by a specialised program which handles the interface between the various programs and the stored data, called the

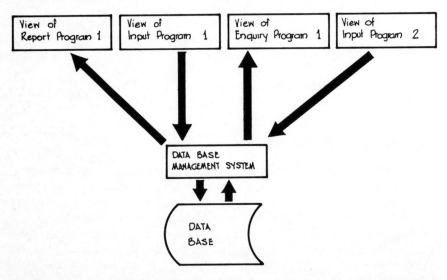

5.1 *Interface between the global database and the local views of programs for input, enquiry and reports*

database manager, as shown in Fig. 5.1. In this way complex systems may develop in a more flexible manner.

3 The greatest benefit of the database approach is that the system can develop in a flexible, logical and structured form, and its users are also able to understand the underlying concepts of the design and hence make full use of the files in retrieving management information.

A technique called *data analysis* has been developed over the last decade by computer systems designers, as a means of exploring the logical structure of the data elements which form the basis of any information system. Briefly explained, data analysis involves identifying the entities (that is the important things: people, events etc.) and the relationships which exist between them. An information system will require many relationships to be established to permit access to the respective entities.

A database contractor's accounting and contract costing system

BIAS (Builders Interactive Accounting System) is a software package developed in conjunction with a small contractor and founded on such a database approach. The package is designed around a database of accounting, contract costing, subcontract management and payroll information, and has a very powerful database manager to handle the interface between the data and the evolving application programs. BIAS is not, therefore, confined to the functions of conventional ledgers for purchases, sales and nominal ledgers but supports all the natural relationships of the data as illustrated in the simplified diagram in Fig. 5.2. A comprehensive open item accounting system which allows part payments and full reconciliation of all types of transactions is supported. It is written in COBOL, the high level business language for microcomputers, and can be run on any microcomputer which operates under the CP/M and MS-DOS operating systems.

BIAS enables different users to set up their own database of accounts flexibly divided between suppliers, subcontractors, clients, nominal and real asset accounts, according to their own requirements and governed only by the total disk storage capacity available. Similarly the number of contracts and subcontracts is defined by the user according to his needs. The system recognises the similarities between invoices, credit notes, payments, journal and cash transactions on both the sales and purchase ledgers, and consequently groups them together in the data base as *transactions*.

A database management system (DBMS) transparently (i.e. unknown to the user) controls the operation of the BIAS database and handles all the storage and retrieval of data for the user. The DBMS also consistently handles security by controlling the access to the stored information.

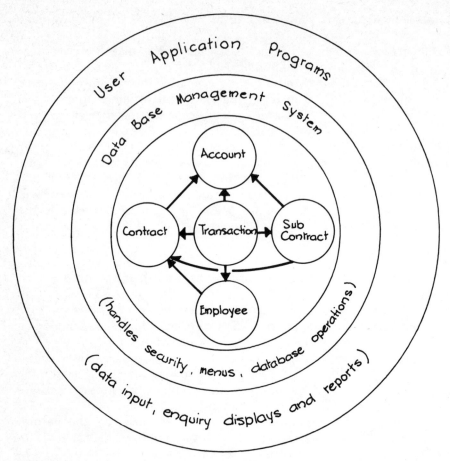

5.2 *A database approach to the contractor's accounting, payroll and contract costing*

The database approach has many advantages for the user:

1 The programs are integrated, enabling the operator to input data once only. It is immediately stored by the DBMS in such a way as to be retrievable whenever and however management would like. This enables all programs to have access to the latest data stored, as there are no temporary files of data waiting to be processed.

2 Data input is handled by the DBMS and, consequently, is made in a consistent and simple manner by filling in forms displayed on the screen. Should the operator make errors, the DBMS in BIAS provides meaningful diagnostic messages and allows the erroneous data to be corrected.

3 Many different enquiries can be made on the database via the DBMS which are displayed on screens representing completed forms, such as the supplier account in Fig. 5.3. Specialised views of the data can be programmed which present the user's own window on the data. This is handled by a report generator which allows the user self-programming facilities.

4 Menus can be controlled by the DBMS, and the BIAS system can be tailored to present each user with an individual menu showing only those operations for which that particular user is authorised.

5 Several levels of security are available, on entry to the DBMS system by password, and on entry to particular sections of the database by authorisation. An operator may be permitted to make only particular selections from the menu, view limited account or contract details, or input data to authorised parts of the database.

6 The storage of data in the database itself is economical, since duplicated data is minimised. The actual amount of data stored in the database is governed by the amount of historical information required by the user and the level of detail which is input, and consequently stored, in the database. Typically a small contractor using BIAS can expect to have available up to 12 months live and accessible data. The user has full discretionary power to transfer information to paper records and delete items from the database.

7 The user can retrieve the precise data he requires from the database via the transparent DBMS. Standard reports and enquiries are available, but very flexible and powerful selections can be made. Information for management may be generated at any time and will be up-to-date with all the data input to date. Contract cost information may be obtained on all or selected contracts in the database in varying degrees of detail, such as:

—a summary of work in progress showing overall profit margins

```
GR15 Rel 2.04            Account Details            30/08/83 [9]

Balance    7353.69 CR                Type 213        Updated 30/08/83

A/c no     2021        Alladin & Co            Cr MTD....   11083.01
                                               Cr Total..   11083.01
                       Long Cavern
                       CASTLETON               Dr MTD....    3729.32
                       DE43 9HJ                Dr Total..    3729.32

   Date    Tr no  Ld    Type          Account              Total
08/08/83    44    S   Invoice   Subcontract Domestic      3729.32
08/08/83    45    S   Invoice   Subcontract Domestic       163.91
08/08/83    46    S   Invoice   Subcontract Nominated     6175.00
30/08/83    57    S   Payment   Bank Current A/c          3729.32-
30/08/83    58    S   Invoice   Subcontract Domestic      1014.78
```

5.3 *A supplier account*

—a contract cost summary showing total costs analysed to nine user definable headings (Fig. 5.4)

—a detailed cost breakdown itemising all lines of invoices, subcontract certificates etc. with descriptions (Fig. 5.5).

In addition to the standard reports provided, an enquiry facility and report generator enables the user to access the database in a flexible manner and design his own reports to extract his required information.

8 Since every input to the database is made via the DBMS, it is able to generate a detailed audit trail by creating a unique transaction number for every item of input which is traceable throughout the system.

9 An important feature of BIAS is that it is evolutionary and allows the user to build up his database gradually, learning from experience and establishing the appropriate level of detail needed to be input for his particular requirements.

10 All information stored on the database is a valuable company asset, and the database is accessible to other software such as word processing packages.

Database systems are suitable for all sizes of data processing requirement and BIAS has features that make it particularly useful to various types and sizes of contractor.

```
QR16 Rel 2.05              Job Expenditure Details              30/08/83 [9]

                    Margin    370.52   Margin  19.00 %  Updated 30/07/83

Job no     101     MJ&C House For Walter Getty    Cost MTD      353.00
Client     1500    Mandell Jenson Co              Cost TOT     1949.48

Retention          Valuation 30/08/83   2500.00   Estimate   120000.00
                   Costs o/s 30/08/83    180.00   Invoiced

              Nom   MTD              Heading              Total
               1    353.00   Materials                    1637.00
               2             Hired Plant
               3             Plant & Transport              120.00
               4             Labour                         192.48
               5             Subcontract Domestic
               6             Subcontract Nominated
               7             Subcontract Labour Only
               8             Site Overheads
               9

  Do you want a breakdown of expenditure (Y/N) N
```

5.4 *A contract cost summary*

```
QR16 Rel 2.05              Job Expenditure Details              30/08/83 [9]

                    Margin     370.52   Margin  19.00 %  Updated 30/07/83

Job no      101      MJ&C House For Walter Getty      Cost MTD      353.00
Client      1500     Mandell Jenson Co                Cost TOT     1949.48

Retention            Valuation 30/08/83   2500.00    Estimate   120000.00
                     Costs o/s 30/08/83    180.00    Invoiced


  Date    Tr No   Nom    Type            Description              Amount
01/07/83     1     1    Invoice    5T OP Cement @ £54/ton          270.00
01/07/83     1     1    Invoice    6000 Heather Mix Facgs @ 149/m  894.00
01/07/83     1     1    Invoice    2000 Trigalv wall ties @ 35/m    70.00
01/07/83     2     1    Invoice    2 rolls 1200g polythene          50.00
20/08/83    51     1    Invoice    33 8x4 wall panelling           353.00
24/07/83    29     3    Dmy Inv    Clear site                      120.00
24/07/83    34     4    Job Tfr    48 hours trades                 192.48



Do you want a breakdown of expenditure (Y/N) N
End of List
```

5.5 *A detailed cost breakdown*

Advantages for the smaller contractor or subcontractor
—storage of detailed descriptions of purchases costed to jobs
—costing of small works and also management of larger contract work
—transferring materials from stock to jobs or between jobs
—the management of subcontracts if required
—costing invoice lines to various jobs or contracts
—part payment of invoices giving full credit control for purchases, sales
  and retentions
—long term data storage of contract details
—flexible selection of reports
—operated by existing staff, either secretarial or managerial
—regular production of management accounting information, including
  VAT reporting, without duplication of effort.

Advantages for the larger contractor with a turnover of up to about £5 million
—flexible accounting and contract structure
—sophisticated subcontract management enabling work to be valued
  by measured work, daywork, variations etc. with details of retentions
  and appropriate tax deductions
—comprehensive contract reconciliation of costs, certificated value,
  internal value and reserves

—the ability to produce remittance advices, subcontract certificates, statements and fully selective reporting of the open item account details

—preparation of final account reports to enable speedy completion of financial accounts.

Advantages for the software house which developed BIAS

—the system can be tailored easily to meet the needs of new customers

—the system is modular in design and can thus be extended to cater for new areas of computing

—consistent methods of input and information retrieval can be maintained, thus economising on the need for user training

—consistent programming design means less problems when training new development staff.

In conclusion, software based on a database approach offers all the advantages of shared data, very powerful flexibility, and expandability to respond to the needs of users as requirements become established. New aspects of data processing can be integrated into the database without affecting the existing programs which have been developed and tested. The benefits of conventional program design such as speed, integration and ease of use are also available to the database user. Such database systems do require larger memory than other systems, but this becomes less significant with each new generation of microcomputer.

6 A Computerised Plant Control System for Medium Sized Building Firms

Paul Barton   David Heath

INTRODUCTION

This chapter is based on recent research conducted by the authors in conjunction with several medium sized building firms in the West Yorkshire region of Britain.

The research involved a detailed study of the data processing facilities of the firms, with particular emphasis on project data, using the structured systems analysis technique. As a result of these studies a general model was developed.

One of the co-operating firms then asked the researchers to devise a computerised plant control system to meet their specific needs. This was agreed with the proviso that the finalised system would be sufficiently flexible to meet the needs of similar building firms.

It can be seen from Fig. 6.1 that the overall system has a subsystem representing information processes associated with plant. Consequently, it was decided to use this model in conjunction with a detailed analysis of the plant department of the firm in question, in order to develop the system.

The remainder of the chapter explains how this was done.

DETAILED ANALYSIS

The first stage consisted of a study of the various processes involved in handling the administration of plant records.

The plant department administrated the hiring of plant from the company's own yard stock or from hire plant companies outside. The department was manned by a plant manager and his assistant: the former handled external orders and the latter managed internal plant movements.

Construction sites requisitioned for plant, usually over the telephone to the plant office, or by memo via the contracts manager. The site manager decided upon the type, size and number of plant items required and when they were needed for work. It was the function of the plant office to meet the demands made, firstly by using plant in stock, then secondly by going to external hire.

Plant purchase

If the site management were aware that an item of plant was to be used for a long period of time, they might propose to the plant manager that the plant in question be purchased. The analysis of whether it would be financially beneficial to purchase plant items was carried out by the

6.1 *A project data/information handling system*

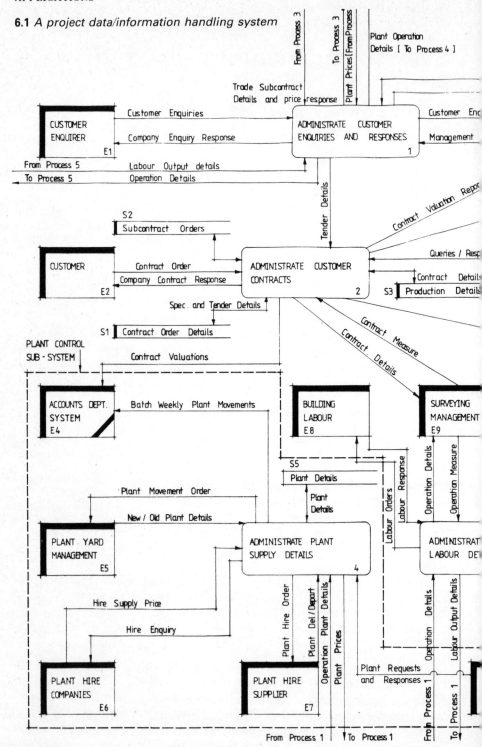

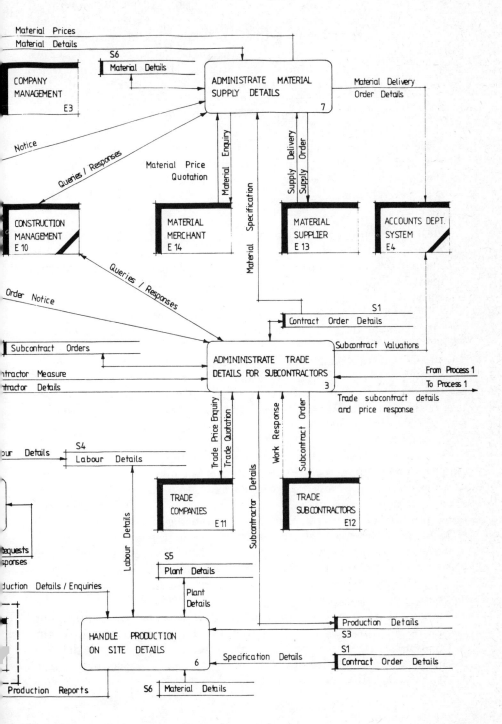

plant manager. Quotations were obtained from manufacturers regarding purchase costs, and corresponding hire charges were collected from the various firms on file. The purchase or hire report was submitted to the company director responsible for plant operations, who would then make a decision as to whether a purchase should be made. Plant purchase orders were assembled by the plant manager and deliveries and invoices verified by him as they arrived. His assistant entered the new plant on a fresh record card for use in the internal plant hire administration. All purchase orders and delivery notes were retained on file until the manager decided that they could be destroyed (usually for the life of the plant).

Trade directories were maintained by the manager as a source of information concerning suitable manufacturers' products and the sources of supply; this was also done for plant hire companies, which were regularly updated.

Internal plant movement

Requests for plant were taken by the assistant if it was believed that the company might own the item. If not, then the plant manager would commence proceedings to obtain a hire agreement with an external company. Usually the request would consist of a plant name, size or capacity, with the number needed and location and date for which it was required. When the order was received it was given a position of priority, and the date, time, and from whom the order was taken were noted.

The plant record book contained the locations for all company owned mechanical plant. Non-mechanical plant was not as rigorously recorded, as its movements were relatively limited. All plant, when not on hire, was returned to the yard. Therefore, by viewing the records under the respective plant categories the assistant was able to identify whether an item was available.

As no records were kept regarding the state of repair or service, a check had to be made before any plant items could be sent out on hire.

An internal plant movement order was written out in triplicate when a hire was made. This listed the intended location, date, plant description and the location from where it was being moved. A copy was retained for reference, the accounts department received a copy for determining a hire charge, and the third copy was sent to the site, or was kept in the plant office if the plant was moved before an order was made out. The general practice was to keep the site copy in the plant office – a policy decision taken by the plant manager.

The yard and transport controller was responsible for loading and unloading the transport wagons with plant. The assistant informed him of the items to be loaded on to specific wagons, together with delivery instructions. Transport costs were recorded for the accounts department, with regard to charges made to each site.

Plant deletion

Company plant no longer serviceable was deleted from the record system and from the yard stock by the order of the plant manager. Plant performance was monitored by the plant manager, who considered the number of repairs and maintenance time. Each plant item had its own number (in a lot of cases this was the original serial number rather than a separate company number). Account records were updated annually, showing which items had been scrapped or sold.

Items which were lost or stolen were recorded as such, although not necessarily immediately, in case the item was returned at a later date or its movement had not been recorded. Confirmed missing items were dealt with by the office manager, although he might supply information for the claim form.

External plant hire

Requests for plant received by the plant manager were placed in order of priority and dealt with individually. Quotations for hire rates were obtained and negotiations finalised usually over the telephone. Order details were kept for invoice confirmation. If a plant request had to be delayed, the plant manager would instruct the site office to make alternative arrangements.

A hire order is a request to supply a certain type and size of plant to a particular location on a specific date and time. This was kept on file for reference. The site which received the plant would also receive an advice note stating that delivery or departure of plant had taken place. Following the order, the plant manager would receive a hire agreement which was confirmation of the hire conditions and charges. An off-hire order was dealt with by the plant manager as a plant request from site.

Invoice vouching

Invoices received by the accounts department were vouched by the plant office before payment. Plant hire invoices were cross-checked weekly with the hire agreements and actual periods of hire. Valid invoices were passed back to the accounts clerk, but if a query existed it was referred to the hire company in question.

Plant reports

The plant department did not provide a reporting facility for construction management regarding plant hire costs, either internally or externally. Also, there was no comprehensive report of available plant in the yard.

THE CURRENT LOGICAL PLANT SYSTEM

Using the structured systems analysis technique, it was then possible to identify the major processes and dataflows relating to the control of plant by drawing a boundary around the appropriate subsystem in the

6.2 *Administrate plant supply details*

general model. From this a more detailed model was produced (see Fig. 6.2).

Within this subsystem, the main processes are to (1) handle internal hire requests, (2) handle external hire orders, and (3) obtain quotations, and are demonstrated in relation to each other by a dataflow diagram (Fig. 6.2). The main datastore is the 'plant details' numbered S5; the external entities to the system are the construction management, the plant hire supplier, plant hire companies, the plant yard management and the accounts department system.

Each process shown in Fig. 6.2 is numbered, and like the overview they can be further defined by lower level dataflow diagrams. Therefore, taking each diagram in turn, an examination was made of the major subprocesses, identifying the various instructions that comprise each process in terms of data input, data manipulation and data output. Fig. 6.3 (Handle internal hire orders), Fig. 6.4 (Handle external hire orders) and Fig. 6.5 (Obtain quotations) are low level representations of the detail in Fig. 6.2 (Administrate plant supply details). For practical purposes of being able further to define the current logical model in terms of programs for computing, the diagrams are at the lowest level. A specification of the function of each process is necessary in terms of written statements in order to be of programming use. The dataflows at the lowest level are analysed for data content, as this is important for designing the computer programs, and the structure of data control and handling requirements such as the volume of data.

REVISED PLANT SYSTEM

In essence the processes identified above are viewed as being those that are necessary for the subsystem handling plant supply details. However, the dataflow diagrams do not take into account the types of query from management requesting plant information and the kinds of responses to be expected.

Revision of the current logical model was then necessary to take into account these management information requirements. Defining the types of report and their content was a problem which had to be solved by interviewing the management users of plant information at one of the companies. It was preferable to use the same company which provided the further investigatory plant control system information, because this company was also willing to support the testing of the computer based system within its office.

The current physical plant management system did not have formal provision of a reporting facility. The construction management members in charge of the building work did not have access to the charges being incurred through internal and external hiring of plant. The plant movement orders were available, but not in any alternative form of presentation. The availability of company owned plant could only be reported upon by applying to the plant yard management for infor-

APPLICATIONS

6.3 *Handle internal hires*

48

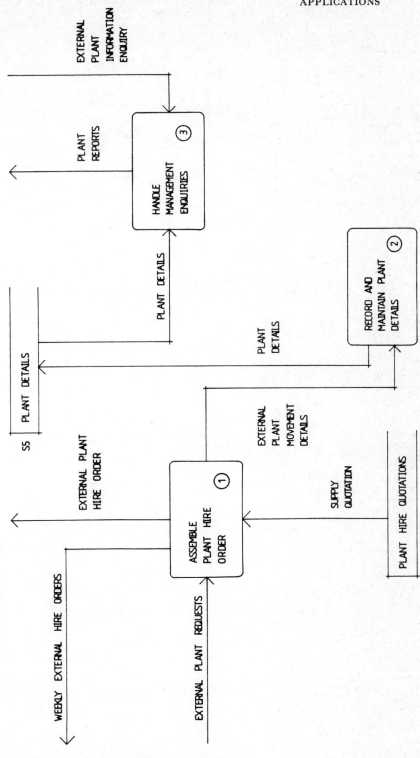

6.4 *Handle external hires*

49

6.5 *Obtain plant hire quotations*

mation. Currently, if a report is required of the items of plant in stock, then the manual abstraction of data from the card record system would be required. From observations of the number of people employed in the administration of plant hire, it seems likely that the manual preparation of reports would consume more than the available time for processing the paperwork.

Therefore, with the potential for introducing a computer based plant control system, providing reporting facilities by electronic means and an understanding of the basic administration processes, the information requirements of management were recorded. It was found that they would like reports upon plant in the following format:

1 Plant stock available in the yard
2 Plant stock of a particular type available in the yard
3 Locations of a type of plant
4 Location of a particular item of plant
5 Listing of plant currently on a site, both internal and external
6 External plant allocated to a site
7 The costs being incurred, cumulative, daily or weekly

The information provided on the reports should include the plant identity, dates of movement (arrival/departure), hire rates, date of the report, the site identity, reference to the external hire company.

REVISED PHYSICAL SYSTEM

A logical system refers to processes which have not been allocated the means to fulfil them, whether they be computer programs, i.e. software, or the computer equipment, i.e. hardware. A physical system, however, is the implementation of these data processes.

The current physical system was found to be essentially manually based. The plant details of inventory and movement orders are recorded on paper forms and cards.

Revision of the physical system took into consideration the alternative availability of a small computer with accompanying peripheral equipment. In order to identify which processes and datastores could be handled more effectively, recourse was necessary to the dataflow diagrams of the revised current logical system.

Design and development of the system software, i.e. computer programs, was dependent upon a detailed specification of the data and processes in terms of their functional use. The dataflow diagrams provided a means to arriving at an understanding of the inputs and outputs within the subsystem but not in sufficient detail for creating computer programs. Each process must be further defined to a specification which can be transformed from a statement of instructions for manual operation to coded computer commands.

From the dataflow diagrams it was possible to identify certain processes which could form the basis for a plant control system and the storage of data required. It was necessary to consider the current

51

physical system of the company where the trial run of the computer was to take place, taking into account the manual production and storage of forms. For example, the assembly of the plant movement orders was designated a manual process because the forms were an integral part of the firm's system with which the study was not allowed to interfere; although, if freed from this constraint, there would be no reason to prevent the computer system handling the printing of orders. The system processes and the datastore are listed as follows:

1 Record and maintain internal plant details
2 Record and maintain external plant details

These processes were combined because of their similarity, the function being to receive data belonging to a plant item, record it, and update the values stored as they change to reflect the movement of plant or the increase in hire charges because of a change in running costs.

The plant details consisted of:

1 Plant number
2 Plant name plus plant type by implication
3 Plant hire rate
4 Plant location
5 Plant arrival date/departure date
6 Plant owner, i.e. company or hire company

As different plant types occurred from new these would form additional plant categories.

The values which were changeable constituted a need for a record of maintenance; plant also may be deleted or added to the total listing. The values are: plant hire rate, plant location, and plant movement dates.

If a plant item was rendered temporarily out of use, then this was a factor to be accounted for in order to give a true picture of plant available.

1 Handle management enquiries (internal plant)
2 Handle management enquiries (external plant)

These two processes share the same function of providing management with information to satisfy their enquiries. They take the form of plant reports, using the plant details listed above as a basis:

1 Plant available in the yard
2 Plant type available in the yard
3 Locations of a type of plant
4 Location of a particular item of plant
5 Plant on a site (internal and external)
6 Costs of plant in total, daily or weekly, to a site

Processes of the revised logical system – computer based

From the dataflow diagram 'Handle internal hires' (Fig. 6.3) are the following processes:

1 Record and maintain internal plant details

2 Handle management queries

From the dataflow Diagram 1.4.2 (Fig. 6.4) 'Handle external hires' are the following processes:

1 Record and maintain external plant details
2 Handle management enquiries

Major datastore of the revised logical system – computer based

This appears on the overview of the project data/information handling system as S5 'Plant details'.

This datastore receives data from the processes mentioned above for internal and external plant, and is accessed for data to produce the information for reporting to management.

The remaining processes on the dataflow diagrams were designated to remain manual.

Design specification of the physical system

The hardware of the small computer system consisted of a central processing unit run by the CP/M operating system with 48K of random access memory, a visual display unit, two disk drives with mini-floppy disks of 70K capacity each, and a matrix dot printer.

The computer software was written in the language of Extended Basic and was in accord with the operating commands of the CP/M hardware system control.

The datafiles stored on the disks were designed for random access; each plant type was given a datafile, then all the files were chained together. This facilitated easy maintenance of the data if changes were necessary by enabling files to be added or deleted without loss of the remaining data files.

The random access allowed fast data input and output from the disks, unlike serial storage, which would have required the whole disks to be accessed for a particular record and the creation of a new file when updating.

Incorporated as a facility for the user was the option of accessing information by the visual display screen or via the hard copy produced by the printer. Input of data was by the keyboard method; no other device, such as a digitising tablet, was used for the tests, although it was possible to alter the system to connect to such devices.

The microcomputer systems that were available for the testing of the system at the development stage were known commercially as the North Star Horizon and the Modular Business Systems Tutor. The latter also had an increased memory capacity of 64K.

The design of the computer programs was in accordance with the modern practice of modular construction, which matches the structured analysis approach of documenting the system under view. That is, the programs were written as modules which could interface together rather than as a rigid single program of instructions which would necessitate comprehensive re-writing when changes were required. The modules enable changes or the addition of more programs to the system by their characteristic of being able to be accessed individually (in a similar fashion to subsystems in the data analysis possessing boundaries which are crossed by dataflows).

Plant control systems software

The name given to the package of programs was the Plant Control System. It consisted of the following sections:

1 Create master datafiles of plant records by data input
2 Update the master datafiles of plant records as the date changes in value by user input of the new information
3 Enquiry options, a facility of report selection and information retrieval for the user

An examination of the data to be used revealed the size of words, the quantity of items to be recorded, the various class types of plant, and the length of lines in the output of the data from the functional specification. It was necessary to match the specification needs with the hardware limits, in order to design the input and output statements in the software to reflect this balance; for example, the printer line length was a limiting constraint.

Create plant datafiles

The plant data is accepted via the keyboard and displayed on the screen; it consists of:

1 Plant type
2 Plant name and reference number and size, if necessary
3 Plant identity reference number
4 Plant hire date to and from the location
5 Site location, contract reference
6 Hire rate per day or week
7 Name of company if externally hired

This takes account of whether it is a company owned piece of plant or externally owned. It is entered into the appropriate plant file, say, for example, 'excavators' or 'compressors'. Editing for mistakes is allowed with this system; if discovered following input, then they must be recalled for correction. The information above constitutes a plant record.

Update the master datafiles

The plant data contains values which change, the most usual or frequent being the current plant location; the system was, therefore, designed to take account of this. A record is recalled to the screen and the appropriate value is changed; if the plant is external then the change would be deletion of the item. Maintenance of all items covers both internal and external plant, and this function combines the two processes shown on the dataflow diagrams of record and maintain internal/external plant.

Enquiry options

Here the user is provided with a menu selection of various types of plant report which corresponds to the specification requirements. By selection of a particular option the user can be provided with a hard copy report printout, or for speed of retrieval, use the VDU screen.

The reports are:

1 Plant allocated to a site or in the yard
2 Location of a particular plant item
3 Location of a type of plant, e.g. all dumpers
4 External plant on hire (with locations)
5 The costs of plant hired to a site, cumulative and daily/weekly

Testing the new plant system

The aim of testing the computer based plant control system was to find out whether it would meet the needs of the user and to what extent the application might affect the current physical system. One of the case study companies agreed to allow the installation of the new system at its Head Office, where the mainstream management was based. The operations of the manual procedures handling plant information were not interfered with, the computer system was tested in parallel providing an alternative source of data.

The small computer system consisted of the CPU, a VDU, and a printer, with disk storage facilities. The location was within the main office rather than the plant department, providing management with ease of access to plant reports when needed. The plant manager used record cards for holding company owned plant data with regard to current location, plant identity and movement dates. These were used as a convenient source of data for creating the master files of plant records to be stored on disks.

The movement records of plant, i.e. internal plant orders, generated by the plant department were available for abstracting the necessary data to update the master plant files. This was done daily, and therefore some of the plan records were out of date if a movement occurred on the same day that a management report was requested.

Similarly, the movement of external plant was recorded on plant orders; although the transaction usually occurred by telephone, the details still had to be noted for future reference. The hire rates could be obtained from the preliminary negotiations of enquiry/quotation. By daily visits to the plant department, the external plant hire data could be abstracted, together with internal orders. As before, the information could change during the time after collection and the next point of updating, so the management's reports had to be read with a degree of caution.

The datafiles were constructed without any problems: the design of the records matched the sizes of descriptions of plant, the alphanumeric coding the quantity of information to be handled, and the speed of retrieval was acceptably quick. The computer programs operated without any major logic problems, and the processing of data was carried out to the requirements of the design and development.

The function of the plant control system to provide information for management depended not on the mere ability to retrieve data but on whether the reports produced were capable of use in practice. Various construction managers requested reports in their different guises, with the result that they were all effective in reporting information about plant.

The main report used was the usage of plant on a particular contract including the costs incurred. This could be taken to the site for checking whether the plant could be released or if it was still where it was expected to be. The managers on site were introduced to the reports, providing information about plant that they previously had not gathered together.

If the construction manager required a piece of plant and it was not shown to be in the yard, he was able to trace its location through the records and then contact the site management to ascertain its availability. This allowed a dialogue about plant usage to take place between managers that had previously only happened between plant management.

The senior construction managers were able to monitor the ratio of externally hired plant to company owned plant used on site, and they were in a position to query the hiring of external plant with the plant management. Under consideration would be the extra costs being incurred and the efficiency of service to repairing and maintaining plant, so that more working hours could be obtained from company owned plant.

Because the computer was running parallel to the manual procedures, it was only possible to note the managers' proposed use of the plant report rather than the action taken if it involved the ordering of external plant. This was because the generation of movement orders was the prerogative of the plant management and they were not part of the testing of the systems use. It was found that if the construction manager knew the availability status of plant in the yard, he could, if the plant was not in stock, place an external hire order. Also, the use of the report which listed the locations of a particular type of plant, such as cement mixers or dumper trucks, was limited because again the plant manager was responsible for moving plant for which the reports information would be necessary.

By observing the operation of the computer and manual plant control systems in parallel, it was seen that if the plant datafiles could be updated at the time of dealing with the orders, then the computer could without difficulty replace the manual procedures. Reporting facilities could be taken advantage of, including the ability to handle data more efficiently. The printer could be utilised to produce movement orders, the VDU to display information immediately without waiting for a hard copy; the keyboard introduced an element of conformity in producing data rather than various types of handwriting which were sometimes illegible.

The record book of plant would be absorbed by the disk storage technology, and the processing of updating records by the central processor. The updating of the plant records and the creation of plant orders need not then necessarily be done by the plant manager – it could be carried out by construction managers. Whether this devolution of authority is within the bounds of the company management policy is another issue.

The dataflow diagrams identified a transfer of information to the accounts department for charging for the use of plant. The system on the computer could be extended to take over this requirement by communicating to the computer held in the accounts department the movement and new locations of plant. Also the arrival and departure of plant at the site could be accounted for if the computer system was accessible.

Following the successful testing of the system within the company, which resulted in meeting the current needs of information upon plant by the construction management, the system was tested for reaction by other building companies. The testing was restricted to a shorter period, sufficient to demonstrate the other workings. Even without the benefits of longer term testing of the computer within the organisation, it was still possible, however, to note the management comments.

Again the reports shown were found to meet the managers' needs if the system was made available to them. There appeared to be a lack of such reports in these firms. In particular the report detailing the plant used on site with hire costs was considered to be currently most useful. The comments had to be viewed in the light of their own plant departments because other reports might be highlighted if a parallel test run could be carried out.

Revision of system development

The structured systems analysis methodology proved itself useful by allowing a view of the development area in relation to the overall system. The major dataflow inputs and outputs could be identified enabling the subsystem of administrating plant hire details to be considered as an overview, partitioned for development purposes from the other subsystems.

By taking a logical approach, the processes of plant hire could be grouped together without the problem of mixing or conflicting job specifications. The different levels of detail simplified the analysis by allowing a route to be taken through a process with the knowledge that other processes would not be affected.

Before drafting the dataflow diagrams it was deemed necessary to record the physical system in a written form so that this might be used for building the overview and subsequent lower levels.

The revision of the current logical model required defining the users' requirements. The diagrams formed the basis for review, enabling the user to understand clearly the extent of the system and the current processes involved. In so doing it was possible to specify the forms of plant reports based upon the available data.

The problem of introducing new technology is to determine which processes and datastores can be selected for application without disjointing the manual procedures. A graphic representation such as the dataflow diagram enables boundaries to be drawn around suitable application processes and then the observation of whether the remaining processes can be successfully handled by manual methods.

The structured analysis approach created a modular view of the system, each subsystem acting as a module which could be selected for further development. The programs, in turn, could be structured as modules to form the computer system software.

Therefore, if any changes to the design specification and computer programs were required, these could easily be carried out by acting upon a particular module – unlike a system where various inter-connected programs are responsible for a group of related processes.

BIBLIOGRAPHY

GANE and SARSON, *Structured Systems Analysis: Tools and Techniques*, Prentice Hall, 1979
T. DE MARCO, *Structured Analysis and System Specification*, Prentice Hall, 1979

ACKNOWLEDGEMENTS

This chapter is based on part of a research project funded by the Science and Engineering Research Council whilst the authors were employed at Leeds Polytechnic.

The co-operating firms were Irwin Construction, Cartwright Construction and Totty Construction.

7 Principal Factors in the Design and Practical Implementation of Computer-based Contract Control Systems *R. H. Neale*

INTRODUCTION

The widespread availability of microcomputers, and the associated publicity, has rekindled interest in the use of computers in the planning and control of construction projects. This has happened 20 years or so after the first enthusiastic experimentation with these aids to project management, the results of which were generally disappointing. It is true that some firms adopted computerised systems and found them useful, but the majority of firms who tried them subsequently rejected them. This is particularly true of construction contractors. Some of the reasons for this have been explained in a convincing way by Pascoe[1] in 1972. Strong arguments against the use of computers in planning and control were also expressed by Levi[2] in 1976. If the views of these practitioners can be expressed in a single generalisation, it is that the techniques and systems available at that time could not be easily integrated within the normal framework of construction project management because of their technical limitations and behavioural unacceptability. This, of course, prompts the question, 'What is so different about the microcomputer that will enable us to overcome all the previous difficulties?' In my view, the answer to this question is that the microcomputer has revolutionised the way in which the non-specialist views computing. An awareness of computing has permeated everyone's daily life, and this has fostered a new climate in the context of project management.

Of course, many of the old, fundamental problems remain, and some of these are discussed in this chapter, which is mainly based on my experience of the design and implementation of computer-based planning systems for construction contractors over the past eight years. From this experience a number of principal factors have been established: hardware, interactive computing, communications, software, the problems of data, integrated systems, planning methods, and some aspects of human behaviour. This selection and sequence of the factors does not imply that they are discrete and independent, because there is considerable overlap and interdependence.

HARDWARE

Hardware has been one of the main and early considerations in system design. Large contractors usually have substantial computing facilities to which they are committed financially and organisationally. Smaller contractors have perhaps only begun to contemplate the use of computers because small computers are now available so cheaply. This approach is understandable because most of the publicity has concentrated on the hardware, and its phenomenal capabilities.

Paradoxically, technological advances have made it possible to relegate the choice of machinery to a relatively late stage in the system design process. Modern computing is so powerful, flexible and relatively cheap that the major requirements of a planning and control system may be analysed and specified before the hardware is considered in detail. This is an important advance because it enables system design to be based on an analysis of the requirements of the firm, rather than on an assessment of machine capabilities.

This change means that the major question for the construction manager is no longer, 'What can the machine do?' but, 'What do I want to achieve, what is to be planned and controlled, and what is our yardstick?' This may be amplified by using a construction analogy – the distribution of concrete on a construction site. Today there is little doubt that the technology and plant exist to place concrete in any reasonably conceivable place in any reasonable quantity. Given a particular concreting problem to solve, the site agent starts by analysing the job to be done. The main factors are the quantity, the time available, the dimensions of the pours, the characteristics of the required concrete mix, the arrangement of the reinforcement, and so on. The selection of the plant – concrete pump, crane and skip, etc. – comes later. These will be evaluated against some criteria of time and cost.

Thus the choice of hardware should be made fairly late in the system design process, but the following associated technical factors must be considered at the start.

INTERACTIVE COMPUTING

The publicity which accompanied the advent of the very cheap computer overshadowed a much more important advance in computing: the interactive computer. Interactive computing has enabled the user to engage in a dialogue with the machine. Computing has therefore become immediate, responsive and flexible.

One immediate effect of this should be a reduction in the amount of paper produced by the machine. The dialogue between the user and the machine takes place via the visual display unit and only the final results of the dialogue need to be printed. If the purpose of the dialogue is to help the user to make a decision, there may be no need for anything to be printed on paper at all.

Not all computing needs to be interactive. Where, however, there are a number of alternative routes through a computation, an interactive program removes the need for the computer to produce the answers to all the possible questions every time it is used. This reduction in paper output must remove a significant cause of user disenchantment.

Interactive computing has led in turn to the development of 'user-friendly' programs, that is, programs that enable the user to use them easily by providing helpful description and advice and limiting the detrimental effect of input errors. Anyone who struggled to master some of the unreadable documents produced in the early days of computing (perhaps the definitive forms of 'user-hostility') must agree that user-friendly software has removed another significant cause of user disenchantment.

Small computers, interactive computers and user-friendly software developed concurrently; in fact, the development was interactive. These three aspects of modern computing have tended to coalesce in the current preoccupation with microcomputers. This is unfortunate because the aim of those concerned with providing a computer service to construction management must be the provision of attractive, useful and economic comput*ing* facilities. These facilities may use a microcomputer or they may not. The decision should be based on selecting the combination of computer and communication most appropriate to the particular circumstances.

COMMUNICATIONS

There are, broadly, three main ways in which construction sites may be provided with computing power: 'stand-alone' small computers, terminals connected to a central computer via a telephone line, and a mixture of these two which is often called 'distributed computing'.

There are powerful arguments for the use of small stand-alone computers on site. Some of these were summarised by Neale and Backus, as follows:[3]

1 '*Cost*. Telephone charges were estimated on the basis of two hours' use per day (ten hours per week), and it was just possible to acquire a minicomputer within this estimate. In fact the computer is currently in use for about twenty hours per week.

2 *Management attitude*. An on-site computer is a fixed or "overhead" cost, therefore there is every encouragement to use it as much as possible. Conversely, the telephone charges for the use of the remote computer increase directly with increasing use, thus provoking restraint.

3 *Novelty*. There was genuine interest in this new example of modern technology; most people were impatient to "have a go".

4 *Efficiency*. An on-site computer is independent from the telephone system; there are no "engaged" signals, breakdowns, crossed lines, or other telephone malfunctions.'

These small machines do many tasks very well – e.g. calculations for the analysis of a reinforced concrete beam. They also enable users to develop ideas informally and confidentially, rather than having to submit their intellectual embryos to the critical scrutiny of computer specialists. This is also the weakness of the microcomputer, in a managerial context: it is an insular and covert means of managerial analysis. Small computers on site which are operated independently of any other systems can therefore only fulfil the limited and perhaps introspective needs of the site itself. What is necessary is a means of satisfying the site's needs and also of establishing an exchange of information between site and head office.

Much of the data that construction management computing requires is derived from construction sites, which will in turn become more involved in the use of computer systems in the future. Construction sites are, of course, distributed throughout the land at varying distances from the contractor's head office and from each other. The capabilities of electronic communication should be, therefore, an important factor.

Thus the most obvious and straightforward alternative to an on-site computer is an on-site terminal connected to a central computer via the telephone system. Leased lines, networks of leased lines and now packet-switching services and similar innovations have made data transmission efficient and relatively cheap.

It may seem old-fashioned to advocate the use of on-site terminals connected to a remote mainframe computer, but in the context of construction management persuasive arguments can be made. The modern interactive mainframe will usually outperform a microcomputer in straightforward computing (depending upon the number of users making concurrent demands), and can also provide important additional facilities. If each site uses the computer for planning and control, the resource demands of each site may be easily aggregated to give the resource demands for the firm as a whole, and the performance of different sites may easily be compared. A similar facility can be used to control plant and optimise its use between sites; it can also be linked directly to computerised systems for charging and costing.

Additional facilities, such as 'electronic mail' and word processing may be offered. Such an arrangement enables the site staff to familiarise themselves with the use of just one set of hardware for all their computing and communication needs, whereas the microcomputer approach may require them to learn to use a number of quite different machines.

'Distributed computing', being a combination of the two approaches described above, is essentially a compromise, but a very sensible one. The following description is taken from a report produced by the Construction Industry Computing Association:[4]

'In distributed computing a central computer can be linked to a number of smaller satellite computers. The processing load and the storage of data can then be shared by the central and the satellite computers. There are obvious advantages in such an arrangement, and contractors have a lot to benefit from it because of the nature of their operations. A small computer installed on each site can solve many problems without overloading the host computer at head office, while still in a position to obtain large amounts of data from it which could not be stored locally. Conversely the storage in the host computer need not be full of data which have a significance only local to the company's individual departments.'

Another alternative is to use microcomputers which are simply interconnected by a telecommunications system. In fact, there is a wide range of alternatives and possibilities, and the selection of the appropriate computing system requires some fundamental analysis of the firm's methods of working and likely future developments. (This may be the main, perhaps sole, benefit from the introduction of a computer system!)

This analysis leads to the conclusion that construction companies need to develop a comprehensive strategy for acquiring and implementing construction management computing. The popular approach seems to be the search for microcomputer-based systems at minimum cost. As a long-term strategy it is inadequate because of its severely limited perspective. Modern computing and communications technology will, in time, completely change the way in which construction companies are administered, partly because so much of what is now done manually will be done electronically, and, as a consequence of this, the administration may be done in a different way.

SOFTWARE

One immediate effect of the introduction of user-friendly programs has been an increase in the cost of writing programs. If computing is to be effective, considerable effort has to be put into it. In the case of user-friendly programs, much of this effort must be put in by the programmer, rather than the user, so the cost of programming has increased as the cost of the hardware has decreased.

Table 7.1 lists some common and possible applications of computing in construction management. The list is arranged with the most common and well-proven applications at the bottom and the more erudite and little used at the top. These programs have been grouped into three broad groups: basic financial functions, management information, and decision analysis. A list of this sort cannot be exhaustive, the precise order must be debatable and the grouping is somewhat arbitrary, but the author believes that it is broadly correct. It will be used as a vehicle for discussion of the practical application of construction management computer programs.

The Basic Financial Functions provide few problems on their own and have been shown to be valuable; few companies do their accounts manually. The problems of application begin about half-way up Management Information. It is here that the design and application of the program become intertwined with management philosophy, so it

63

Table 7.1 Applications for construction management programs

Probabilistic and other advanced planning and scheduling packages	DECISION
Modelling and simulation	ANALYSIS
Investment appraisal	
Claims analysis	
Cash flow forecasting	
Estimating	
Contract planning and scheduling	MANAGEMENT
Plant control	INFORMATION
Internal valuations	
Contract costing	
Labour costing	
Applications	
Plant invoices and cost records	
Plant asset register	BASIC
Subcontract ledger	FINANCIAL
Sales ledger	FUNCTIONS
Bought ledger	
Payroll	

becomes difficult to achieve a consensus of opinion about what the program is expected to do and the way in which it must be done. There is little argument of this nature at the lower end of the list. For example, the method by which a site payroll must be prepared is well defined.

The natures of the tasks performed by the programs listed in Table 7.1 differ significantly. Those that appear at the lower end of the list offer straightforward numerical processing of accepted and necessary management functions. Those in the middle and above have to enshrine a specific management philosophy so that the machine can be given an unambiguous set of clear instructions. Such programs will be useful only if both the program and the enshrined philosophy are properly applied. The suppliers of such programs must therefore be prepared to provide substantial and continuing consultancy and training support. Ideally software would be written for each individual company's needs but, because software is expensive, this may only be seen as an 'economic' solution for the large company who will expect to use such a system extensively or where the magnitude of the problem justifies the expense.

Although the 'economic' solution will often be to acquire ready-made software, this will only be approximately compatible with the firm's existing (manual) systems. The process of adjustment may cause severe organisational problems, and it is from such problems that many computer 'horror stories' originate. The resulting imperfect implementation negates the original 'economic' decision, and thus gives economic weight to the organisational approach to system design. After all, a specially designed but expensive system that 'works' will give an infinitely higher return on investment than an 'economic' system that does not.

Thus an argument can be developed that, almost regardless of expense, the specification of a system should evolve through highly participatory discussion with potential users. Such an approach is argued cogently by Eason.[5]

The weakness of this approach is that most potential users do not know how to design a computer system, and may not be sufficiently experienced in the use of systems to predict future problems. They have no alternative, therefore, but to press for a minutely detailed replica of the current manual system. This gives rise to various problems, some of which are caused by data.

THE PROBLEMS OF DATA

Computers are ideal for finite element analysis and analyses with similar characteristics: that is, using extensive, repetitive and tedious methods of calculation which require relatively little input data. They are also suited to financial analysis such as payroll calculations, where a relatively large quantity of basic data is used repeatedly – weekly or monthly – at the initiation of relatively trivial current data.

Managerial analyses usually have quite different characteristics. Most managerial analyses are of complicated and interrelated managerial issues, usually involving the relationship of resources and time. If the issue were not complicated and interrelated it could be resolved without using a computer, but to use the computer the necessary data must be assembled and input. This may be an immense task, giving rise to the well-known management-science contrivance that these data can then be used repeatedly to explore a large number of alternative possibilities.

In theory, the management-science approach is sound; it is only by diligently generating and evaluating alternatives that the 'best' managerial decision may be made. In practice, managers have neither the time nor the mental energy to generate a large number of alternatives and, if they did, few would need a computer to analyse their important and crucial effects. Many could be quickly rejected on the grounds of human acceptability, obvious costs or delays, or for other simple and obvious reasons.

The surviving alternatives may then proceed for computerised analysis, and here the management-science contrivance is exposed because it is unlikely that the alternatives will all use the same data. Some will be common to all, but in the author's experience a substantial proportion will be specific to each. Only fairly simple alternatives can be simply generated: using fewer resources on an activity and so extending its duration; delaying one or a number of interrelated activities; or varying the planned length of the working week, are all examples of simple alternatives.

Any real alternatives usually depend upon alternative *construction* methods rather than alternative *scheduling* methods, and consequently each alternative method requires some input data that must be specifically acquired. To generate the input data for a detailed analysis of a number of alternative methods requires more time, effort and diligence than is generally available in construction firms: engineering analyses, discussions with colleagues, sub-contractors and perhaps the engineer; estimation of outputs and durations; estimation of the costs of resources, with the attendant meetings and telephone calls in the search for information; these are all examples of the necessary activities. It is, in the author's view, one of the major reasons why computer systems fail to provide the benefits they should.

Any review of the published literature on this subject would show a predominance of the management-science viewpoint, with a few strident exceptions. Principal among these is a paper by Lindblom,[6] 'The science of muddling through', which argues that the generation and analysis of wide-ranging alternatives is only possible for small, simple problems, and otherwise would consume disproportionate time and resources. His practical conclusion is that most people work towards a decision by appraising a limited number of alternatives, which adopt familiar and well-proven methods.

The generality of the author's view on data is supported by Professor D. C. Hague in his text-book *Managerial economics*.[7] The following is an extract from a section entitled 'Problems of information':

'On the one hand, a firm should not be expected to collect *all* the information which might possibly be relevant to its decisions. Information is expensive to collect; the right information may be even more expensive to collect. On the other hand, even when information has been collected, it still has to be used. The businessman taking a decision needs the right information at the right point in the firm at the right moment. This does not always happen. Those who research into business problems are often surprised how much information, expensively collected, is left unused when the decisions on which it has a bearing come to be taken. This explains a fear that one has about the advent of large, high-speed computers. One wonders whether in future even more information will remain unused in the computer's memory store than at present lies unused in the firm's filing cabinets and on its punched cards.'

Further problems occur with input and validation. Input problems may be simply but perhaps expensively overcome by delegating the task to those who are employed specifically to undertake such tasks: typists and data preparers. The validation problem is much more difficult to overcome, and it exists on two levels. The first level is when the data are validated managerially and technically, e.g. does the sum of the estimated labour and plant costs allocated to each activity equal the expected total? The second level is to determine whether any errors occurred during the preparation or input of these data. This may be such a time-consuming and tedious task that it is not uncommon for an exasperated engineer or manager to introduce a fictitious activity into a plan to absorb these errors, thus contriving 'validated' output from erroneous input!

Earlier in this chapter it was argued that system design should begin with a study of the major, functional, requirements of planning and control; it should not begin with a study of the hardware available. The immediately preceding discussion has established that the major constraint is the acquisition, preparation, input and validation of data. This problem is fundamental to most management systems, because they generally require the drawing together of diffuse but interrelated data. A system for the planning and control of construction work is typical of such systems, requiring information about progress in terms of time and value, and resources in terms of wage, plant, materials and other costs; it is clear that the preparation of such data will involve most departments in a construction firm.

The major practical constraint of data forces the construction manager to make a fundamental choice between two system design strategies:

1 *Simple system and simplified data.* The use of a simple system reduces the data problem because it demands fewer data; in addition, the simplicity of the analyses done by the system may make it unnecessary for the data to be minutely realistic, with consequent savings in the effort and time required to acquire and prepare them. The advocates of such systems argue that management decisions are ultimately about making a fairly crude choice between alternative courses of action, all of which are based on some analysis of uncertain future events. Thus simple systems are adequate.

2 *'Realistic' system with 'realistic' data.* Such systems attempt to model the actual complexities of the activities involved in the management of construction sites, and thus demand actual costs, values, etc., as input data. They are conceived in an attitude that 'we have to get it right'. They require a frontal attack on the data problem.

Strong supporting arguments can be made for both strategies, but the deciding factor is behavioural rather than technical. The technical, computing, factors are nevertheless important, because they involve the arguments for and against integrated systems.

INTEGRATED SYSTEMS

Returning to Table 7.1, there is obviously some merit in linking some of these programs. Data used and produced by the payroll program, for example, could be useful as input to the labour costing and contract costing programs, and in this way the idea of the integrated system was born. This is obviously difficult: if anyone doubts this let them try to draw it out on a piece of paper, using only the most obvious interactions. Integrated systems also create difficulties because all sorts of things will be happening which are entirely beyond the user's immediate and direct control, e.g. the act of entering information relating to the change of location of an item of plant may also generate an invoice and an accounting entry – automatically. There are thus sound reasons for keeping all the programs quite separate, which match fairly conveniently with the use of independent small computers: 'stand-alone' programs on 'stand-alone' small computers. In this way many of the problems of integration may be eliminated.

The counter-argument is that the data used by these programs are related and this must be accepted by the system designer. A very simple example of this may be taken from the work of Neale and Backus.[3] The on-site minicomputer was used for short-term planning and control, and required the calculation of the cost and value for each activity. The section engineers were required to use this system and were also required to calculate the operatives' bonus manually. Many of the calculations done in the planning and bonus analyses were very similar and used the same data. The section engineers felt that it was unnecessary for them to have to do two sets of essentially similar calculations which used the same input, and in response to this pressure the research team wrote a program for bonus and then integrated the two systems. The section engineers were thus relieved of a chore in return for using the short-term planning and control system, which they therefore found more attractive.

To quote again from the CICA report referred to above:

'Systems which are not integrated may involve substantial duplication of work. However efficient a program may be, it cannot do anything without data which at some stage will have to be given to it by the user. Data preparation can be a formidable task. Ironically there is a tendency for simpler programs to be more demanding in data preparation than more complicated ones.* The Design Office Consortium has found in previous evaluation reports that the cost of data preparation ranges from one to four times the cost of computing. This suggests that data preparation should be made as easy for the user as possible, even if this means a more expensive program. It suggests, furthermore, that it is worth integrating groups of applications' programs so that the results from one program can be passed on as data to the next one with as little interference by the user as possible.'[4]

The solution must be to adopt some reasonable middle road between 'stand-alone' programs and a fully integrated system. The clue to how this may be done is given in the passage from the previous paragraph, 'it is worth integrating groups of applications' programs'. Full inte-

---

* Author's note: this is because the data have to be pre-processed manually before the program will accept the 'simple' data.

gration of all programs will be difficult and costly. Integration of groups of closely related programs is more feasible. Other, less closely related programs may only need to be linked loosely and sparsely.

PLANNING METHODS

Barnes and Wright have stated the fundamental principle:

> 'Experience has shown that, in project management systems, it is important to use the computer only to do simple things. The computer should add only the ability to do these things on a scale and at a speed which is superhuman. Computation using unfamiliar or sophisticated mathematical relationships, although acceptable in design work, prevents a management system becoming widely or confidently used.'[8]

This approach truncates the hierarchy of application shown in Fig. 7.1. The vital aspect of a planning method is that it be accepted by its potential users.

There are a dozen or so 'new', interactive, small-computer-based planning and control systems currently available. Most of them make full use of modern computing facilities – graphics, split screens, 132 character-wide displays and so on. Conceptually, however, they are disappointing because they have concentrated on making the existing techniques easier to use, rather than using this advanced computing power to develop those techniques further to fulfil the user's real needs. This may be illustrated by considering some aspects of network analysis, a common planning technique.

Most of the planning and control systems available are based on network analysis more or less as described in text-books. Formal network analysis produces a list of the earliest start, latest start, total float, free float and perhaps independent float and other analyses. The objective of this is to enable the user to identify which activities are critical (i.e. have no float) and those which are not (i.e. those that have float). Thus the manager may concentrate his attention and resources on critical activities, and manipulate the timings of the non-critical activities to make the best use of available resources. In some circumstances this information will be most useful: if the construction manager intends to adopt the management-science approach and explore all possibilities; if the job being analysed is extraordinarily complex or novel; or if the construction manager is extraordinarily inexperienced. None of these circumstances occurs in the general run of construction work. By the time a competent and experienced construction manager has prepared the basic plan, including the logical relationships between activities, he will have acquired a fundamental understanding of the project. By the time he has completed the extremely difficult task of estimating activity durations, he will have acquired most of the knowledge available to him in the float listing referred to earlier. He will do this intuitively, perhaps with a few elementary calculations, but, because he has 'built the job in his mind', he will have acquired a deeper understanding of the project than he can obtain from a listing of float calculations.

Such a listing will therefore contain a large quantity of data that, at best, is largely redundant. Because it ignores the manager's experience and ability, it may be insulting, and because of the way in which float is calculated and listed, it may be misleading. To illustrate this a float analysis of the network shown in Fig. 7.1 could result in the listing shown in Table 7.2.

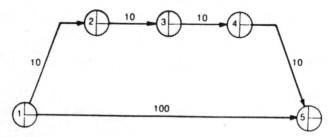

7.1 *Network with unconstrained chain of non-critical activities*

Table 7.2 Float analysis of network in Fig. 7.1

Activity	Duration	Early start	Latest start	Total float	Free float
1–2	10	0	60	60	0
2–3	10	10	70	60	0
3–4	10	20	80	60	0
4–5	10	30	90	60	60
1–5	100	0	0	0	0

Activity 1–5 is obviously critical; activities 1–2, 2–3, 3–4 and 4–5 are obviously not, and each has a total float of 60. This total float sums to 240 units in a project of 100 units duration. This is clearly impossible, and occurs because the four non-critical activities are in an unconstrained chain and so share the 60 unit float; if 1–2 is delayed 60 units, the four 'non-critical' activities of 10 units' duration must be completed in the remaining 40 units of time, so the total float has obviously evaporated. Although the calculations have been made correctly, according to current practice, an important anomaly has occurred. In the case of this simple example, it is obvious, but if the network shown had been merely part of a large network, it is quite possible that the events could be numbered as shown in Fig. 7.2. The float calculations would not then be listed in the sequence of the 'chain' which gives rise to the anomaly, but would occur scattered throughout the listing according to some rule related to the event numbers. This presents the construction manager with an unnerving problem in interpretation.

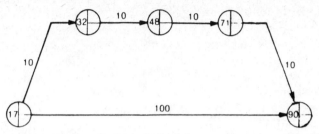

7.2 *The network of Fig. 7.1 renumbered as it may appear as part of a large network*

The end result of this analysis is not ideal for resource management. The overall inference is that the logical construction sequence portrayed by the network diagram is paramount, and the non-critical activities are then shuffled around to minimise the resource demands. This may be the case in complex construction work, and is usually the basis for the initial, strategic, planning of all construction projects. However, once the commitment has been made to a particular strategy, the emphasis changes from construction logic to resource utilisation. At the critical level, the logic – i.e. the construction methods – will be changed where possible under the fierce pressures of cost and resource availability. Thus the computer system must allow plans to be 'resource-driven', rather than 'logic-driven'.

This discussion on planning methods has been developed to make the point that implementation of planning and control systems is made much easier if the system itself is devised to suit the real needs of the potential users. A modern computing system should be based on an analysis of the manager's job and the way in which he analyses and solves problems. This analysis would reveal where the manager has to make decisions based on intuition, which would benefit from computational analysis. Systems could then be devised which use the existing mandatory system as a source of basic data, to give the manager the information he actually needs.

SOME ASPECTS OF HUMAN BEHAVIOUR

One of the objects of the system discussed in this chapter is control, and this implies the exercise of managerial power. Implicit also is the likelihood that the exercise of this power will be resisted, and this is, of course, a reason why systems are unsuccessful.

At its most naïve the philosophy behind the introduction of a planning and control system is based on the concept of the site manager as a decisive and strong person who continually strives to maximise profits. Therefore, he should have a good system to help him in his work. Naturally, the system will be used to monitor the site manager's performance, and will thus help senior management to identify the good site managers and generally to control the company. (An interesting result of this is that site managers tend to favour self-contained micro-computer systems, whereas senior, Head Office, management may find centralised computing more attractive!).

In practice, such an approach to site management would be unbearably abrasive for the site manager. Instead, he will endeavour to turn in a reasonable profit rather than the maximum possible profit. This will enable him to deflect the most intractable managerial problems rather than attack them directly. This behaviour is perfectly natural, sensible and mature, but an overtly rational and analytical control system will expose it. The manager's traditional defence of this has been to attack the obvious technical inadequacies of the system, because this is much safer than an explicit defence of the cause of his resistance. Thus we have the traditional criticism of manual control systems: 'I'm here to run the job and make a profit, not to sit filling in forms while we make a loss'. The computer systems of 15 years ago gave site management wonderful extensions of this argument, because the form-filling was perhaps increased and resulted in reports which were both cryptic and voluminous. Modern computing offers facilities to overcome most of the technical objections. Thus, the fundamental managerial problems become exposed, and on the modern construction site these problems may be very real and very difficult to solve. The main point to note is that modern computing may resolve some apparent problems but expose some fundamental ones.

It is very likely that the conflict inherent in control systems cannot be satisfactorily resolved. Instead, the system has to provide the users with some tangible benefits which may be set against the unattractive aspects. In this way, the system may have an *overall* attraction to the users. An example of this has been previously discussed on p. 68, where site engineers undertook to use a computer-based planning and control system, and in return were relieved of much of the tedium of bonus calculations. This simple example also served to illustrate a further development of this approach. Bonus calculations have to be done: they are part of the system of making wage payments, and consequently the timely performance of this task is mandatory. The pressures on site management are such that only tasks such as this will be done regularly and reliably. The chances of a system being used are enhanced if a substantial proportion of it derives naturally from mandatory functions – wages, valuations, and plant charging.

Eason[5] describes the human aspects of these systems in detail. The following passage is taken from the abstract:

'An essential point is that it is not enough to understand the technology; effective implementation demands the ability to establish organisational needs and to choose a form of technology which will meet them.

The paper examines three ways of designing systems. Firstly, a technology-led approach which leads to "fire fighting" when the negative organisational effects become apparent. A second method has tried to compensate for this by involving users in the design process. Unfortunately, by the time the users have come to terms with their new task and are able to make a contribution, the system has usually been designed.

The third method of design expressly seeks to give users the time and opportunity to learn how to contribute to design, by making the design process evolutionary, i.e. by building slowly from small systems to large ones and retaining the flexibility to change. Within this concept user learning and adaptation is promoted by pilot systems, user design exercises, user support and evaluation procedures. It is only by these methods that users can be given the confidence and knowledge to exploit the potential of the new technology.'

Such an approach places great emphasis on the development of an understanding of modern computing in the system's users. It is here that the microcomputer-based system can make a tremendous contribution. The author has on several occasions been involved in training courses where the participants were given an opportunity to use these small systems themselves, and they aroused strong interest and motivation.

The most popular microcomputer-based systems cost about the same as the most popular company cars. Seen in this context, they are not a large capital investment which must be agonised over, with careful research being done on the likely financial returns. Rather, they should be seen as a cheap way of promoting understanding in the firm, so that subsequent investment in a more extensive system, that suits the firm's needs more specifically, is well spent. This learning process may be enhanced by the intermediate use of more substantial 'ready-made' packages that may be leased, rented or obtained from a bureau service.

As a final behavioural note, the introduction of BS 6046[9] is a significant indication of the importance of behavioural factors. Part 1 of this document is entitled 'Guide to the use of management, planning, review and reporting procedures', and is very nearly a British Standard on project management.

CONCLUSIONS

This chapter argues against the current preoccupation with 'stand-alone' microcomputer-based control systems. It nevertheless recognises that these small systems have generated great enthusiasm for this important computer application, and this enthusiasm should be encouraged. They have been found to be very attractive to participants on training courses, and the principal benefit to be gained from their use may be educational. This will help to overcome an obvious and vital human obstacle to the practical implementation of contract control systems: the potential users' lack of technical understanding.

The point has also been made that the systems which predated interactive computing and its concurrent developments 'could not easily be integrated with the normal framework of construction project management' (p. 59). The practical weaknesses of the classical management-science approach have been exposed, particularly in regard to their requirements for the generation and systematic analysis of a number of alternative strategies. The disconcerting practical inadequacies of 'text-book' techniques have also been illustrated.

A pragmatic approach has therefore been advocated, which aims to provide conceptually simple systems which facilitate the natural way in which construction managers naturally work. A major effort has to be made to provide the user with systems that respond to his real needs, and consequently to seek a real and substantial user involvement in the design and implementation of the system. This should ensure that each potential user derives tangible benefit from the use of the system to compensate for any discomfort. This implies that each company has to develop its own systems, otherwise this involvement and commitment cannot be mobilized. This approach demands some considerable knowledge from the user, and further emphasises the educational potential of the microcomputer. It also suggests that more substantial 'ready-made' packages may be used as a further means of acquiring computing knowledge and experience. These may be acquired from a bureau, or leased or rented, and may thus be readily disposed of when the company is ready to produce its own system.

One of the major constraints is the preparation, input and validation of meaningful data. This inherent problem is magnified by most users' preference for using 'real' (i.e. actual, detailed) information rather than some simplified but approximately valid data; and by the natural pressures of construction management which provide little time or incentive for the preparation of data specifically for use by a planning and control system. The elimination of this major constraint is beyond the power of any conceivable computer system. The most practical way forward is to devise a system that links together data that are currently used for other, mandatory purposes, so that relatively small sets of data are required to fill the 'gaps'.

This solution to the data problem is compatible with the conclusions on p. 73, and thus completes a general strategy for the design and implementation of computer-based contract control systems.

ACKNOWLEDGEMENTS

The author wishes to express his thanks to E. Bates, G. Bull, S. J. Backus and D. A. Morrison of Bovis Civil Engineering Ltd; Dr M. E. Fleming of Construction Computing; A. Lester, Foster Wheeler Power Products Ltd; Mrs Brenda Wroe, Leicester Polytechnic; Professor E. G. Trimble, Loughborough University of Technology; D. E. Neale, May Gurney and Company Ltd, and Dr Martin Barnes of Project Software Ltd. The author has also benefited greatly from a regular involvement in training courses on this subject at the Cement and Concrete Association Training Centre, and wishes to offer his sincere thanks to C. A. R. Harris and R. V. Watson of their staff, and to the participants in these courses.

REFERENCES

1   PASCOE, W. A., *The use of network analysis in practice, a personal view* (Internet (UK) seminar 19 September 1972). A transcript is held at Department of Civil Engineering, Loughborough University of Technology.
2   LEVI, A., The human factor in network analysis, *Project Manager*, 1976, **1**, 10–14
3   NEALE, R. H. and BACKUS, S. J., Short term planning and control using an on-site minicomputer. *Small computer systems and their applications in construction*. Institution of Civil Engineers, London, 1980, 41–53
4   CONSTRUCTION INDUSTRY COMPUTING ASSOCIATION. Computer programs for construction management, *User Report No. 4*, Cambridge, 1979
5   EASON, K. D., The process of introducing information technology. *Behaviour Inf. Technol.*, 1982, **1**, No. 2, 197–213
6   LINDBLOM, C. E., The science of 'muddling through'. *Business strategy* (ed. I. G. Ansoff). Penguin Education, London, 1969
7   HAGUE, D. C., *Managerial economics*. Longmans, London, 1969
8   BARNES, N. M. L. and WRIGHT, Q., Project cost model on site. *Small computer systems and their applications in construction*. Institution of Civil Engineers, London, 1980, 31–40
9   BRITISH STANDARDS INSTITUTION. *Use of network techniques in project management*. BSI, London, 1981, BS 6046

8 Interactive Graphics in Project Planning and Control
M. Jackson

PLANNING AND CONTROL AS A DESIGN PROCESS

Design has been defined in an authoratative book on the subject as 'decision making in extreme uncertainty with high penalties for failure'[1] and this definition would certainly be seen by most project planners as applying exactly to their risky occupation. The project planner is concerned with the fixing of construction method, he does it before the event occurs and therefore in a state of uncertainty.

The decision making concerning project method does not, of course, stop when the work actually starts on the construction site. There is a very real limit to the amount of detail which can be given to the plan before activity starts, for much depends on the particular conditions of the project, and this detail is added as the day-to-day decisions concerning the running of the project are made. This adding of detail after the start of construction work is often carried out by different people from those responsible for the initial planning and is given a different name: project control. This separation of planning and control within organisations is to be regretted, for it masks the fact that planning and control are each part of one continuous process, the formation of a construction method in increasing detail as data flows to the decision

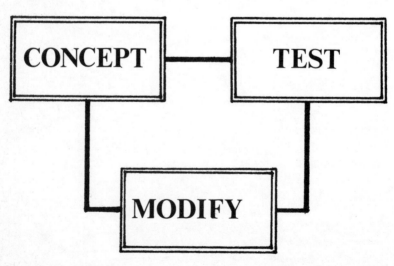

8.1 *The design cycle*

maker first from the contract documents and pre-tender investigations and later from the records of the project itself.

Planning and control are, then, one operation, and consideration of the classical diagram of design shows that they are design operations. Fig. 8.1 shows how the design process works: an idea is modelled in some way, the model is tested and, if found to be less than satisfactory, is changed. The cycle is repeated as many times as is required to enable the designer to reach a satisfactory solution.

For the project planner/controller, the same iterative process is necessary. He must be able to model the project and must be able to apply a test of the acceptability of the solution. The analysis of the model, although important, is only one part of the design cycle. Equally important is the ability of the designer quickly to understand the results produced by the model, and also the ease with which he can change the model in order to develop his ideas.

THE EARLY USE OF COMPUTERS IN PROJECT PLANNING

Computers were applied to construction planning some twenty years ago. In the early 'sixties the invention of the Critical Path Method and PERT coincided with the installation in many of the larger companies in the construction industry of computers for Head Office accounting. Critical Path Analysis is a simple arithmetical technique and it seemed obvious that the arithmetical power of the computer should be used to do the analysis. Such applications of computers usually proved to be less successful than had been hoped and one of the reasons for this lack of success can be seen in Fig. 8.2. Fig. 8.2 shows for a notional 100 activity network the proportions of time spent on different tasks by a planner producing a project plan. As can be seen, the analysis of the network constitutes less than 5 per cent of the time spent on the operation and, as most project planners are highly numerate, this 5 per cent consists of work which is quite enjoyable.

If the analysis work is carried out by centralised computer, as shown in the second diagram in Fig. 8.2, then there is a new activity, that of 'keying in' the planning data, and the analysis activity becomes of negligible duration. Often the input of data for one of the early programs would require more time than would the analysis of the network by hand, and thus there was a net increase in time and, what was worse, the analysis, which was pleasant, was replaced by an error-prone and unpopular data input phase.

Fig. 8.2 shows that confining computer applications to analysis is inefficient in that it provides help where it is not needed, the data input is unpleasant, the machines are frequently inaccessible, the output is often presented in acutely indigestible form, and the computers cannot make a significant contribution until the whole of the design cycle, not merely the analysis, is computer aided.

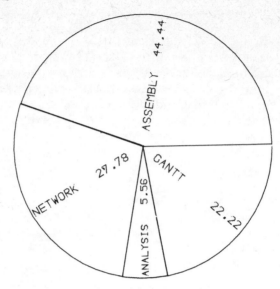

a) Manual Analysis

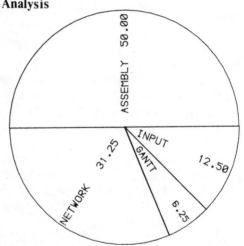

b) Simple Computer Analysis with Graphical Output

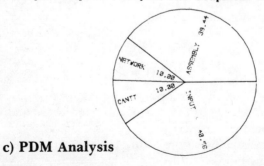

c) PDM Analysis

8.2 *The effect of computerisation*

THE NEEDS OF INTERACTION

Design is, by its nature, iterative, and the most efficient way to use a computer for an iterative process is through interactive programming, using the machine to provide the background for decisions which the designer must take. Interactive programming requires two features: it requires that the machine should be easily accessible, preferably in the designers' normal work space, and that the information produced by the machine should be such that it is quickly and accurately assimilated by the designer.

It is only in the last half decade that these two features have begun to become widely available in the project planning environment. Firstly, the rapidly reducing cost of computer hardware is making computers available to even the lowest levels of design staff and site management, and, secondly, the increasing power of even very small and cheap computers is making the use of graphic techniques, confined until recently to the more prestigious research establishments, commonplace. Thus, the new generation of computer hardware, cheap and with the capability of high quality graphics, is making real interactive design possible for the project planner and for his colleagues in the other engineering design disciplines. The planner is now in a position to use the computer throughout the design cycle, not only in the analysis of the model, but also in the building of the model and the presentation of the results obtained. It is helpful, therefore, to consider in detail the way in which interactive graphics can contribute to data output, data input, the direction of the computer program itself, and to data capture.

DATA OUTPUT

The early computer programs produced output consisting of columns of numbers produced by a line printer. Although the construction industry has traditionally used charts (notably Gantt Charts) as its means of communication, only rarely were the computer-produced figures converted by draughtsmen into charts; too often the user of the planning information was expected to glean what information he could from the printed output. Not surprisingly the communication was neither good nor popular.

Today the situation has changed and the need for understandable output is universally recognised. Usually this need is being met by some form of graphics. Hard copy graphical output will normally be produced by plotters, although line printers are sometimes used for this purpose on low budget installations.

The use of a line printer for the production of hard copy output has the obvious advantage that the line printer is a cheap and universally available tool. Line printers have been successfully used for the production of Gantt Charts on several packages, particularly those written for use with microcomputers. They do, however, suffer from

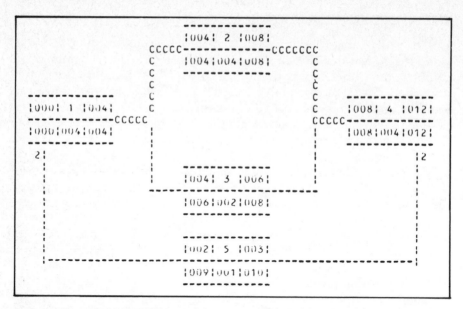

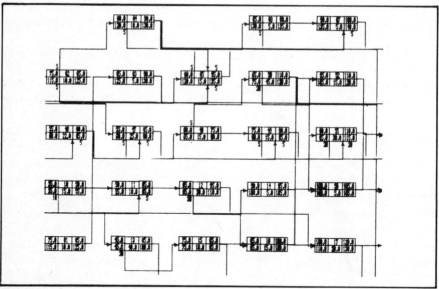

8.3 *A comparison of printed and plotted networks*

the major disadvantage that the charts they produce look significantly different from those produced by a draughtsman. Experience in the use of such charts in industry suggests that the appearance of the chart creates some resistance. It is clear, however, that a chart produced in this way is far superior to the purely numeric output of the past.

The alternatives to the line printer are the increasing number of hard copy devices which are now available to the graphics market, including sophisticated printers and pen plotters. The price of these devices is now falling rapidly and thus the major disadvantage to their use, that of inaccessibility and cost, is rapidly disappearing. The major advantage of these devices is the quality which they provide. Fig. 8.3 contrasts a network diagram produced on a line printer with one produced on a pen plotter.

If planning is to be interactive, the output of information from the analysis of the model must be presented not only as hard copy, normally required only for the presentation of the results of the last design cycle, but also as screen displays. Here again the rapid reduction in the cost of computer power has brought a dramatic change. Graphical screens can now present information very quickly and with the same quality as produced by a pen plotter, but the strengths and weaknesses of the two media must be understood if they are to be effectively used.

The plotter can produce very large diagrams either through the use of a drum feed or through the (rather inconvenient) piecing together of separate sections. These diagrams are of high quality but are produced relatively slowly. In contrast, screen displays are limited to the rather small size of the normal terminal screen, but they are produced with great speed. Thus, if a large diagram is to be presented on a screen, it is both necessary and possible to examine it section by section either through continuous or stepwise scrolling.

The Gantt Chart is well suited to examination by scrolling: the user can either scroll vertically, examining the various activities which are to occur within a period, or horizontally, examining the position of a group of activities within the project. Scrolling is not as successful for network displays, where neither the vertical nor the horizontal position of a particular activity is either known or significant. Experience has shown, therefore, that for interactive use the most useful form of output is a scrolled Gantt Chart, while for the presentation of the results of design, the final project plan, a diagram consisting of both a Gantt Chart and a network is desirable. Fig. 8.4 shows such an output.

Although the Gantt Chart has been found to be the most suitable form of output for interactive use, it has the disadvantage of not showing explicitly the dependencies upon which it is built. Clearly a linked bar chart would remove this disadvantage, but a linked bar chart is difficult to read if the project is complex, and doubly difficult if vertical scrolling is required. To overcome this difficulty, it has been found convenient to give the operator the facility of interrogating the displayed Gantt Chart. A display such as shown in Fig. 8.5 is produced, and the operator is given the option of being given further information which, if taken, produces a display such as that in the lower section of Fig. 8.5. This device produces the information the planner needs in great detail if and when he requires it.

A final area of interest concerning output is the use of colour. Colour graphics have been available on pen plotters for several years and are now also available on the screens of graphics terminals of quite modest

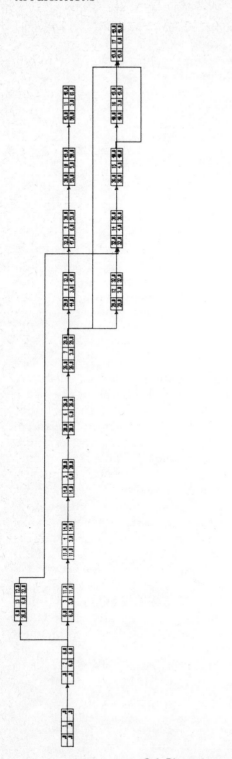

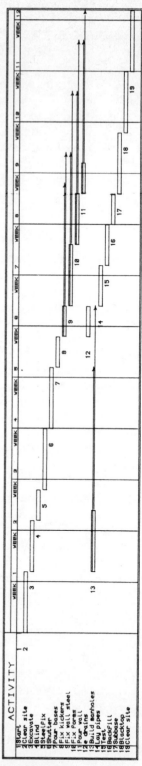

8.4 *Plotted output for a simple network*

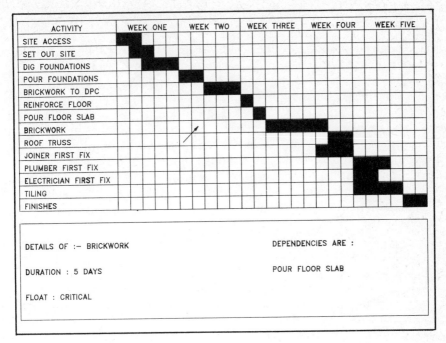

ACTIVITY	WEEK ONE	WEEK TWO	WEEK THREE	WEEK FOUR	WEEK FIVE
SITE ACCESS					
SET OUT SITE					
DIG FOUNDATIONS					
POUR FOUNDATIONS					
BRICKWORK TO DPC					
REINFORCE FLOOR					
POUR FLOOR SLAB					
BRICKWORK					
ROOF TRUSS					
JOINER FIRST FIX					
PLUMBER FIRST FIX					
ELECTRICIAN FIRST FIX					
TILING					
FINISHES					

DETAILS OF :— BRICKWORK   DEPENDENCIES ARE :

DURATION : 5 DAYS   POUR FLOOR SLAB

FLOAT : CRITICAL

8.5 *An enhanced Gantt display*

price. Our experience at Newcastle, where the use of interactive graphics in project planning has been the subject of research for several years, is that the use of colour for the presentation of data is so effective as to be virtually indispensable. The simple device of picking out the critical path through a network in a contrasting colour can transform a diagram which is so complex as to be almost useless as a means of support of managerial decisions, into an almost self-explanatory medium. Coloured bar charts can show not only the critical and non-critical activities, but also those which have been carried out, or those which use a particular resource.

If the key to interaction is the rapid assimilation of the data produced by the model, then graphical output has provided a major step forward in the true CAD of project plans.

DATA INPUT

The brief analysis of the tasks comprising the establishment of a project plan, which was illustrated by Fig. 8.2, showed how the early computer programs required considerable effort for the assembly and input of data. Two factors have combined to reduce the need for this expensive preparation. They are the development and introduction of the Precedence Diagram Method (PDM) of network representation and

83

analysis, and the increasing availability of good quality graphics displays.

Although, superficially, PDM and CPM are similar, both modelling the project as a network of linked activities and both being analysed by the same arithmetical technique, they are in fact markedly different, for the CPM links represent both activities and also the flow of logic, whereas in PDM the links represent logic alone. This difference becomes most apparent when the structure of the network is being defined – as at the input stage of a computer analysis – for CPM requires the prior drawing of a network so that the network nodes can be numbered. PDM, on the other hand, requires no prior drawing of the network, and the structure is unambiguously defined by the specification of precedent activities. Using PDM it is possible, therefore, to list the various activity parameters, the duration and the precedent activities and to analyse the network without actually drawing the network diagram. Clearly this reduces the work of the planner and is to be welcomed.

This reduction in the preparation time has been exploited by the many excellent PDM programs which are now available. Most of these programs continue to rely on alphanumeric input of data, but in most cases care has been taken to ensure that the input phase is as user-friendly as is possible in an environment which must of necessity include a typewriter keyboard.

The second factor to affect data input is, of course, the low cost, high quality graphics now available. The use of graphics as a basis for data entry brings the advantages of user-friendliness: operators enjoy using graphical input, the work is now interesting and the operator is less error prone, and the ease of checking gross errors becomes immediately obvious. Two data input routines will be described in detail: the input of activity names and durations, and the input of dependencies.

Activity input

A recent program[2] has used a horizontal histogram display for the input of activity details; the display is shown in Fig. 8.6. The column to the left side gives the names of the various activities, while the bar opposite each name represents the activity duration. Similar charts could be used for other activity parameters, cost and resource use perhaps being the most obvious. The input to the chart is controlled by some form of digitiser, a cursor or a lightpen.

To operate on the chart, the user indicates either a blank line or an existing activity, if he wishes to change or, perhaps, to delete it. Depending upon his choice between these alternatives, he will be instructed either to type in a new title and then to indicate the duration on the chart with the lightpen, or to indicate the new duration of an existing activity. If the graphics display is of the raster type and indepen-

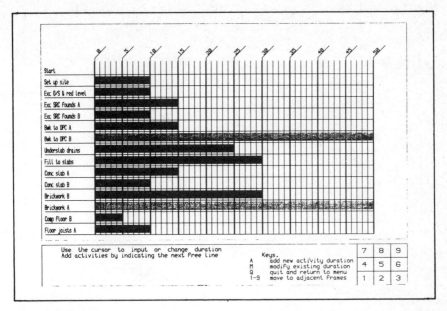

8.6 *The duration histogram*

dent windows are available, then these instructions can be displayed in a window separate from the main display.

Clearly a display of this form cannot give information concerning all the activities in the network. Similarly it may be that the duration or cost of some activities may require a wider grid. Both these problems are overcome by scrolling. Stepwise scrolling, where the new origin is indicated on the chart using the lightpen, and the chart is redrawn, has been found to be effective, particularly where the speed of drawing is such that a continuous rolling scroll would be very slow.

The histogram input has been found to be pleasant to use and error free. The freedom from errors emanates, it is thought, from the fact that what was previously a chore is now a relatively pleasant task, and that the display is such that errors are immediately apparent.

The dependency matrix

It was noted above that, using PDM, it is possible fully to define a network without constructing the network diagram. The property is exploited in the second of the input devices to be described, the dependency matrix. In order to use a lightpen to indicate a link between activities, a displayed activity list is required and the user should indicate first the dependent and then the precedent, that is A, the first, is dependent and B, the second, is precedent. Although such a system of specifying links is possible, it is clumsy: the user must indicate two points on the screen for each link and it is difficult to indicate on the screen those links which have previously been specified. An alternative method is to display lists side by side and to indicate first the dependent

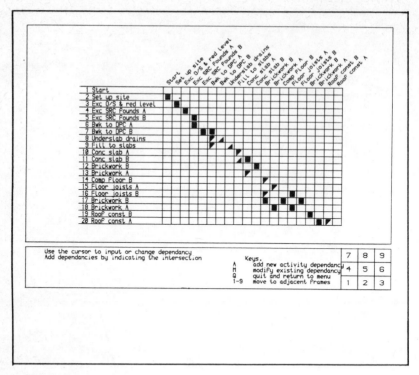

8.7 *The dependency matrix*

on the right hand list and then the precedent on the left. Existing links can be indicated by plotting lines between precedent and dependent. Again, two points must be indicated and, although links can be shown, the display becomes difficult to scroll.

A solution to this problem of easily specifying and reporting links comes through the turning of the precedent list through 90° and representing the possible links as points on a square matrix. Such a display is illustrated in Fig. 8.7.

Having created an activity list using the histogram display described previously, the user is presented with a square matrix, each row and column representing one of the activities. To specify a link between activities, the user indicates the intersection between the row representing the dependent activity and the column representing the precedent. The display registers the existence of the link by blocking in the intersection; some links are shown in the figure. The specification of links using this method is very quick and accurate – only one point is required completely to specify a link, and the display is easy to read and to scroll. As with the histogram display, scrolling will be necessary and, again, stepwise scrolling has been found to be suitable and convenient.

Within precedence networks it is possible, of course, to have links which are other than direct finish of precedent/start of dependent links;

these complex links may link the start of activities (leads) or their finish (lags) and constitute extra data dimensions which must be handled by the graphics display. Two extra dimensions are required representing the type of link (lead, lag or lead and lag) and the duration of any delay built into the link (for example that activity A may start two days after activity B has started). These two dimensions can be conveniently condensed to one indata storage by storing the link duration as either positive or negative, depending on whether it is a lead or a lag, but their display causes difficulty.

A solution to this problem, which has been successfully adopted in one program, is to represent the type of link by either a different colour block or, if the colour is not available as part of the graphics display, as different symbols.[3] The duration is displayed only if the user interrogates the diagram. Thus if the user wishes to find the stored link duration for a link reported as complex, he indicates the block with his lightpen and, on receiving instructions from the operator, the screen display gives him the information he requires.

The linkage of activities within a network is one of the design variables available to the project planner, for although many of the links are based on pure logic and thus cannot be changed (for example concrete must be poured before it can be cured), many are based on management decisions (for example that only one set of abutment shutters are to be bought and therefore that the two abutments cannot be built simultaneously). It is thus important that the project planner should easily be able to identify the links he has built into his network and to change them or add to them. Previous methods of building networks have not encouraged this 'what if' approach because the changes involved the time-consuming altering of networks. The dependency matrix is, by contrast, easy to change and to understand and thus makes a valuable contribution to the interactive design of project plans.

PROGRAM DIRECTION

Computer Aided Design consists of more than analysis and thus the use of computers in the design cycle for project planning requires more than an analysis subroutine. The designer will wish to input data, examine it, analyse the network it represents, consider the results (both of time and, perhaps, of cost) and alter data. Detail will be added either by replacing activities with their constituent sub-networks, or by the use of hierarchically structured programs. The designer will rarely wish to proceed directly from data input to hard copy of the results. Interaction implies involvement and involvement direction of the processes within the program.

This need for direction within interactive programs is well recognised and has been met by the use of questions and answers through the screen and the keyboard and of menus. Computer graphics presents the

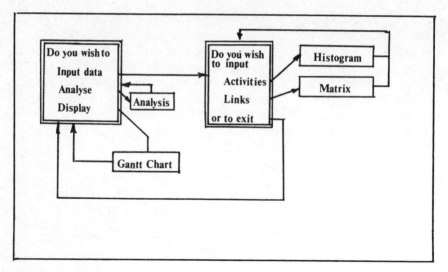

8.8 *Menu control*

programmer with a new and pleasant medium of communication. Menus can now be accessed not by requiring the typing of the answer to a displayed question but by requiring the user to point to the answer using the lightpen. Even the most keyboard-illiterate user can thus very quickly find his way through quite complex structures.

The use of graphics for program direction brings with it, in addition to high speed, the possibility of using the graphics displays themselves as part of the program direction. Thus if the user wishes to interrogate the dependency matrix, he is asked to indicate the link which interests him, the display forming part of the menu; similarly the Gantt Chart can be interrogated or hierarchical structures built.

The sophistication of the menus depends, of course, on the wishes and tastes of the programmer and his client, the eventual user. Experience suggests that, although needlessly 'fussy' menus will not be appreciated, attention should be paid to the aesthetics of the displays and that users will respond well to well-designed and elegant menus. It should be remembered that, lying as they do within an iterative process, the menus are to be used very many times, and what may be a minor annoyance to the programmer who is writing the package, may become a major irritation to the planner who has to use the package for the next five years. Fig. 8.8 shows a possible array of menus for a simple interactive planning package.

HARDWARE REQUIREMENTS

It is clear that a minimum requirement for the use of interactive graphics in the way that has been described is a high quality graphics display together with a user-controlled cursor. Hard copy facilities, while not essential for the interactive and iterative phase of the design, are highly desirable for the communication of the design to those who are to implement it.

Cursor control is available in various forms: as a lightpen, as a mouse, as a target on a digitiser pad, or as a keyboard driven cursor. Each has its strengths, but the keyboard driven cursor is perhaps the least suitable for the interactive design of project plans. The high accuracy it gives is not necessary for either program direction through menus or for the alteration of planning data, whilst its slowness of operation can lead to the frustration of the operator who wishes to proceed quickly through a series of menued options.

The lightpen has the advantage of speed and directness, although some users may feel that a graphically based program such as has been described requires so much interaction via the cursor that the use of the lightpen, pointing the pen at the vertical screen, may be physically tiring. The two remaining options overcome this difficulty, for both the mouse and the digitiser pad consist of devices which operate on a horizontal surface, enabling the operator to remain with his arm relaxed for most of the time he spends using the program. The lightpen, however, is a cheap device which is increasingly becoming a standard peripheral in microcomputer installations.

The digitiser pad has an additional advantage: the facility to use 'paste on' menus, menus which are printed on card and which fit over the digitizer board. Such menus bring the advantage of freeing the screen from the need to display the menus essential for program direction. The only disadvantage to their use is the loss of directness which is a guaranteed feature if the menus are part of the screen display.

The program which has been used as an example throughout this chapter is written for the ICL PERQ, which has a digitiser pad as a standard peripheral. Screen-displayed menus have been used. This is, however, an expensive hardware option and gives power which is perhaps not necessary for this application. A cheaper but satisfactory solution would be a lightpen or a mouse.

THE CONTROL PHASE

The techniques which have been described above fit most easily into that part of the planning/control continuum which has traditionally been called project planning. The data for this phase flows from the experience of the planner, the contract documents and the additional pre-tender investigations which the planner may feel it prudent to carry out. During the control phase, further information flows to the decision maker, the source of the information now being the project itself.

This source of information brings special difficulties for the project manager, who is usually concerned with activities which are unique. Information which flows only slowly to the decision maker is of limited value because the activity to which it refers is completed. Thus the data capture and the response time of the system are profoundly important.

There have been attempts to increase the speed of response of construction control systems by the use of computer. The control cycle illustrated in Fig. 8.9 includes a reanalysis of the project model. It has been thought that committing this reanalysis to the computer would increase the speed. Unfortunately, as in the case of project planning, the introduction of the computer often resulted in a worsening of service rather than its improvement.

This discouraging result should not, however, be seen as reason to abandon the attempt either to control construction operations or to gain data from site. Two approaches seen to be worthy of investigation, short-term forecasting and graphical data capture, are both simple in concept but both capable of providing significant progress.

Short-term forecasting[4] is a device to formalise the forward view that all managers must take. Traditional control systems have looked to the past and have required managers to report on progress. As has been seen, such retrospective systems are in danger of failing to provide data which can be acted upon because of the long response time which seems to be inevitable in control systems in large organisations. Short-term forecasting asks the managers, in addition to reporting on the past, to forecast for the future either the anticipated cost of activities (as used by Trimble *et al* at Loughborough) or the time they will require. These forecasts are used as the data supporting decisions and thus decisions are made prior to the activities to which they refer.'

The second technique recognises one of the difficulties of construction control, that is, the need for accurate reporting by low level supervisors. As has been remarked earlier, the construction industry is familiar with graphical displays and hostile to alphanumeric data. It is usual on

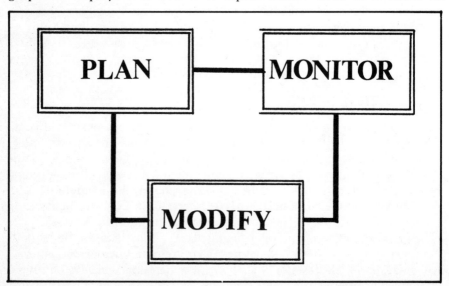

8.9 *The control cycle*

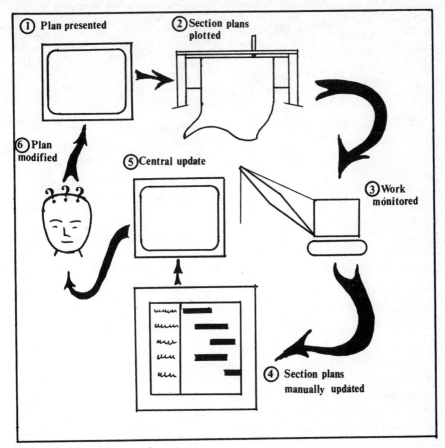

8.10 *A 'mid tech' control system*

construction sites to present information in graphical form; bar charts may be costly to produce by hand, but are used because they are effective. The computer fitted with graphical peripherals can easily produce bar charts and certainly should be used to do so from the project plan; but these bar charts can also be used for data capture.

DATA CAPTURE

There is a possibility that in the future the capture of data for construction control systems will be by direct input through site cabin-based graphical display units. This situation is, however, still firmly in the future, and the designer of control systems must realise that the site environment is far from conducive to the maintenance-free working of computer equipment and that the agents doing the reporting, the first level supervisors, are not familiar with the hardware which would be necessary for the operation of such a system.

It does seem possible, however, for improvements to be made to control systems without the risky investment which is included in this

PLAN FOR WEEK TWO				
ACTIVITY	WEEK TWO	WEEK THREE	WEEK FOUR	

8.11 *The updated Gantt chart*

futuristic strategy. The combination of the concepts of short-term fore-casting and individually computer produced bar charts could lead to a system such as is illustrated in Fig. 8.10. At the start of each week each supervisor is given a computer produced bar chart illustrating his program for the next three weeks (Fig. 8.11). Throughout the week he plots the daily progress of his section and, at the end of the week, he sketches his forecast of the work to be done in the next two weeks. This forecast, together with his record of actual progress, is used to update the central plan, and the updated plan is used to produce the charts for the next week. It is important that the transfer of data chart/machine is as efficient as that (machine/chart) which is used to produce the weekly charts. For this reason a graphics terminal display must be used and the display should exactly duplicate the section chart as originally drawn. The computer operator can then alter the displayed chart in exactly the same way that the hard copy chart has been altered, but using a lightpen rather than a pencil.

A system such as this achieves two important objectives: with little cost in terms of hardware investment or supervisor time, it provides the central planning system, and thus the central site management, with details of the short term expectations of the supervisors and also, through the regular use and storage of hard copy, a permanent record of the events on site. The techniques which have been described previously can be used to update the planning data.

This system is being tried in prototype within a nationally known building contractor's organisation.[5]

THE WAY FORWARD

The techniques which have been described in this chapter are now available for use on relatively low-cost computer installations and thus the interactive design of project plans through both the planning and the control phase is possible even at the lowest levels of the industry. The key to this development has been the reduction in the cost and the increasing availability of graphics. Throughout the engineering design disciplines, interactive graphics has been found to be a vital ingredient to CAD, and project method design is no exception to this.

The extent to which it will be found desirable to link project planning/control with other management systems remains to be seen. Work is proceeding with the development of a link between a system such as that described and a unit costing system, and it is clear that such a system could, in turn, lead to support for estimating and tendering. Experience of attempts to produce 'all singing, all dancing' programs in the past tends to counsel caution, but it is inevitable that such development will continue.

As with all applications of new techniques, it is important not to freeze the methods of the past into the systems of the future. A particular case in point is the artificial division which has built up between planning and control, a division which restricts the flow of information within the management structure and which, at its worst, encourages a damaging antagonism between 'planner' and 'controller'. The new systems will contribute to the efficiency of the industry if they can remove this barrier.

REFERENCES

1 ASIMOW, M., *Introduction to Design*, Prentice Hall, 1962
2 JACKSON, M. J. & CLARK, A., *The Design of Project Plans*, CAMP '83, Berlin
3 JACKSON, M. J. & CLARK, A., *Interactive Graphical Planning*, Eurographics '83, Zagreb
4 TRIMBLE, NEALE & BACKUS, *Effective Control of Project Costs*, Internet '79
5 HARRISON, J. P. & PEARS-WALLACE, N. J. A., 'The Role of Micros in Construction Planning & Control', *Engineering Software for Microcomputers*, Venice, 1984

9 The Simulation of Construction Projects
Richard N. Ormerod

THE CONSTRUCTION PROBLEM

A construction project presents a unique situation to those involved in managing the construction process. Each project is different from all others, and must be carried out at a different location each time. The project must be formulated and executed by integrating the efforts of a large number of different organisations and individuals, all of whom have different and often conflicting priorities and objectives.[5] The manager of the process must consider and assess different technologies and alternative combinations of labour and equipment. While the manager knows what must be done, he has considerable latitude in how it is to be executed. Furthermore, he must consider the effects of imponderables such as weather, material shortages, labour problems, unknown subsurface conditions, and inaccurate estimates of duration and cost. All these considerations combine to form a complex, dynamic problem.[10]

The construction manager must assess this dynamic problem in the context of future events and performance. Estimates and predictions must be made which attempt to forecast the future. Inevitably the forecasted value will deviate from the actual outcome, due to a lack of complete information about future events.

Another major effect common in construction projects is that the initial definition of the project is changed in scope due to modifications in the basic plan to incorporate changes. Quite often it is these unknown factors which create surprises for the client who commissions the construction project.[12]

All managers face a certain amount of unknown possibilities which can affect the process they are attempting to control. However, the construction manager is likely to have to confront and resolve problems of a type and magnitude not found in other industries. Every manager engaged in construction, at whatever level, encounters these problems in the course of every working day. The problems are readily identifiable and are accepted in the industry at large – a few typical examples are listed below:[8]

—the actions of external agencies (e.g. Government)
—unknown or unassessed elements of the work to be performed
—errors and omissions in working drawings
—delays in obtaining management approvals
—the effects of the weather on construction operations

—late delivery of purchased material and equipment
—unknown results of testing and commissioning complex services systems
—unknown rates of inflation
—the normal highly-variable performance work rates
—mechanical breakdown or malfunction of equipment
—rejection of poor quality work and re-work

All these factors and the complexity of the construction problem have long been recognised. This recognition led to the establishment of the Project Management discipline and the adoption in recent years of computerised, critical path network based systems to provide assistance in planning, budgeting, scheduling and controlling projects. Yet the availability of such sophisticated management tools and the establishment of a construction management profession has not generally provided the hoped-for improvement in project performance. Total project cost and time overruns are still commonly reported[9] and clearly the use of sophisticated management techniques has not eliminated project estimating or performance problems. In view of this track record the client, who must use the facility provided by the construction process, has become increasingly critical of the ability of construction managers and has come to view the industry with mistrust – as highlighted by the recent BPF proposals.[2]

A major reason for this perception has been the many changes forced on projects by the external, uncontrollable forces described before. However, this perception has been unwittingly nurtured by the tendency to characterise projects by single-value measures – a single cost, a single duration – which give illusions of certainty. The economist, Ken Boulding, has said, 'an important source of bad decisions are illusions of certainty'.

UNCERTAINTY

The many contributing factors to the construction problem – some of which are outlined above – are referred to collectively as *uncertainty*. The purpose of this chapter is to consider the construction process in the light of uncertainty and to describe an effective management tool to assess its impact.

The management tool which will later be described more fully is the Construction Project Simulator (CPS), and its underlying hypothesis is that this global uncertainty can be subdivided into two major components, namely *variability* in the performance of a task, and *interference* from outside the task which frustrates its progress. This categorisation is supported by evidence from the direct observation of the construction process and by evidence from other construction academics.[1,3,13]

When making decisions, managers cannot be certain of good outcomes, because they cannot completely control external events or

95

have total foresight. Therefore, management should try to increase the probability of good outcomes by making good decisions. Where there is uncertainty as to which events might occur, the logic of the decision process should include that information.

There is a basic need to be able to quantify and assess the impact that uncertainty can have on a project, and to incorporate this knowledge in the project brief and the management of the project. This expanded awareness of the project gives executive management and the client a more complete view of the project and a basis for decision making. It provides a much higher quality of information on which to base a decision, and allows an assessment of both uncertainty and risk while incorporating the manager's own value judgement into the decision. The inclusion of uncertainty further supports the efforts of management in concentrating on the essential elements of the project. If construction project prediction and performance are to be improved, uncertainty and its sources must be dealt with seriously and specifically. Not as a final rudimentary 'contingency item' (whether explicit or not), but detailed systematically as an integrated part of the management process.[8]

Variability and interference

The use in the simulator model of variability as a component of uncertainty is based on the factual observation of the construction process. However, neglect of this factor is often proposed by texts of 'classical' network analysis, with statements such as 'only an occasional construction project will have variances in activity durations',[7] while observation of the construction operations leads to the conclusion that it is pervasive and very large.[6]

Variability can be defined as the range and frequency distribution of possible durations in the execution of a particular task.

This arises as performances are subject to wide variation since, in any given discipline, there is a wide range of capabilities. Different skill levels, degrees of motivation and fatigue, and other behavioural factors will affect worker performance and produce the normal variations found in practice. In addition, certain construction tasks are inherently uncertain due to the nature of the material, e.g. excavation with variable ground conditions. Also, in practice, an appreciable and uncertain amount of repeat work is carried out.

It is important to stress that the variability referred to here is specific to a particular task. It is necessary to compare like with like and ensure the quality and quantity of work carried out, and the method of execution should be identical or at least very similar.

It is also important to account for the effort expended in completing the task at the workplace and not to account for any time when the activity was suspended through inclement weather, lack of information etc. There is considerable evidence that in building work typically many

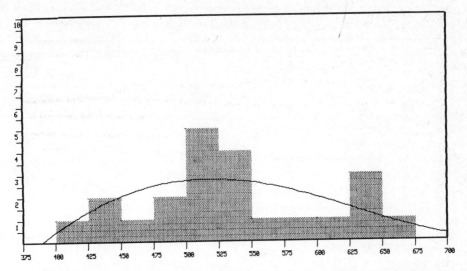

9.1 *Brickwork superstructure (half walls only), variability of output for all gangs, one site*

visits are needed to complete a task,[11] and so it is important to account only for the time actually spent on the task.

When these factors are considered, they lead to a range of possible results which are typically presented as a frequency histogram, and represent the potential range of productivity outputs at the workplace. An adequate amount of data for the construction industry exists to make the existence of variability inescapable. A typical distribution for brickwork is illustrated in Fig. 9.1.

That interferences exist in the construction process – as external influences on the progress of site works which cause stops to production – is readily apparent to all practitioners in the building industry. They stem from a wide variety of sources – such as the structure and work of the industry, acts of God or human and social factors, risks outside the contractor's control, integrating the effort of a number of different organisations and individuals (many not under direct control), legal impositions, and environmental factors.

These give rise to specific events which prevent work starting or continuing. The most frequently mentioned are: the weather, planning permission and building codes, lack of design details, non-availability of materials and components, non-attendance by subcontractors, labour strikes and shortages, equipment breakdown and theft and vandalism. Occurrences of interferences on any one project can be found in abundance.[1]

Previous work in this area has been sparse, but it is postulated that the general classification of interference is made up of four major components, each of which affects to some degree the progress and cost of actual construction activities. These components are: interferences

97

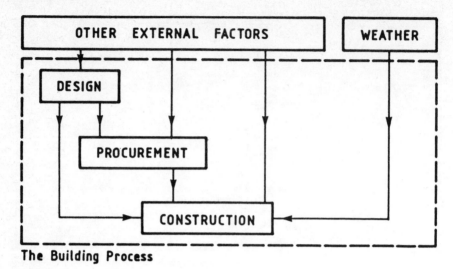

The Building Process

9.2 *The components of interface and their interaction*

originating from the design process; interferences originating from the procurement process; interferences originating from the weather, and those other external human and social factors remaining. This classification is illustrated in Fig. 9.2.

The recognition of interference as a separate category of uncertainty is an important step for practical as well as theoretical application. By focusing attention on the external influences, it redefines the strategic and tactical management of a project to encompass the control of external events and the mitigation of their effects. The concentration of management effort on reducing the impact of interferences may have a greater beneficial effect than the control of production variability, which is essentially a site-operational management task.

SIMULATION

As well as an awareness of uncertainty, a manager requires a management tool to use in quantifying and assessing the impact this uncertainty may have on the project. The manager must be aware of the effects uncertainty may have so that he may make a rational decision as to what level of risk to accept in the light of the circumstances at the time. A management tool incorporating uncertainty will not make decision making easier, but it will present more and better information than is currently available on which to base a decision and, therefore, arguably improve the possibility of a good decision.

The technique which is employed to form a management tool in an uncertain environment, to augment the decision maker's intuition and experience, is *simulation*. Simulation is also referred to as the Monte Carlo technique – due to the gambling aspect of the process; or as a stochastic technique – due to the presence of random processes. Stochastic simulation typically generates durations and costs for each activity in a plan by randomly calculating a feasible value for each from a statistical probability frequency distribution – which represents the range and pattern of possible outcomes for an activity. To ensure that the chosen values are representative of the pattern of possible outcomes, a large number of repetitive deterministic calculations – known as iterations – are made. The result is typically presented as a cumulative distribution plot and a frequency histogram.

Due to the repetitiveness of the process and the handling of large amounts of numerical information, it has only been feasible to implement this technique since the advent of computers. The current practices of industry, in using single-value, deterministic methods, are a legacy from the era before computing liberated people from laborious calculations. Also it allows a deeper investigation of problems – like construction – which do not have a single-value solution that can be represented by a set formula, nor operate in a totally random environment which can be represented by statistics, but have a limited random component (i.e. stochastic) which can only be investigated through simulation.

It has been claimed that the introduction of simulation methods for construction management is likely to have as great an impact on the construction industry as did the introduction of network planning and scheduling methods some two decades ago. Some of the advantages claimed for the technique are summarised below.

1 The major advantage is that the results of such a simulation, given the validity of input assumptions, provide an unbiased estimate of the project completion distribution. This is particularly important in the light of evidence of inherent bias in deterministic network techniques.

2 Simulation provides an almost unlimited capacity to model construction operations, which permits the construction manager to evaluate quickly and at moderate cost many different combinations of equipment and methods under varying conditions of operation.

3 Simulation can give the manager an insight into which factors are important – and hence where to concentrate his effort – and how they interact.

4 Simulation allows the user to experiment with different strategies without the risk of disturbing the real project and incurring costs. Simulation also enables the user to study dynamic systems in much less time than is needed to study the actual system.

5 Additionally, if a person can interact with the computer simulation in a gaming environment, experience can be gained under realistic conditions before the work is started. This should lead to better management through a deeper knowledge of the problem.

6 Finally, and most importantly, simulation models often predict things which are not specifically incorporated into the model. Simulation of repetitive processes has shown that, when uncertainty exists, there are large penalties rather than benefits of scale. There is some evidence that, in the construction industry, it is the larger projects which go wrong most frequently. Also, most work study experts talk about the benefits of specialisation. Simulation shows that, for large projects subject to uncertainty, there are penalties of specialisation. Further, most models of construction processes assume that the cost of a project is the sum of the costs of the activities. Simulations of repetitive processes show that costs are largely generated by the uncertainties that exist, and that simple additive models like the Bill of Quantities seriously under-estimate cost. Finally, the traditional approach to construction would expect financial benefit to accrue from productivity increases and would direct effort towards increasing the speed of production. Simulations incorporating uncertainty direct attention towards obtaining benefits from reductions in interferences. The benefits to be gained by these reductions in interference can be shown to be very much larger in magnitude than gains made possible by productivity increases.

The only disadvantage of simulation techniques is that they are time-consuming and expensive in computer time, due to the requirement to perform many iterations of the same calculation. This has been true in the past when the only computers with the required capacity were large mainframe computers with high operating costs. Presently, however, due to the pace of technological development, relatively cheap micro-computers with sufficient capacity are readily available. The objection that the process is time-consuming is also overcome by allowing a fully automatic operation and by carrying out the processing at times when the microcomputer would not normally be used (i.e. at lunchtime or at night). Looking into the near future, if even some of the promises of the 'fifth generation' computers are realised, then even these drawbacks will be nullified.

The use of computer simulations for construction applications is a recent development dating from the early 1970s. However, in this time nearly 30 different simulation models have been developed. All have their inherent strengths and weaknesses, and they were reviewed during the course of the research. The objective in developing a new computer program was to overcome many of the shortcomings of previous techniques. Specifically the CPS includes processes to model the two components of uncertainty – variability and interference; it operates on a relatively cheap, easily available microcomputer; it has an increased capacity over earlier models in being able to accommodate more variables such as activities, costs, weather, resources and preliminaries in one package; and, above all, it is a model which is simple to operate, being designed for use in industry by managers who are not computer-literate.

COMPUTER PROGRAM DESCRIPTION

The development of the computer program known as the *construction project simulator* (CPS) was undertaken during a research contract and is based on the ideas and theories outlined before.

The software philosophy has been to make the operation of the programs as easy and simple as possible (user-friendly). This was accomplished by the extensive use of computer graphics, the inclusion of many checks for errors and error messages, through minimising the use of the keyboard, and the inclusion, where practicable, of 'help' screens to prompt the user in the correct operating procedure. Also the structure of the programs is based on a hierarchical approach to allow ease of use and present a choice of levels for answers to increasingly complex questions, as schemes and strategies for a project develop.

The suite of programs is driven by a menu to which all program operations must return before another function can be chosen. The suite of programs is basically configured into two different categories: the series of programs allowing the entry of data describing a project, and two programs where this data is used to perform simulations and produce the end result as output.

The programs have been coded in compiled Basic, and operate on a 512 kbyte ACT Sirius I microcomputer with twin floppy disk drives providing 1.2 Mbyte of data storage.

DATA INPUT PROGRAMS

The following programs and facilities require input from the user and all provide data in one form or another to the simulation programs described later. Some programs can be used only after another program has been successfully completed and saved on disk, as they draw on information produced earlier – program operation automatically checks for these conditions.

Commencing a project

Two floppy disks are required: one containing the CPS suite of programs is loaded into drive A, and a data disk is loaded into drive B.

The programs are then initiated by entering the three characters 'cps'. This starts an automatic process which loads the graphics software and checks the data disk for existing data. If the data disk is blank, a program is entered which allows the entry of the project title, start date, anticipated end date, and a time unit to be used in the primary bar chart. If the data disk already has project data present, then the menu program is run – through which the user moves from one program to another.

Bar charts

The bar chart programs represent the heart of the CPS data input routine. The bar charts are arranged as a hierarchy, which is reflected in the structure of most other programs, and also models the way effective managers plan. The first bar chart to be presented is the primary level bar chart, in which the user defines separate activities known as *primary work packages* (PWPs). Each one of these PWPs may subsequently be 'exploded', or magnified, to define a secondary level bar chart which allows the constituents of the PWP to be planned in detail. Within the secondary level bar chart, the user defines separate activities known as *secondary work packages* (SWPs). The SWPs are the sub-operations of the PWP; thus a primary bar chart with PWPs must exist before a secondary bar chart program may be entered.

The primary bar chart is presented from the data entered previously – the start and end dates, and the time unit (weeks or months) – and a calendar of dates and time unit numbers is calculated and presented on the screen along with the project title. The time unit and the length of the project defines how large the steps are between cursor movements on the screen, as the cursor moves horizontally in steps or jumps of one time unit. Thus activity durations have to be in whole time unit lengths. All of this process is carried out automatically and the user is presented with a titled, dated and scaled blank bar chart screen, ready for the entry of PWPs.

The maximum number of PWP bars permitted is 39; however, only 15 are displayed at one time on the screen, but the screen scrolls up or down, one bar at a time, so that all bars may be viewed. The user enters a bar by typing its title in the title panel, and by defining the start and end positions, using one function key and two direction keys, the bar is automatically presented. Only one bar per line is permitted. Once a bar has been set up, the start and end dates may be changed, and the bar redrawn in the desired position. Changes to bar charts can thus be rapidly executed. Bars may be inserted or deleted from the bar chart, and bar titles may be retyped.

The PWPs are interconnected by the device of logical links, entered by the user and drawn on the screen as thin lines. The maximum number of links is 250. The links act as logical restraints to progress and are entered by setting the cursor at the desired position on one bar, pressing one function key and moving the cursor, by four direction keys (or one day by the use of a mouse!), to the desired position on another bar and pressing the same function key again. Certain strict rules govern link arrangements, as these are the basis of the logic employed during simulation. Basically all links must pass down the screen when drawn, and are sorted by 'rescheduling', so that at least one link between any two bars is vertical and none slopes from right to left. Links may be erased by placing the cursor on their origin and pressing one function key on the key board.

The combination of rapid data entry, graphic display, and the ease with which changes can be made provides a powerful tool for investigating the effect of logic or duration changes, as, at the throw of a

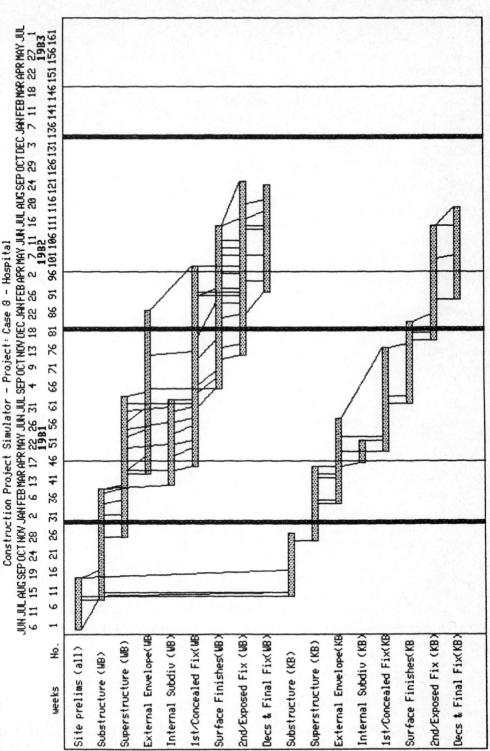

9.3 *Typical primary bar chart*

switch, the logical effect of any change is seen – much as the non-graphical and un-timescaled critical path analysis performs. An example of a primary bar chart is illustrated in Fig. 9.3.

Holiday periods may be entered and deleted in much the same fashion as bars are entered. The maximum number of holiday periods permitted is nine. It is assumed that holiday periods have no effect on the time taken to complete an activity and they are treated as 'dead' periods. As the cursor moves in time unit steps, the duration of a holiday period must be a whole number of time units.

After a session of data input to the bar chart, whether initial input or as the result of some change to the plan, the user must press the 'reschedule' function key before he is permitted to save the bar chart details permanently on disk. The reschedule checks, and if necessary rearranges, the logical links to ensure the plan is logically correct. The requirement always to reschedule before the save function key is enabled is to ensure that all plans contained on disk are correct ones.

Once a correct primary bar chart has been created and saved, each PWP of this bar chart can be expanded to form the basis for a secondary level bar chart, when the more detailed constituent SWPs can be entered by the user.

The secondary level bar chart program takes the PWP title and calendar (and week number) start and end dates, and the presence of any holiday periods from the primary bar chart program. The user then has to select a time unit, equal to or less than the primary bar chart time unit – in weeks, half-weeks, or days – and the computer presents a titled, dated and scaled blank bar chart screen with any holiday periods in the right place, ready for the entry of SWPs.

The processes used to enter SWPs and logical links are exactly the same as those used in the primary bar chart, and described above. The maximum number of SWP bars permitted is 39, but the maximum number of logical links is set at 200. Thus in the unlikely event that all PWPs were expanded, the maximum number of SWPs in the entire plan would be 1,521 and they would be restrained by a maximum of 7,800 logical links. It is not expected that this facility will ever be fully utilised, but the upper limit was set to accommodate the largest possible number of SWPs and links in one PWP which are likely to be found in practice. During use of the CPS, the largest number of SWPs found in practice has been 410, with just less than 2,000 secondary logical links, contained in 28 PWPs. This was for a complicated £9 million, 1.8 year project.

A typical secondary level bar chart is illustrated in Fig. 9.4 and represents the expanded plan of PWP3 – Superstructure (WB) – in Fig. 9.3.

Cost entry

The direct cost in labour, materials and small plant needed to carry out the operations described by a PWP or a SWP must be entered into

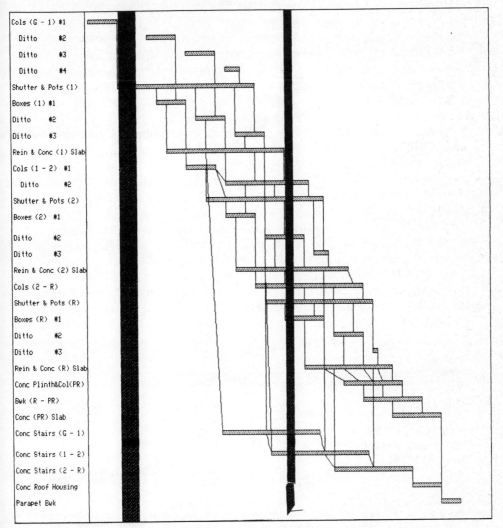

Construction Project Simulator - Case 8 - Hospital ⁞Activity - Superstructure (WB)

9.4 *Typical secondary level bar chart – expanded plan of PWP in Fig 9.3*

the relevant cost program. The cost program takes the work package titles from the relevant bar chart and presents them in a table. Against each title are two fields defined by brackets, one for the labour cost of the work package and one for the material cost. By using the edit function key, the cursor is placed in the first defined field, and the cursor is moved around the table by four direction keys. Once in the desired field, numbers up to eight characters in length may be entered.

105

A running total of the labour and material costs is displayed on the screen along with a grand total.

As the bar charts are arranged as a hierarchy, the structure of the cost information is arranged in a similar manner. Thus, there are as many cost tables as there are bar charts, and the cost totals for a PWP are made up of the sum of the constituent SWPs. The totals from a secondary cost table, when saved, are automatically placed in the primary cost table, thus removing a potential source of user error. A typical cost screen, as it appears to the user, is illustrated in Fig. 9.5.

The costs discussed so far are those for the materials and effort required for incorporating them in the building. In construction, however, a significant element of the cost is contained in cost centres which will not be permanently incorporated in the building, but which are nevertheless essential for the construction of the building. These are the 'preliminaries' costs for a building project, and the most significant elements are: supervisory staff, plant, scaffold access, temporary accommodation, temporary services, and materials-handling/cleaning. These costs are often shared by more than one activity on the plan, and they are specifically dependent on the duration and logic of certain elements of the plan. For example, the tower crane may be erected when a certain SWP in the substructure PWP has been completed, and may be dismantled when a certain SWP has been completed in the superstructure PWP. The timing and hire period of the item of plant is linked to the logic of the plan, and, if the durations of activities are extended in

PWP No. 3	Superstructure (WB)			
Activity	Labour Cost	Material Cost		
Cols (G – 1) *1	<3330 >	<6120 >		
Ditto *2	<3330 >	<6120 >		
Ditto *3	<3330 >	<6120 >		
Ditto *4	<1660 >	<3055 >		
Shutter & Pots (1)	<2295 >	<6810 >		
Boxes (1) *1	<610 >	<150 >		
Ditto *2	<610 >	<150 >	LABOUR TOTAL	
Ditto *3	<610 >	<150 >	<	121680>
Rein & Conc (1) Slab	<11020 >	<17660 >		
Cols (1 – 2) *1	<3330 >	<6120 >	MATERIAL TOTAL	
Ditto *2	<8320 >	<15290 >	<	216935>
Shutter & Pots (2)	<2105 >	<6240 >		
Boxes (2) *1	<665 >	<165 >	GRAND TOTAL	
Ditto *2	<665 >	<165 >	<	338615>
Ditto *3	<500 >	<125 >		
Rein & Conc (2) Slab	<9645 >	<15455 >		
Cols (2 – R)	<11100 >	<20395 >		
Shutter & Pots (R)	<1915 >	<5675 >		
Boxes (R) *1	<600 >	<145 >		
Ditto *2	<600 >	<145		

9.5 Typical cost screen

practice, then the crane will be required for a longer period and the cost will increase.

This logic has been modelled in the CPS by the provision of a preliminary schedule where up to 15 separate 'preliminary categories' may be attached to the logic of the primary bar chart. Once this program is engaged, all the information entered into the primary bar chart is reproduced, except that the majority of the logical link graphics are omitted for clarity and the link positions merely marked by short vertical lines. The user may then enter preliminary categories by the use of one function key and four direction keys to define the start and end of a category, using the same procedure as drawing logical links in a bar chart. The only difference is that the cursor moves from link position to link position, rather than in time unit steps, and the start and end can thus only be attached to a logical link position. Heavy dashed lines are used to represent a preliminary category on the screen. Categories may also be deleted, if required.

The effect of setting up a preliminary category is that the logical links associated with the start and end positions are specifically identified, or 'flagged', to allow computation of the number of weeks between the start and end position. This information is then presented in a preliminaries cost table where a title, a weekly cost, and a fixed cost can be entered for any preliminary category – to form the basis of the indirect cost calculation. A typical preliminaries schedule and cost table are presented in Fig. 9.6.

Resources

Where resources are desired to form the basis of resource restraint or cost calculation, then three stages of data entry are required. However, the structure of the data entry has been designed to minimise the typing of resource titles, etc. many times. The first two stages are the creation of a library of standard trades and then of trade gangs, which, once created, need only be occasionally updated. Thus the entry of resource data is particularly rapid.

The first stage is to enter typical trades and their cost per time unit into a table of 100 available categories. This is accomplished in much the same way as direct costs are entered, with the user moving between defined fields to enter trade descriptions and costs. The number associated with a particular trade is then used as the trade reference number. This data entry takes place in the top half of the screen, and although there are only 10 trades on display at any one time, the top half of the screen scrolls independently.

This information is then used to build up typical trade gangs in the lower half of the screen. A gang title is entered and up to five different trade members may be assigned to any one gang. It is common for there to be only one member of a gang, and the average number is two or three. In this way a library of typical gangs is built up, although without any quantities of members, to allow a gang to be used in many

107

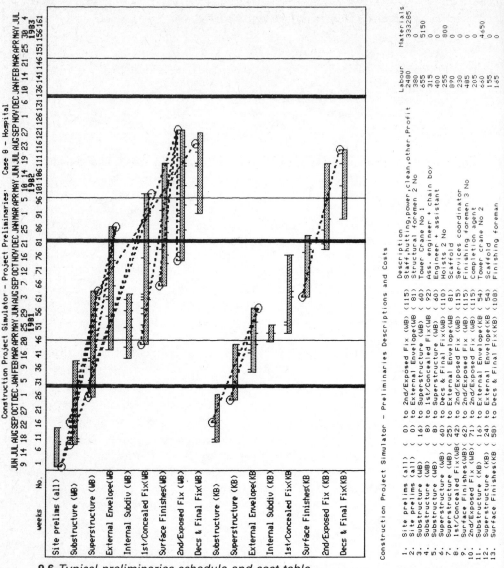

9.6 *Typical preliminaries schedule and cost table*

different instances and then have different quantities added later. The number associated with a particular gang is then used as the gang reference number. The data entry takes place in the lower screen, and, although only 10 gangs are displayed at one time, the lower screen scrolls so that all the 100 available gangs may be viewed. A typical resources screen, as it appears to the user, is illustrated in Fig. 9.7.

Once the library of resource gangs has been assembled, the business of applying them to particular activities can proceed. Resource restraint can only apply to the more detailed secondary level plans. Thus as many resource screens as there are secondary bar charts may be entered,

```
       CREATE RESOURCE SETS
   TITLE              COST
23. <Grdwk bricklyr >   <150    >
24. <Grdwrk plantdvr>   <120    >
25. <Drainlayer    >    <105    >
26. <Formwork Carp >    <125    >
27. <Steelfixer    >    <120    >
28. <Concretor     >    <100    >
29. <Conc. finisher >   <105    >
30. <Scaffolder    >    <165    >
31. <Bricklayer    >    <185    >
32. <Bricklyr Labour>   <190    >
```

RESOURCE SET		CODE REFERENCES				
11. <RC Stairs : TC/P	> <27>	<26>	<28>	< >	< >	
12. <RC Stairs : H/ D	> <27>	<26>	<28>	< >	< >	
13. <RC Foundations	> <26>	,<27>	<28>	< >	< >	
14. <Formwork	> <26>	< >	< >	< >	< >	
15. <Steel fixing & concreting	> <27>	<28>	< >	< >	< >	
16. <Structural steel erection	> <60>	< >	< >	< >	< >	
17. <Asphalt roofing	> <35>	< >	< >	< >	< >	
18. <Tiled roofing	> <36>	< >	< >	< >	< >	
19. <Scaffolding	> <30>	< >	< >	< >	< >	
20. <Brickwork	> <31>	<32>	<90>	< >	< >	

9.7 *Typical resources library screen*

although if resource restraint is desired in only a few PWPs, then only these require data entry.

For the selected PWP, expanded into a secondary level plan, another program presents the user again with a screen split horizontally, with each half again containing a table. In the lower screen the table of resource gangs is presented again for reference, and may not be changed. The upper screen displays the SWP titles from the relevant bar chart

```
              ALLOCATE RESOURCES AND COSTS
     ACTIVITY       RESOURCE SET      [TRADES]+<NUMBERS>
17.[Cols (2 - R)        ] <9 >*27<2 >:26<2 >:28<3 >: < >: < >:<  790>
18.[Shutter & Pots (R)  ] <14>*26<8 >: < >: < >: < >: < >:< 1000>
19.[Boxes (R) *1        ] <14>*26<2 >: < >: < >: < >: < >:<  250>
20.[Ditto     *2        ] <14>*26<2 >: < >: < >: < >: < >:<  250>
21.[Ditto     *3        ] <14>*26<2 >: < >: < >: < >: < >:<  250>
22.[Rein & Conc (R) Slab] <15>*27<4 >:28<5 >: < >: < >: < >:<  900>
23.[Conc Plinth&Col(PR) ] <9 >*27<2 >:26<2 >:28<3 >: < >: < >:<  790>
24.[Bwk (R - PR)        ] <20>*31<4 >:32<1 >:90<1 >: < >: < >:<  955>
25.[Conc (PR) Slab      ] <3 >*27<2 >:26<2 >:28<3 >: < >: < >:<  790>
26.[Conc Stairs (G - 1) ] <11>*27<2 >:26<4 >:28<3 >: < >: < >:< 1040>
```

RESOURCE SET		CODE REFERENCES				
11. [RC Stairs : TC/P	][27]	[26]	[28]	[ ]	[ ]	
12. [RC Stairs : H/ D	][27]	[26]	[28]	[ ]	[ ]	
13. [RC Foundations	][26]	[27]	[28]	[ ]	[ ]	
14. [Formwork	][26]	[ ]	[ ]	[ ]	[ ]	
15. [Steel fixing & concreting	][27]	[28]	[ ]	[ ]	[ ]	
16. [Structural steel erection	][60]	[ ]	[ ]	[ ]	[ ]	
17. [Asphalt roofing	][35]	[ ]	[ ]	[ ]	[ ]	
18. [Tiled roofing	][36]	[ ]	[ ]	[ ]	[ ]	
19. [Scaffolding	][30]	[ ]	[ ]	[ ]	[ ]	
20. [Brickwork	][31]	[32]	[90]	[ ]	[ ]	

9.8 *Typical resources allocation screen*

in a table. Each SWP title has twelve fields displayed against it. The second, fourth, sixth, eighth, and tenth fields are displayed in reverse video, and the user is not permitted to enter these fields. The rest of the fields are defined by brackets and are allocated for user input. The upper screen is used to enter the number of a resource gang and to enter quantities against each constituent trade member.

In the first field of the upper screen, the user enters a resource gang reference number. This has the effect of automatically displaying the trade members in the reverse video fields. This presents the user with details of gang members and an adjacent empty field in which to enter the quantity of members required. Member quantities may only be placed in fields with an adjacent trade reference number. Thus the same gang structure can be used for all similar activities, e.g. brickwork, but the numbers varied to reflect relative resource usage. In the last field the cost per time unit of the whole gang is automatically computed from the data entered previously, and is displayed when the data is saved. A typical resource allocation screen, as it appears to the user, is illustrated in Fig. 9.8.

Once all the resource data for the desired SWPs has been entered, one final data input procedure is necessary to set the upper limit of resource availability for this PWP. The program displays all the separate trade members used in all the gangs employed and this information is displayed as a table. The user can then enter the maximum number for each resource type and the computer validates this to ensure it is not less than that entered previously. These totals act as the upper limit for resource restraint during simulation, and the user, by manipulating these figures, can experiment with different combinations and quantities to determine the best mix.

Creating and allocating distributions

Frequency distributions, or histograms, must be created and assigned, so that variability and interference routines in the simulation programs have the correct information. Certain areas of the distribution program are reserved for specialist purposes: 1 to 50 are available to the user to save created distributions, 51 to 62 are reserved for the weather, and 63 to 140 are reserved for secondary simulation results.

The four most common distributions used in simulation – namely uniform, triangular, normal, and beta – are permanently available. The user can also create skewed distributions for the triangular, normal, and beta – to model pessimistic or optimistic production rates. Bimodal distributions can also be created in a wide variety of shapes, and actual histograms of real data can be entered and saved as the histogram or as a *best fit curve* (see Fig. 9.1). Some typical distributions are illustrated in Fig. 9.9.

The distributions created in this program are contained in a library or database which will rarely require updating once compiled. The distributions in this database should be regarded as a library to aid the manager in applying his intuition to the simulation processes. Each can be regarded in a similar manner to the familiar PERT three-point estimate, and the different shapes used express feelings about an activity, e.g. it is optimistic – thus allocating a distribution with a pessimistic skew. Some familiarity with this concept is obviously required; however, there is evidence that it coincides with how people view the real world.

All the activities, at whatever hierarchy level, must have certain parameters defined pertaining to a particular activity before a simulation may be executed. Values for interferences, productivity variability, and relevant distributions must be assigned to each activity by the user.

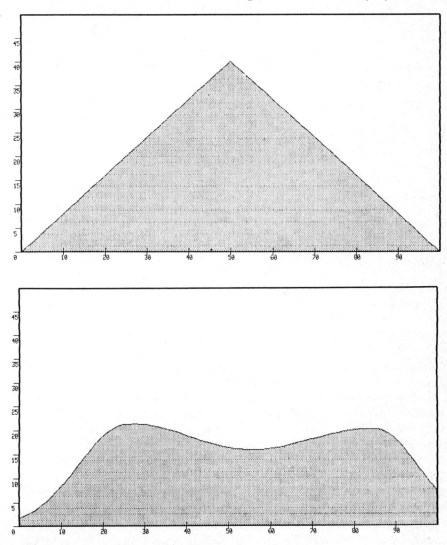

9.9 *Typical frequency distributions (Cont. overleaf)*

111

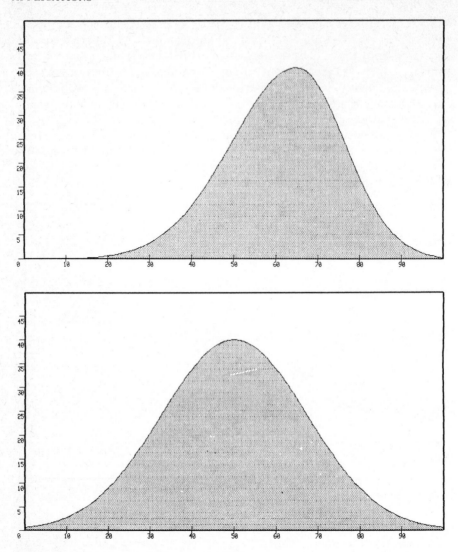

9.9 *Typical frequency distributions (Cont.)*

The structure of these programs follows the same hierarchical structure as the bar charts, so there is one for the primary bar chart and one for each PWP. The structure of the screen display is similar to the cost programs, with the activity title displayed along with fields to accept user input. In this program three fields are defined for use by the user.

The first field defines the interference factor acting upon the activity. A figure between 0 and 99 first defines the percentage chance that an interference will occur at any link position on the activity bar. This is separated by an oblique stroke (/) from an optional frequency distribution number between f1 and f50, which is held on file in the distribution program. This, if entered, is used to select a period of an interference from a user input distribution. If no distribution number is present, the simulation programs will assume an interference period of one time unit.

The second field defines the range of the variability amount affecting an activity. A figure between 0 and 99 defines the plus and minus $(+-)$ percentage variation about the midpoint of the distribution, which defines the range of possible activity durations that may be chosen during simulation. The third field defines the number of the frequency distribution which applies to an activity.

Weather data

The inclusion of weather processing in simulation is particularly suitable, as the basic problem with weather data is that typical weather behaviour may be known historically, but the actual weather which will be encountered during construction is not known. The effect is qualitatively detectable, but not enough knowledge exists to assess the risk quantitatively. However, weather data is a classical stochastic problem[4] where a frequency distribution can be obtained from reliable historic records and repeatedly sampled randomly to reflect the possible weather effects on a project. The treatment of weather information is thus an ideal candidate for simulation.

The availability of data is excellent and can be purchased from the Meteorological Office for a very modest fee. The data used in the CPS is based upon a combined plot when the rainfall during the working day was greater than 0.1 mm/h *and/or* the wind was gusting greater than 10 m/s *and/or* the air temperature was less than 2° C *and* the mean wind speed is greater than 4 m/s. This combined plot is then available for each month of each year for the last 20 years, to provide a frequency distribution for the hours per working month lost through the effect of the weather. Two such distributions are reproduced in Fig. 9.10 to illustrate the difference between February and July when the data is presented in this format.

The twelve histograms for the weather for each month of the year are entered into a separate program. The weather data is specific to one location, so that new data should be collected for projects in different parts of the country as well as other countries. This program also allows the identification of each PWP on the primary bar chart as being sensitive to weather effects or not. Thus the 'substructure' would be designated as weather sensitive while 'decorations and final fixes' would not. In this way, the likely effect of the real weather can be included in a simulation.

SIMULATION PROGRAMS

Once the data input procedure has been completed, then the simulation of the project can be carried out. However, the CPS has been designed as a hierarchy to facilitate the simulation of schemes at various stages,

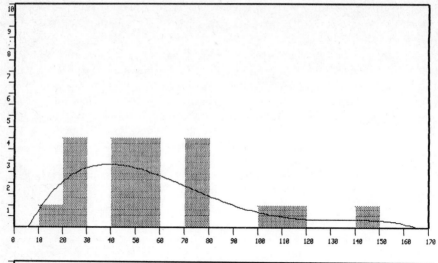

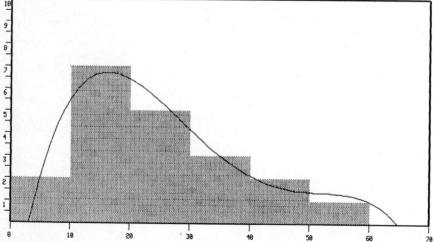

9.10 *Typical weather frequency histograms*

so that data input can have different degrees of detail and simulations still be performed.

A simulation of the primary level only may be carried out after the primary bar chart and weather data, and, optionally, the preliminary schedule and primary cost table have been entered. This allows a quick assessment of schemes at an early stage in their development, or at a tendering stage.

A simulation of one or more secondary plans may be carried out after a secondary bar chart, and, optionally, the secondary cost table and resources details, have been entered. This allows an assessment of single PWPs when design details become available as the scheme develops, or allows re-assessment of a PWP after some change to the construction method.

A full-scale simulation of all the secondary plans, followed by a simulation of the primary level, can be carried automatically. This allows an assessment of the whole scheme, at a level consistent with a good contract programme, to produce the most reliable simulation result. The duration of this most detailed simulation procedure is one and a half to three hours, depending on the size of the project plan.

Simulation method

The purpose of simulation is to imitate the conditions of a system with a model or simplified representation of the system, so that the model mimics important elements of the system under study. The end result is to produce a prediction of the likely range and pattern of contract duration and cost which are feasible under the conditions and constraints of a specific project.

This is carried out inside the computer in a mathematical process using the data provided by the user. The basic problem is to choose from the range of possible durations for one bar of the plan – represented by the assigned frequency distribution and variability percentage – in a manner which is representative of the original data.

The manner in which this is achieved is via the use of random numbers (RNs). Random numbers are generated by the computer and are applied to the assigned distribution to see if the chosen value is representative of the original data. If it is representative, then this is the value which is used in the simulation. If it is not representative, then the value is rejected and more RNs are generated – the whole process being repeated until a feasible value is chosen. The random numbers are used in conjunction with a frequency distribution which limits the randomness to that found in practice. Thus the process is not totally random, but has a random element – hence the term 'stochastic'.

The use of random numbers is really only a device to produce unbiased choices of duration, and, although we cannot say precisely what the duration will be after any one choice, we can say what the pattern and range will be after a sufficiently large number of choices. So it is necessary to make a large number of choices to produce the confidence that the resulting choices are representative of the original data. The number of choices are referred to as *iterations*, and the number of iterations performed is critical to the final accuracy of the whole process. The minimum number of iterations acceptable is 100, and this produces an accuracy of $+-$ 2 per cent. For an increase in the number of iterations to 200, the accuracy can be improved to $+-$ 1 per cent. However, there is a penalty to be paid for increasing numbers of iterations, as the simulation takes progressively longer. Thus the number of iterations chosen is a balance between accuracy and processing time.

115

The CPS has the ability to perform any number of iterations between 100 and 200 – the final decision being left to the user.

Briefly, the procedure on one iteration of a simulation is to take each bar in turn and to choose an actual duration via RNs, the assigned distribution, and the variability amount. This actual duration will not be the same on every iteration, but will reflect the possible values and their frequency of occurrence found in practice. The logical links associated with this bar are then repositioned along its length in the same proportion as entered on the original plan. Each link position is then examined to see if an interference occurs there. This is governed by the assigned interference amount and the use of RNs. The duration of the interference is chosen by RN if an assigned interference distribution is present. The cost of the bar is then calculated from the ratio of the actual bar duration to the original bar duration multiplied by the labour cost and added to the material cost, or, if resources are involved, the labour cost is calculated from the resource costs. The next bar is then taken and the same process followed until all bars have been considered. The whole bar chart is then 'rescheduled' by the logical restraints. If resource restraint and cost calculation are desired, then the resource usage is compared to the available resources to see if progress is impeded. The final duration and cost are then recorded. The whole process is then repeated up to another 199 times to complete the simulation.

Each iteration of the simulation creates a result. Due to the presence of RNs and the duration of each bar being chosen from a feasible range, there is a bewildering combination of possible bar durations and interactions which leads to a range of results being obtained rather than one single result. The results are also presented as a frequency distribution giving the range and pattern of outcomes.

The process just described is true of the general simulation process at whatever hierarchy level. However, two further facilities are employed to feed the results of the secondary level simulation into the primary level and to include weather and preliminaries processing in the primary level simulation. Each secondary level barchart can be simulated to produce a distribution of results for the duration and costs. These distributions are saved on to disk to be used as data input to the primary level simulation process, and to allow the fine detail to affect the overall result.

The effect of the weather is included in the primary level simulation, where the start and end dates of a bar are known after the actual duration has been chosen in a stochastic manner. The actual weather delay each month is chosen via RNs from a distribution of feasible weather delays, and this period is added to the bar to extend its duration. In this way a slightly different amount of weather delay is experienced on every iteration of the simulation. Thus the likely effect of the weather can be analysed, although nobody can predict what the actual weather will be, except perhaps a day or two ahead.

Project name: Case 8 - Hospital

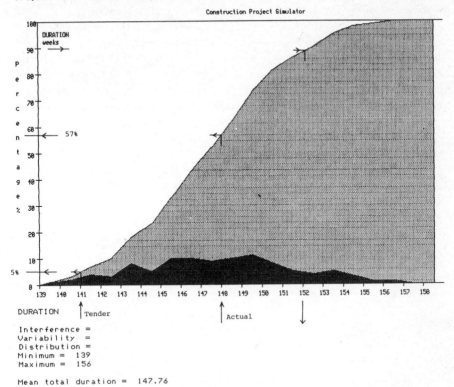

Construction Project Simulator

DURATION

Interference =
Variability =
Distribution =
Minimum = 139
Maximum = 156

Mean total duration = 147.76

9.11 *Typical simulation result, including weather, for project completion*

The costs of the preliminary categories are also calculated at the primary level. As the start and end dates of each logical link are known, it is an easy matter to calculate the period between the start and end of a preliminaries category and multiply the weekly hire rate by this figure. This is added to any fixed materials costs to arrive at a total preliminaries cost. As the position of the start and end links will rarely be the same in the simulation, a range of preliminaries costs will be produced.

This, then, briefly represents the process which occurs during a simulation. However, the myriad choices of duration and the combination of these factors is almost inconceivable to the human mind, and it is only through the use of computers that problems of this nature can be assessed. Thus the computer has brought techniques to the aid of human affairs which would not be applicable without it.

Simulation results

Typical results produced by a simulation are illustrated in Fig. 9.11. The results are presented in two forms: as a frequency histogram (darker shading) – which gives the user an impression of the pattern of results

117

– and as a cumulative frequency curve (lighter shading) – which allows the user to read off risk levels or confidence factors from the vertical scale. This vertical scale is labelled 'percentage' and represents the chance of a certain result occurring. This represents the 100 (or more) simulation results sorted into ascending order – so the lowest one had a small chance of occurring (or is a high risk), while the highest result had a very high chance of occurring (or is a small risk). The cumulative frequency curve is often the most useful as it is possible to read the risk associated with a particular result (or vice versa) directly from the graph. Work is also currently under way to produce cashflow curves as output.

The CPS has been used with several projects, and the results for a hospital project are presented to indicate the use for which the output may be employed. The tender period for the project was 141 weeks, and the tender cost (not including an allowance for inflation) was £4,856,115. The actual period for the project was 148 weeks, and the

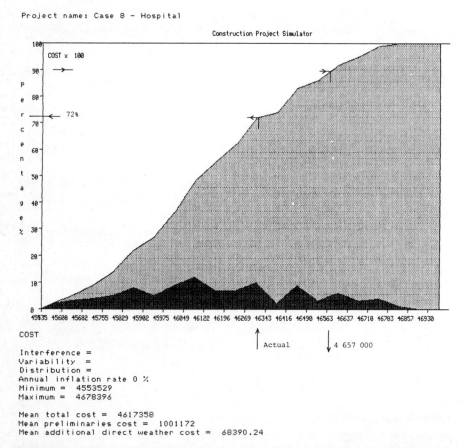

Project name: Case 8 – Hospital

Construction Project Simulator

COST

Interference =
Variability =
Distribution =
Annual inflation rate 0 %
Minimum = 4553529
Maximum = 4678396

Mean total cost = 4617358
Mean preliminaries cost = 1001172
Mean additional direct weather cost = 68390.24

9.12 *Typical simulation result, including weather, zero inflation, for project final cost*

Project name: Case 8 - Hospital

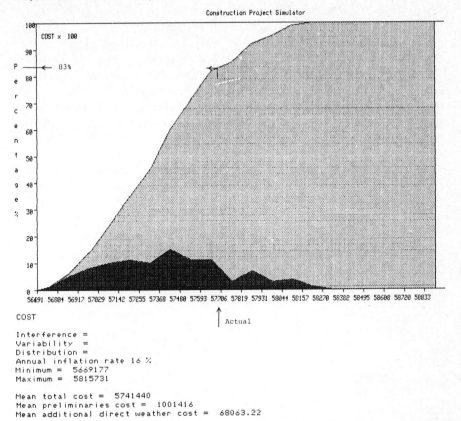

Construction Project Simulator

COST

Interference =
Variability =
Distribution =
Annual inflation rate 16 %
Minimum = 5669177
Maximum = 5815731

Mean total cost = 5741440
Mean preliminaries cost = 1001416
Mean additional direct weather cost = 68063.22

9.13 *Typical simulation result, including weather, 16% inflation, for project final cost*

final uninflated cost was £4,631,785, with the final cost including inflation being £5,769,600. The inflation rate affecting the project was 16 per cent.

The result of the most detailed simulation, including weather, for project completion is presented in Fig. 9.11, and the associated project uninflated final cost is presented in Fig. 9.12. From these figures it can be seen that the tender period only had a 5 per cent chance of success, i.e. it was very risky, while the actual period had a 57 per cent chance of success, i.e. it was very much less risky. This indicates that the contract period fixed in the tender documents was too optimistic, and, if the client was serious about obtaining completion in 141 weeks, then the design solution should have been reviewed or extra management effort expended. However, if the client could accept some later completion date, he would have been aware from the output of the upper limits to his risk, and so planned accordingly. If a risk judgement had been made based on a high confidence level of 90 per cent, then

119

the client would have been aware that a possible time contingency of 11 weeks would be advisable – of which seven weeks was expended. The tender cost was not feasible and was £224,330 higher than the actual cost, even though the project was extended seven weeks.

The professional advisor to the public client clearly overestimated his project contingency, which in this instance was included in the building budget. However, if a risk judgement had again been based on a high confidence level of 90 per cent, then the client, or his professional advisor, would have set the building budget at £4,657,000. This would have represented a reduction in the overall budget of £199,115, or 4.1 per cent, which could have been crucial in the viability assessment of the scheme by the client. The contingency amount then built into the contract budget, assuming a feasible tender cost at the 5 per cent confidence level of £4,564,130, would have been £92,879 or 2 per cent, of which £67,655 would have been expended.

The effect inflation can have on a project can be included in the simulation, and Fig. 9.13 illustrates the cost graph with the anticipated inflation amount included. No estimate of the inflated tender cost was available, but the actual value had an 83 per cent chance of success.

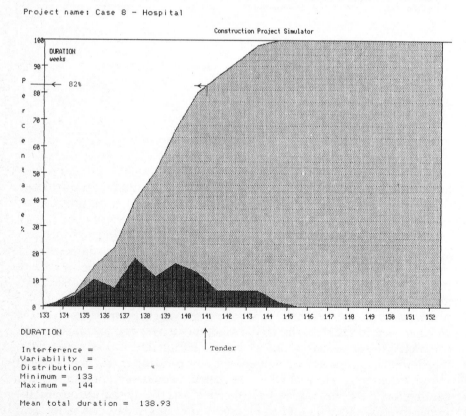

9.14 *Typical simulation result, excluding weather, for project completion*

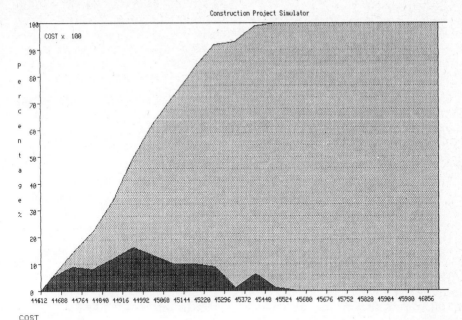

Project name: Case 8 - Hospital

Construction Project Simulator

COST

Interference =
Variability =
Distribution =
Annual inflation rate 0 %
Minimum = 4461245
Maximum = 4544869

Mean total cost = 4500928
Mean preliminaries cost = 953947.2

9.15 *Typical simulation result, excluding weather, zero inflation, for project final cost*

As the weather routine in the simulator is an additional feature, to model a specific component of interference, it is possible to simulate the project behaviour as if it had not been subject to the effects of weather. The results of the simulation omitting the effects of weather are illustrated in Figs. 9.14 and 9.15. These show that the tender period had an 82 per cent chance of success, while the actual period was not feasible. The increase in mean project duration solely attributable to the effects of the weather is 8.8 weeks, or an increase of 6.4 per cent. The increase in the mean total cost is £116,430, or an increase of 2.6 per cent. The increase in the mean project preliminaries cost due to weather is £47,225, or an increase of 5 per cent. This indicates that the preliminary costs are more sensitive to the weather than the total cost.

As well as judging a project's vulnerability to weather, it is possible to judge a project's sensitivity, through changing the project start date. To this end, the actual start date of 9 June 1980 was changed to 9 January 1981. The holiday periods in the primary bar chart were adjusted, but otherwise everything else was unchanged. However, in

121

this case, the risk levels were not significantly changed through starting the project at a more unfavourable time of year for construction operations, and the conclusion was that the project was not significantly sensitive in time or cost to a change in the project commencement date.

Risk

From an overview of the facilities in the CPS, a brief review of the results and the use they may be employed for, it should be apparent that the successful use of the CPS requires an appreciation and a desire to manage project risk; for, where there is uncertainty there is also risk. Due to uncertainty, a number of possible outcomes to one project is possible, the range of which sets the extreme values of major project variables and defines the impact uncertainty has on a project. However, in a commercial environment it is necessary to set single-value objectives, so that a set sum of money may be raised through capital or loans to pay for the project, or an end date is set so that the project can start earning income. When making such a decision in an uncertain environment, a manager must be aware of the range of possibilities and the probability of occurrence, since, in the light of his objectives and constraints, he must make a decision as to which set of outcomes is acceptable and which is not. Any one choice or decision has a certain probability of success – how many times this result or more acceptable results occurred, out of the total number of possible outcomes – and it is this probability which represents the risk the manager is willing to bear.

The risk level chosen will depend on the attitude of the manager in the light of the circumstances under which he operates. Organisations, and hence their managers, may be averse to taking risks or they may be willing to accept higher risk. An institutional client – such as a pension fund – may be unwilling to take much risk due to the possible danger this could present to its investments and funding. However, a smaller, more dynamic, commercial property speculation company, may be willing to accept a higher level of risk, as this may also offer a possibility of higher profits.

The nature of the project may also influence the attitude to risk. For a retail store it may be vitally important that a construction project is completed prior to the Christmas spending season, so that the maximum revenue may be taken. Under such circumstances they would be willing to take only minimal risk, requiring that completion by the start of the Christmas period or before had a high probability. In such circumstances it is also possible to insure against risks through insurance policies for specific events, or to impose the risk on other parties to the contract through damages clauses for non-completion.

In a construction company the costs of the labour, materials and plant could be calculated as being affected by uncertainty, and the minimum overheads and profit required to keep the company solvent added. The resulting range of outcomes for a project could be used to judge the likelihood of success – and hence the risk – a single figure bid for the project would represent. The company's attitude to the acceptable risk level would be influenced by the market, the workload of the firm, and its internal resources and constraints. The risk accepted could vary depending on the circumstances of the firm. If the company had full order books, it might not want to accept much risk for any further projects, and, if a bid were successful, it would desire a high probability of success and profits. However, if the company needed work to reach a minimum turnover, the success of a bid might be vital to the continued existence of the organisation, and high risk levels would be accepted in those circumstances.

In all these instances a risk assessment is made even when operating in the normal deterministic framework of the industry. However, an assessment of risk in such circumstances is more subjective, based on intuition, 'gut-feel', 'seat of the pants', and experience. When uncertainty is specifically included, more information is available on which to base a rational judgement, and it is not confined to those skilful, or lucky enough to be successful 'intuitive' managers; and the configuration of contingency allowances and mark-ups is placed on a more objective footing. The likelihood of success is known, and greater management efforts can be devoted to those projects carrying the most risk, to improve the chances of success.

The advent of powerful microcomputers, and the promise of better hardware in the near future, opens the door to the adoption of these mathematically-intensive techniques which could never have been carried out effectively prior to the computer age. However, it also raises the need for professional managers to be more flexible in their working practices and attitudes if the benefits of these techniques are to be reaped.

REFERENCES

1 BISHOP, D., 1966, 'Architects and productivity – 2', *Building*, vol 272, No. 1229, pp. 533–563

2 British Property Federation, 1983, *The British Property Federation system for building design and construction*, The British Property Federation Ltd, London

3 CRANDALL, K. C., 1977, 'Scheduling under uncertainty', *Proceedings of the PMI/INTERNET Symposium*, pp. 336–43

4 DRESSLER, J., 1974, 'Stochastic scheduling of linear construction sites', *ASCE Journal of the Construction Division*, vol. 100, No. CO4, pp. 571–87

5 FEILER, A. M., 1972, 'Project risk management', *Proceedings of the Third International Congress on Project Planning by Network Techniques*, vol 1, pp. 439–61

6 HALL, B. O. and STEVENS, A. J., 1982, 'Variability in construction: Measuring it and handling it', *Proceedings of the INTERNET Symposium*, pp. 559–66

7 HARRIS, R. B., 1982, *Precedence and arrow networking techniques for construction*, J. Wiley and Sons, London

8 LICHTENBERG, S., 1981, 'Real world uncertainties in project budgets and schedules', *Proceedings of the INTERNET Symposium*, pp. 179–93

9 NUNNALLY, S. W., 1981, 'Simulation in construction management', *Proceedings of the CIB Symposium on the Organization and Management of Construction*, vol 1, pp. 110–25

10 RIGGS, L. S., 1979, *Sensitivity analysis of construction operations*, PhD Thesis, Georgia Institute of Technology, USA

11 RODERICK, E. F., 1977, *Examination of the critical path methods in building: Current Paper 12*, Building Research Establishment, UK

12 TRAYLOR, R. C., *et al*, 1978, 'Project management under uncertainty', *Proceedings of the PMI Symposium*, vol 2, pp. F1–F7

13 WOOLERY, J. C., and CRANDALL, K. C., 1983, 'Stochastic network model for planning scheduling', *ASCE Journal of Construction Engineering and Management*, vol 109, No. 1, pp. 342–54

10 Computer Graphics in Construction Management
B. L. Atkin

INTRODUCTION

Today, computer graphics plays a significant role in such diverse fields as aircraft design and television advertising. Its use is now expanding into other areas, as organisations begin to recognise the commercial benefits of employing this technology. Although there is still much to be done to make computer graphics systems more accessible, there are indications that the opportunities they will provide are likely to have a considerable impact upon society in general and industry in particular. Before we proceed further, a definition would be helpful: computer graphics are *the creation, editing, storage, retrieval and output of symbols representing some real world entity by electronic means*. They may range from simple monochrome line drawings and charts to full colour animation.

This chapter is intended to examine the many benefits that can be gained from the use of computer graphics systems. In the case of the U.K. construction industry, the acceptance of computer graphics has been slow but it is beginning to be thought of as a medium of great potential. Specifically, it is considered to have much to offer the entire construction industry as an aid to both the design *and* construction of building projects. The applications for this technology, traditionally-regarded as costly, are reviewed in the light of the more recent developments in hardware and the advances in software engineering likely over the next few years. An extension of the present use of computer graphics systems to take account also of the physical processes involved in construction is examined. Finally, an indication is given as to the possible effects of the widespread use of computer graphics upon the structure of the construction industry.

Undoubtedly, there is much genuine interest in the use of computer graphics as the primary medium for communication within the construction industry. This is evidenced by the number of user and special interest groups which have been established to date. Indeed, progress *is* being made towards developing a better understanding of industry-wide needs. On an international scale, a C.I.B. (Conseil International du Batiment) working commission, W78, has been set up to encourage research and development in computer-aided design; to organise co-operation, and to carry out work in computer-aided architectural and engineering design. A programme of work has been planned to include the collection and exchange of information internationally and to relate this work to that of other C.I.B. working commissions.

Another collaborative effort has been established in the form of F.A.C.E. (The International Federation of Associations of Computer Users in Engineering, Architecture and Related Fields) of which Britain's C.I.C.A. is a member organisation. F.A.C.E. exists to promote the establishment of technical user associations in countries over three continents; to seek international co-operation; to act as a central source of information, and to disseminate that information.

The C.I.C.A. offers three publications[1,2,3] of interest to the subject area covered by this chapter, one of which examines the *state of the art* of computer-aided design applications in Japan. It is from Japan that significant advances in computer-aided design with *intelligent* interfaces are likely to come into our midst. The systems that the Japanese are proposing may enable designers to integrate some form of intelligent knowledge-base, built from many man-years of working experience.

BACKGROUND TO COMPUTER GRAPHICS

Early history

Ever since visual display units were first developed, pundits have been forecasting the development, one day, of highly sophisticated techniques of visual representation such as animation, image processing, solids modelling etc. To some extent these techniques are all possible now, although they are still a long way from the advanced state often proclaimed. However, it is possible to imagine how far these techniques will develop, since investment in the technologies that support them is the largest of any sector within information technology. The ultimate convergence of these enabling technologies will produce a single source out of which man will be able to visualise most present-day phenomena. Until that day there is still much to be done·to improve the understanding of all sectors of society about the wider uses of information technology. To show where computer graphics fit in is not a simple task, since the technology inevitably presents us with many overlaps. Fig. 10.1 is an attempt to place computer graphics in a wider context, but even this is far from being as clear as it may seem. None the less, it illustrates the various technologies which we are about to consider and their relationships with one another. To aid the appreciation of the current state of the art in both the technology and applications for the construction industry, it is worth presenting a brief overview of the origins of computer graphics.

Some of the earliest work in computer graphics was undertaken at the Massachusetts Institute of Technology (M.I.T.) in the 1950s where, for the first time, lines were displayed on cathode ray tubes. The first really serious work in the research and development of computer graphics began in the early 1960s.[4] However, it was not until the early part of this present decade that acceptance of this technology reached into working practice. Much of this apparent delay in the take-up of the technology can be attributed to the gap between technically feasible

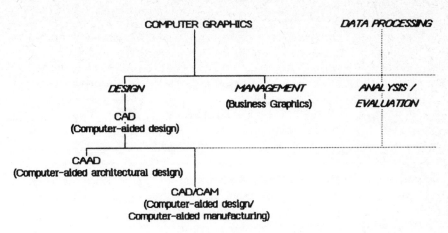

10.1 *Overview of computer graphics technologies*

solutions and commercially acceptable ones. If we were to analyse the cost effectiveness of any so-called computer-aided design system of the 1970s, it would be difficult to see how it could be justified on cost alone. In most cases the technology was introduced to automate the existing manual process of drawing production and, in this scenario, was not expected to have any effect upon existing infrastructures. A major cost/pay-back threshold has now been reached, due primarily to the significant fall in hardware costs and refinement of software tools. We should now be able to predict, with some confidence, the resolution of some long standing problems.

Over the years, the major breakthroughs in computer-aided design have been attributed to advances in three main areas, namely very large-scale integration, display and storage technologies. Each of these areas is covered in more detail later in this chapter.

International standards

The exponential growth in microelectronics has spawned many solutions to man-made problems but equally has caused as many new problems to arise, some of which remain unresolved. Here, we are referring to the duplication of standards in one form or another of anything from operating systems to local area networks (see Chapter 11). It would be naïve to suggest that all this has been caused by the failure of governments and their respective Standards' organisations or institutes to agree on common codes. The gains arising out of the adoption of one particular standard in any field could be substantial for a commercial organisation with the rights to it. Suffice to say, there are many options open to users wishing to install a computer graphics system. The trick, for the user, is to select the most appropriate system from all those available.

Protocols are an essential part of the communications process, since, without them, little successful transfer of data would be possible:

computer graphics are no exception to this rule. In fact, over the last few years there has been increasing activity in the area of an internationally agreed graphics standard. Currently, there is one such standard vying for domination, namely I.G.E.S., Initial Graphics Exchange Specification. I.G.E.S. became available in the U.S.A. in the early part of this decade and is now widely used by both government and private industry. Presently, 2D and 3D information, including surfaces and mesh data for finite modelling, can be exchanged under I.G.E.S. 1.0 and/or 2.0 processors. I.G.E.S. is now supported by most major vendors of computer-aided design systems and, under the proposed version 3.0, it is possible that there will be sufficiently advanced techniques to allow the kind of data exchange discussed later in this chapter. (I.G.E.S. 3.0 is primarily intended to support solids modelling.)

Essentially, I.G.E.S. is a format for communicating information about product design and manufacturing. It is considered to be of particular

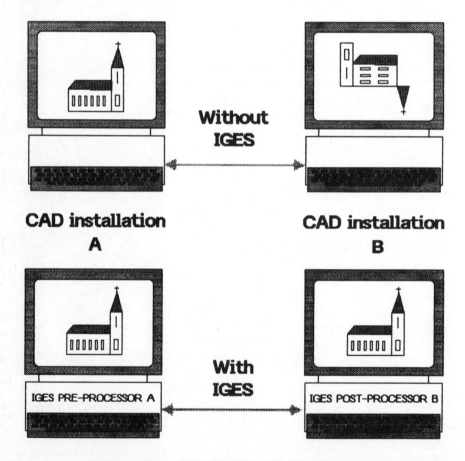

(After an idea by the National Economic Development Office)

10.2 *The need for an internationally agreed graphics standard*

128

interest to organisations using either a number of sub-contractors and/ or a variety of computer-aided design systems. It is designed to link otherwise incompatible installations and will, therefore, dispense with the need to re-input or update data. Fig. 10.2 illustrates the concept of I.G.E.S. in a fairly simplistic way. I.G.E.S. is invoked by the user of the first machine creating a special file using the I.G.E.S. pre-processor: the data is then transmitted in I.G.E.S. format to the second machine. Here, the data is post-processed and read into the second system where it can be used in the normal way, that is to say, interactively. In practice, this procedure necessitates prior agreement on the format of the information to be transmitted, and a number of iterations of the process are likely before the results could be regarded as acceptable.

In the U.K., N.E.D.O.'s Engineering Construction and Process Plant Economic Development Committee has declared I.G.E.S. to be a valuable tool for British industry and, through the Department of Trade and Industry, a pilot project is being supported to examine five areas of working:

1 Transfer of drawings and annotation
2 As 1. above but to include bills of quantity, lists etc.
3 Transfer of models
4 Transfer of a full database
5 Computer-aided manufacturing, CAM

It is not clear what benefits will accrue to the construction industry, but it is obvious that none will if little or no interest is shown by the industry.

ENABLING TECHNOLOGIES

Generations of technology

With the benefit of hindsight, we now see that progress has been linked to the emergence of a handful of discrete components. In fact, it is now accepted that there have been three previous generations; there is still one to come, and so we must now be in the midst of the fourth generation of this technology. If we examine all the generations of the technology with respect to the needs of computer-aided design systems, we have:

1st: Mainframes and refreshed vector displays
2nd: Minicomputers and storage tubes
3rd: Super minicomputers and raster graphics
4th: Networked systems
5th: Knowledge-based engineering systems

Each of these generations has its own combination of technological advancement relative to electronic components and software engineering. Although integration was a term unassociated with first generation technologies, the main driving force has always been to increase the circuits to size ratio and reduce the unit cost of production in the process. Hence, the present concern with very large-scale integration

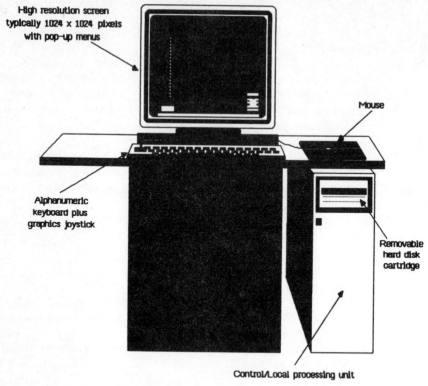

High resolution screen
typically 1024 x 1024 pixels
with pop-up menus

Mouse

Alphanumeric
keyboard plus
graphics joystick

Removable
hard disk
cartridge

Control/Local processing unit

10.3 *Single user computer graphics workstation with network capability*

which will further increase the power and capability of the hardware base.

Very large-scale integration

One of the four main areas identified by Alvey[5] is that of very large-scale integration (VLSI) which is seen as the major enabling technology for fifth generation computer systems. The packaging of many hundreds of thousands of discrete components into one single unit, less than the size of a finger nail, hints at the demise of some of the larger computer systems. However, this assertion is not completely true, since large-scale processing and storage is still likely to be required as a supplement to localised transacting.

Most of the currently installed computer-aided design systems still rely on a substantial central processor for computation and file storage which is augmented, when required, by a variable amount of local processing in the workstation. Here, the central processor is normally a time-sharing super minicomputer such as a DEC VAX or a PRIME. However, this technology is likely to be replaced by dedicated single user workstations over the next five to ten years (see Fig. 10.3). Much of this advancement has been brought about by the very large-scale integration of microprocessor and memory chips.

Display technologies

The familiar cathode ray tube, based on raster-scan display, is becoming a preferred alternative to storage tube technology for graphics work. Some limitations still persist, such as difficulty with certain interactive features – dragging, elastic-banding etc. – but the advantages would seem to outweigh any of the apparent disadvantages. Certainly, solids can be drawn more easily and effectively with raster-scan displays, and this should open up the possibility of different, if not better drawings than current practice seems content with. Moreover, raster-scan technology has created many new opportunities for visual displays: multi-windows, icons, pop-up/pull-down menus, are all associated with this technology. (See Chapter 11 for a more detailed description of workstations using this technology.) Optical/pointing mouse devices are an integral part of this technology, since they allow the user to interact more directly with the processes available within the machine. Together with multi-window and multi-tasking, they will allow the user to pursue concurrent activities which the real world demands, instead of the sequential methods offered at present by system vendors.

Software engineering

The second and most important of the four areas identified by Alvey[5] is that of software engineering, which has emerged in recent years as a discipline in its own right. Software engineering is *the embodiment of the good practice of developing and applying appropriate tools to the systematic analysis of problems, and the design of the software solution.* Part of the work of the Alvey Directorate is concerned with the implementation of projects into the development of advanced programming languages. The newer, or fifth generation programming languages, of which PROLOG is a good example, are thought to have a lot to offer computer-aided design. In particular, they enable systems' designers to construct code structures that will allow a greater amount of logic programming. This will then assist the end user in the generation of design solutions by virtue of the system being able to infer certain conditions from a given set of rules and constraints. These will be applied to a knowledge-base which will be constructed in a manner similar to relational data bases of the present.

Integrated graphics systems

Howard[6] expressed the view that integration, to computer people, meant linking programs, that is to say, running different applications from the same data base. To people in construction it is more likely to mean getting the architect, engineer and contractor to work more closely together: this implies exchanging information more freely. Fig. 10.4 shows, in a generalised way, how these two ideas are fundamentally the

131

An integrated computer system

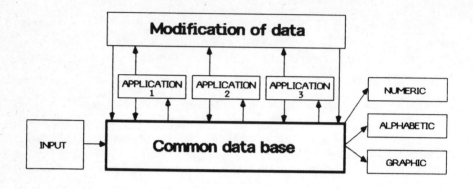

An integrated building design system

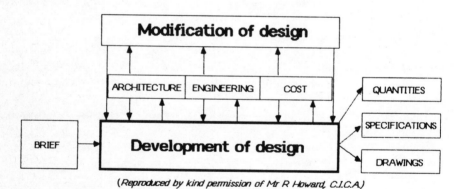

(Reproduced by kind permission of Mr R Howard, C.I.C.A.)

10.4 *Integration as two different but closely related concepts*

same. The computer industry has a basic view of computers, in that it perceives them as *universal* machines, whereas the construction industry is simply concerned with their application to solve real world problems; in both cases the concern is with defining precisely the nature of the information to be handled by the system.

There are many obvious benefits from the use of integrated systems, but the major penalty is the large overhead which these systems must carry. Like so many other innovative technologies which must rely on public sector backing, integrated systems cannot support themselves.

They must enjoy the type of financial backing which can only be provided by large public sector construction programmes, such as housing, schools and hospitals. Since this backing has not been forthcoming in recent years, and since the overheads have continued to rise, the integrated system has given way to draughting systems whose use can be justified solely by the output produced in the immediate term.

For the time being, graphics systems are physically large and very demanding of the software required to support any worthwhile application. Current practice usually means computers being used for the automation of existing manual processes. In many design offices, the packages used to generate production information, that is to say, drawings, schedules, specifications and even bills of quantities, are often separate. The desire to link individual packages gives rise to the notion of integration which, in the context of architectural applications, implies not just draughting but also design. It seems that the term CAD is invariably taken to mean computer-aided design when, in fact, it rarely extends beyond draughting. Perhaps the term computer-aided design and draughting (CADD), would be more appropriate in these circumstances.

Integration may occur in many forms and at various levels of sophistication but does not suffer from quite the same problems as *compatibility*. In keeping with the concept of the workstation at its various levels (see Chapter 11), this chapter now considers four levels of integration from which it will be seen that there are, indeed, some similarities.

Level 1

This is essentially an unintegrated system, but one which offers the potential for sharing data. All the software or *tools*, as they are normally referred to, are widely applicable and, therefore, require configuring to suit individual solutions. Consequently they are likely to be low cost packages which have a proven track record. They might well include:

Drawing – for generating and editing sketches, diagrams etc.

Writing – typical word processor for creating and editing text

Modelling – financial and/or numeric manipulation; the familiar spreadsheet

Graphing – for creating graphs, charts etc. from numeric data

Level 2

This relates to those tools which offer some degree of interconnection so that data can be moved across from one application to another. In simple terms this may involve the cutting and pasting of, say, a spreadsheet into a section of word processed text, or the transfer of modelled costs to a business graphics package in order to show trends etc. In some instances it may be possible to place, say, cost and resource data on to drawings to provide links or interfaces to other programs.

Level 3

Greater amounts of data transfer are possible here and a number of quite separate users may be able to work on an evolving design. Here the major problem is one of ensuring that individual users are working on the correct version, especially as the latest offering from the designer may well be little more than initial sketching. In this scenario, it is usual for the architect to be working on one layer, the structural engineer on another and the services engineer on a further, different layer. Each of these layers can be thought of as overlays to the general arrangement plans etc. In a manual system these overlays sometimes create their own problems of co-ordination.

Level 4

These systems rely on large-scale data bases to drive the design through to completion of production information. Data driven design systems exist in a variety of forms, depending on the amount of data captured within the data base. They may range from a *parts model*, where the building is represented by a collection of parts or components (each one a 3D solid), to a sophisticated database where all facets of the building are present. Obviously, the latter is extremely difficult to achieve in all but those cases where designers are working with a fairly narrow range of possible solutions; for example, industrialised buildings where the data to drive the design is within known bounds. No doubt as databases expand, the opportunities for exploring a wider range of possible building solutions will increase accordingly.

Database management systems

The term 'database' is inevitably associated with computers, even though most databases are physical constructs. Essentially, a database can be thought of as *any organised, integrated information structure which will permit a number of different users to gain access, retrieve and store information.* Naturally, most databases found in general usage are paper-based. On a small scale, a project file is a database and, on a larger scale, a building product/commodity filing system is another; for example, Barbour index etc.

Many of the current database systems could be more accurately described as information retrieval or electronic filing systems. However, when data is held in a large system and more than simple accessing is involved, a more appropriate term would be a *database management system*, DBMS. Unfortunately, traditional attitudes associate the term DBMS with large numbers of programmers swarming around masses of computer print-out paper; this is no longer the case. Trends in database design have produced more compact solutions which are infinitely more user-friendly, well designed and packaged to suit the user and not data processing personnel: the small computer market is geared to self-sufficiency and off-the-shelf sales. In this marketplace, buyers and users are one and the same, and therefore products have to be geared to appeal to non-computer minded people.

Traditionally, there have been three main types of database for large computers: hierarchical, network and relational. In a hierarchical system, records are linked in a top-down or parent-child relationship. Network based structures expand the concept of hierarchical by allowing records of information to have many owners rather than one. The relational concept comes closest to the ideals of flexible access and simplicity of design. Relational databases are structured as a series of 'flat' sequential files with data repeated in different files (or *tables* as they are often known) to form logical links which may be supplemented by pointers or index tables. Locating the data, therefore, relies upon the data in one table being related to another. Some relational database structures also permit a degree of mathematics and analysis to be performed, and so the possibility of constructing powerful knowledge-bases becomes more of a reality.

Some of the databases linked to computer graphics systems incorporate a query/report utility, restructuring capabilities and data description languages to avoid much of the tedium and lack of user-friendliness often associated with many of the earlier systems: an ability to generate output in a form which the user can comprehend is paramount. Screen formatting, selection criteria and sort parameters are now commonplace, and prospective users should look to these factors when evaluating a system or package. Other systems may include a data dictionary, which permits the user to maintain a coherent assemblage of terminology, essential if there is to be no chance of misinterpretation. But the major use of a data dictionary is to apply itself to the problems associated with data such as size, characteristics, relationships within files and records.

In most *turnkey* situations the database has already been configured and, as a result, the user is often presented with a less flexible system. Where a complete computer-aided design system is to be brought together by the user, there may well be distinct advantages in spending greater time and effort in specifying the database management system. Graphics are probably comparatively easy to judge, but database structures may contain subtle nuances which may later constrain fuller use of the system. Therefore, prospective users should carefully consider the nature of the information which the system will be expected to provide during its lifetime.

A number of external databases are now currently on offer to the construction industry. They hint at the probable direction of developments in the provision of the extensive databases needed to drive the computer-aided design systems of tomorrow. Currently, these include both public and private systems in which the user is normally responsible for maintaining a dedicated microcomputer or workstation as a terminal and the costs of telephone connection charges, computer time etc. Typical of a public networked system is British Telecom's PRESTEL, and, in the case of private networks, the R.I.C.S. offers an on-line cost database facility through their Building Cost Information Service. Ultimately, it may be possible to incorporate the data from this source into the parameters of a relational database held on a user's computer-aided design system.

APPLICATIONS

Business graphics

The presentation of data in a medium which can be readily assimilated by the recipient is a powerful aid and one which is likely to improve decision-making processes. For instance, the trends implicit in most cost indexes are often difficult to perceive if they are in a purely numeric

1. Contract Cash Flow

Valuation No.	Cummulative Valuations	Net
1	40,000	40,000
2	90,000	50,000
3	150,000	60,000
4	260,000	110,000
5	470,000	210,000
6	710,000	240,000
7	850,000	140,000
8	920,000	70,000
9	970,000	50,000
10	1,000,000	30,000
11	1,020,000	20,000
12	1,045,000	25,000

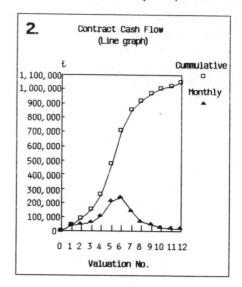

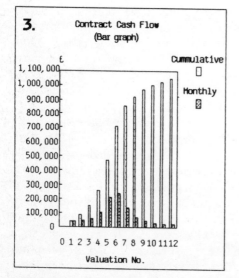

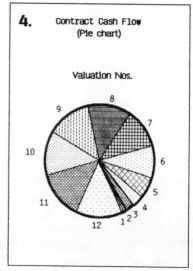

10.5 *Four ways of presenting the same data*

form. However, if this data is used to generate graphs, the trends can be identified immediately by simple visual inspection. Fig. 10.5 demonstrates four different ways of presenting the estimated cash flow for a construction project. The numeric data has been transformed into a choice of three graphical forms, of which the last is the least meaningful. This illustrates the point that computers can be used, without much thought, to produce something that may be taken as useful even though it is little short of nonsense.

Computer-aided engineering (CAE) and computer-aided design (CAD)

In much the same way that information technology is the generic term for all computer-based equipment, computer-aided engineering is the term nowadays applied to all forms of computer-aided design systems. However, this does not give any clue as to the applications being brought under the control of the computer, except for those that are concerned with engineering *per se*.

Currently, there are over 200 systems claiming to provide computer-aided design in one form or another (2D, 2½D, 3D, solid modelling etc.). Some of these systems are really little more than draughting machines and unlikely to be capable of actual design. Accordingly, many of them still fail to provide the full package of information that would benefit the entire design/construction team. In fact, the sole aim of some manufacturers is to convince would-be purchasers (mainly designers, of course) of their system's ability to produce drawings in such a way as to make them indistinguishable from manually prepared ones. High quality graphics which appear to represent *real* forms often have very little to back them up: the system's knowledge of the symbols used rarely extends beyond the name and the location of the object it represents.

There are good reasons why system vendors are as yet unable to provide a more complete package. This is due, in part, to the fact that graphics place enormous demands upon software design and computer power. Therefore, it is to be expected that the full potential of these systems should be limited in some way. Hence, the main thrust of development in recent years has been the refining of existing systems to produce greater cost effectiveness in the drawing office. Apart from obvious increases in processing and storage, improvements have been achieved by the introduction of more rapid means of data input such as the use of tablets (for menus and locating), lightpens (for pinpointing), mouse devices (for menus and locating) etc. Another reason for the reluctance of vendors to expand their systems is the limited market into which such systems could be sold. Obviously, until the demand for more broadly-based systems becomes clearly evident, vendors will continue to make progress by increments, that is to say, offering systems which can be fully utilised by customers only at a particular time.

Before proceeding with specific examples of construction industry-based applications, it would be helpful to have some understanding of the way in which computer-aided design systems are used. The workstation is normally the hub of the system and is likely to comprise the following (see also Chapter 11):

Monitor	– video display for viewing graphics, text and menu selection
Tablet	– surface for entering (digitising) graphics and standard menu selections
Pen or puck	– electronic stylus for digitising graphics and for menu selection `
Keyboard	– alternate command entry device
Printer	– local hard copy of displayed graphics or text
Control unit	– workstation manager for control of characters and of geometry. This device may be a semi-intelligent terminal or a super microcomputer

The above outlines the more obvious features without examining some of the more crucial issues, such as those pertaining to the domain of user interface. Firstly, there is the on-line documentation which is needed by the user whenever a prompt is sought. Documentation which is entirely paper-based is likely to be a cumbersome means of receiving assistance. Moreover, the response is needed within the system not outside it. Secondly, command structure can have a demoralising effect upon the user if it is illogical or complex. To overcome these problems, a number of system vendors have constructed their own command languages based on conversational English syntax. Lastly, function selection can be achieved without laborious keying-in using menu overlays on tablets. Fig. 10.6 illustrates the principle. Menu overlays can be designed to suit an organisation's individual requirements and so can reduce the total number of inputs. Macro-commands are sometimes possible – these link multiple commands – so that complete operations can be performed by a single action.

A computer-aided design system is fundamentally a graphics system and should be expected to incorporate fast, flexible graphics manipulation. The graphics capabilities of a typical system should include the following:

Multi-layering to emulate overlay draughting
Grids for referencing; auto-grids for snapping-to
2D and possibly *3D* capability
Zooming and scrolling locally and globally
Stretching, deleting, partial deletions and blanking out
Grouping and locking objects
Mirroring, rotating, translating etc.
Multiple views and independent scaling

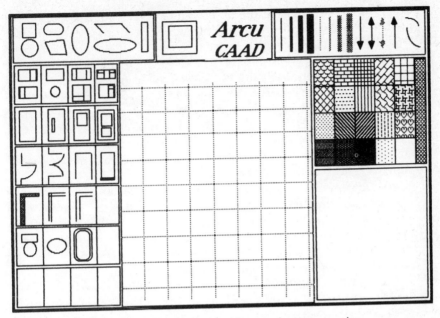

10.6 *Typical graphics tablet showing architectural menu overlay*

Automatic dimensioning
Measuring capability – distance, lengths, areas and angles
Graphic elements – lines, arcs, circles, splines etc.
Text and line fronts selection

Any system must have, at the very least, a library of symbols, representing elements or components which can be called up from the database as required. In practice, it is usual to have a range of libraries relative to the individual disciplines using the system, for example, architectural, H.V.A.C., electrical etc. Elements within a library may include such items as lines, text and texturing. They may be simple or complex depending upon the object being represented. In addition to graphics, library elements may sometimes incorporate non-graphic attributes. These may be any kind of information the user wishes to associate with the element, such as part numbers, wall finish types, cost codes, suppliers etc. It is these non-graphic attributes that are central to the system's report generation capabilities. These features are only made possible by the system's database management system. Ordinarily, libraries can be modified quickly, in the case of adding elements, by the digitising of manually prepared templates or by using the inherent graphic capabilities of the system. Library elements are normally independent of scale and so the inserted elements automatically adjust to the scale of the drawing.

Creating drawings is achieved by the conversion of sets of digitised locations into lines which can be made to represent walls etc. By specifying a thickness, or, if a double line facility is available, by selecting that from the menu, it is possible to create 2D plans. When wall height is added, the two-dimensional drawing can be used to create either a 2½D model or a 3D one.

Doors and windows are inserted into wall segments by menu selection: the walls are then automatically cut back and trimmed to the dimensions of the inserted element. By the successive generation of wall segments and the enclosure of space, the system should be able to store all the information pertaining to the ownership of elements within that space. It may then be possible to perform measurement exercises as well as a number of report generation facilities such as *where found* for components, and schedules of finishes etc.

Interference, overlay, clash and consistency checking etc. are now fairly well-established features in computer-aided design. The system's knowledge of the complete model of the building should ensure that the warning bells sound when, say, an attempt is made on one layer to introduce pipework through a column or when a door is positioned on an external wall above the ground floor.

Visualisation is a most powerful aid to the designers' work, in that it will permit concepts to be presented in an infinite variety of perspectives. Isometric and perspective drawings provide the user with the ability to visualise from an unlimited number of views. Coupled with this ability must be one of hidden line removal and, with the more powerful systems, it may even be possible to use colour renderings from a vast palate to give the design texture and presence.

Computer-aided architectural design (CAAD)

Computer-aided architectural design (CAAD) and computer-aided building design (CABD) are essentially one and the same, although either term may be used in preference to the other so as to infer some subtle distinction or special slant. Fig. 10.7 presents a simplified schematic view of the individual packages that may well constitute a working computer-aided architectural design system.

Early work in this area tended to focus upon the general functional activities in building design with the intention of isolating those functions for which a relatively simple software solution could be found. These early applications ranged from structural design and environmental analysis to spatial design. In the case of the latter, complex algorithms were involved in addition to the more obvious computational effort. The four basic functions which a typical computer-aided architectural design system should exhibit are:

1 The storage of some form of digital representation of the building, or part thereof

2 The ability to input data, edit it and thus modify the building

3 The measurement of the performance of the building in terms of its engineering and cost

4 The generation of graphical, quantitative and qualitative documentation consistent with the needs of the users of the system
There are other requirements that could easily be added to this list,
but it is suggested that the full list would preclude from consideration
many of the systems currently on the market. A total system could well
be described as a fully integrated system and this is, perhaps, where
current development should be aimed, if it is not already. Today, four
discrete areas of application are recognised:

1 Spatial planning
2 Architectural detailing
3 Environmental design and building services
4 Building performance appraisal

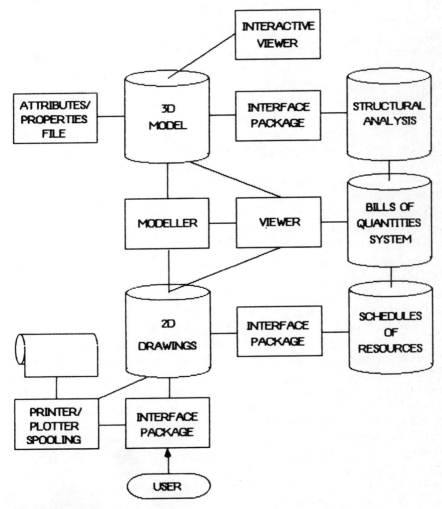

10.7 *Schematic representation of a computer-aided design system*

A number of computer-aided architectural design systems are now commercially available. They range from a low cost spatial modelling package to fully integrated design and draughting linked to manufacturing. Some of these systems are now reviewed with the intention of outlining their typical features rather than providing any detailed comparison between them.

Ecotech's SCRIBE (Space, Cost, Resources and Integrated Building Evaluation) is a microcomputer-based graphics system for the detailed modelling and evaluation of the form, cost and thermal performance of building designs. It permits a building's dimensional form to be modelled from a plan layout for the presentation of elevational, isometric and perspective views. The system is built around a three-dimensional graphics module which was designed as a general drawing and spatial modelling program. SCRIBE also has the facility to measure forms when elemental materials have been defined, for total thermal performance and elemental cost. This is achieved by giving every drawn line and plane a unique code number that classifies it as a spatial element with specification or attributes in terms of cost, thermal conductance, capacitance or mass. SCRIBE is also able to compute the area of walls, roofs, floors or other planes, as well as volumes of mass elements and spaces. From this data it is then possible to calculate the total fabric cost, heat loss and steady state energy consumption. With the further development of the complete SCRIBE system many additional routines could be undertaken. Current applications for SCRIBE, apart from its obvious architectural usage, include interior design, urban design, engineering and construction planning. In fact, it is known that SCRIBE is presently in use as an aid to the laying out of houses on sites for a speculative builder. Fig. 10.8 illustrates the use of SCRIBE in the design of housing on a live project.

GMW's RUCAPS is a draughting system linked to a database which provides for building forms to be developed in three dimensions. In addition, there is a choice between 2 and 2½D working which provides a good deal of flexibility for the designer, permitting concepts to be developed in the most appropriate dimensions. The RUCAPS database is a fundamental part of the total system as it provides the basis for maintaining a coherent body of data that can be drawn on to generate both graphic and non-graphic output. A library of building elements and information on cost can also be built up within the database for use on any project. This library allows the user to schedule lists of building components and, if required, undertake costing exercises.

ARC's BDS and GDS are two related systems, with the former working in three dimensions and the latter in two. BDS, or Building Design System, deals with a building form by storing it as a 3D model from which any plan, elevation, section or perspective can be generated. BDS subsystems provide the means for handling evaluation data for cost and environmental analyses, and for detailed design and documentation including bills of quantities. Although appearing to offer more to the designer, BDS is used less extensively than its 2D relation, GDS. However, the two systems can be used to complement one another such that BDS models the geometry and physical components of a building in three dimensions. It is then used to organise, analyse and reproduce

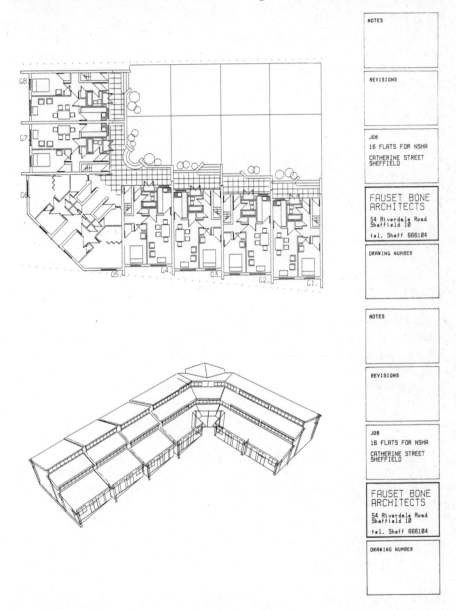

10.8 *SCRIBE in use on a live housing project (reproduced by kind permission of Mr. C. Green, Ecotech Design Ltd and Fauset Bone, Architects; both of Sheffield, U.K.)*

the kind of information normally associated with building design. GDS will accept drawings from BDS and produce fully-annotated detail and production drawings. In addition, GDS can also be used as an input facility to systems which produce tapes for numerically controlled (N/C) machine tools. This opens up the opportunities for a continuous computer-aided design/computer-aided manufacturing capability, CAD/CAM.

Intergraph offer a system which combines an interactive graphics design system with a data management and retrieval system to support architectural design and draughting. The complete system, which is based upon DEC's PDP 11 and VAX series, is capable of generating fully interactive 3D models of building designs. At the user interface of this system is a workstation which is normally configured to provide two displays, one in monochrome, and one in colour. Together with a large tablet and menu overlays, the user is able to drive the system. Visualisation techniques are particularly impressive, using this system through the design and draughting stages.

CIS's MEDUSA and CV's DESIGNER systems have recently been brought together into a full range of computer-aided design systems. These systems provide the usual range of graphics capabilities including 3D display, visualisation, analysis and reporting from its database facility. Included in this range of systems is a single user workstation known as the CDS 3000, which is based on the MC68010 microprocessor with virtual memory support and UNIX operating system. Individual workstations are linked via an Ethernet local area network, and multi-tasking is available. This workstation also has the benefit of multi-window management, icons, pop-up menus and mouse devices, thus making it a strong contender as a common construction industry workstation (see Chapter 11). It represents a complete distributed CAD/CAM system which may also be linked to an IBM 4300 series computer to provide large-scale data management capabilities.

Computer-aided manufacturing (CAM)

In Sweden, one particular design and construction company has developed its own data driven computer-aided design system. It is based on a commercially available computer-aided draughting system which interfaces to other applications' packages, such as computer-aided manufacturing. The complete system is possible only because of the fairly limited range of products that are offered: the system is geared to producing standard housing units, although some variations are possible.

A number of computer-aided design vendors already offer links to manufacturing for other industries. It is suggested that, in the short term, the opportunities for links through to computer-aided manufacturing will be few and the gains limited. However, in the long term, factory production techniques may well demand closer ties between design and manufacturing, thus forcing designers to fall into line.

IBM's CADAM (Computer graphics Augmented Design And Manufacturing) has a dual personality in that it is both a computer-aided design and draughting system, and a computer-aided manufacturing system. The keystone of the CADAM system is a large-scale database which is created by the user generating the necessary graphics at the terminal and then storing each under a distinct drawing identity. Access to this database permits any number of personnel involved with the project to call up drawn information to suit his/her specialist needs. This might include the designer, production engineer, N/C programmer, tool designer and a product support specialist. It is known that CADAM is being used extensively by a major, public sector, multi-disciplinary organisation to generate architectural production drawings, and an industrialised buildings design/constructor offering a well-defined range of products.

Simulating the construction process

To date, computer-aided architectural design has been preoccupied with producing drawings more rapidly than was previously possible by traditional manual methods. Consequently, it tends to deal with the design component only of the design and construction continuum. Existing design practice is essentially geared to producing graphical representations of the completed building form; invariably, it takes little account of the actual fabrication and assembly processes involved in its construction. In fact, current design practice, which concentrates upon 2D detailing, seems to have little regard for the construction process. Taking account of actual construction implications in the design of any building is believed to offer one way of overcoming many of the deficiencies in the existing process. People with experience of other industries, particularly on the fringe of the construction industry, will be aware of the integrated, inseparable nature of design and construction: design is sometimes regarded as a subset of construction. Fig. 10.9 contrasts the attitudes of two other industries towards design and construction.

The requirement that design must reflect most if not all construction implications is, in practice, difficult to achieve since many of them are unknown prior to work commencing on site. It is suggested that an ability to simulate the physical construction of the built form should lead to better designed buildings. By the testing of alternative strategies, it should be possible to determine the most appropriate method of construction having regard to both time and cost. In this regard, design is considered incomplete unless it has been tested in some way.

The possibility of effecting a worthwhile improvement within the existing framework of design is likely only if all those factors attributable to the physical construction process are incorporated into design principles and practice. Such factors would include temporary works, plant

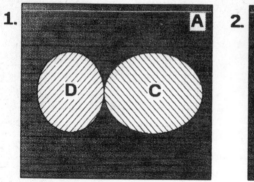
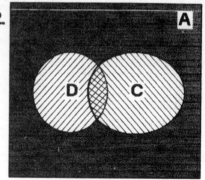

CONSTRUCTION INDUSTRY
(TRADITIONAL BUILDING CONTRACT)

CONSTRUCTION INDUSTRY
(WITH CONTRACTORS DESIGN)

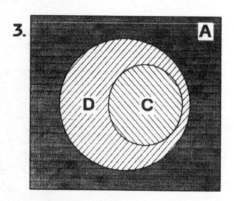
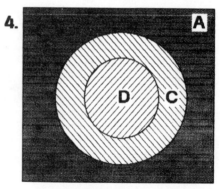

AEROSPACE INDUSTRY (AIRCRAFT)

OIL INDUSTRY (OIL PLATFORM)

A - Total Project; D - Design; C - Construction

10.9 *Contrasting project systems*

and machinery, storage and hutting etc. Although these factors are hardly ever associated with the final built form, they are of no less importance than the material fabric and are a significant part of the total cost of any project.

In practice, taking account of the above constructional factors would be difficult if the processes were of an entirely manual nature. However, the use of powerful computer-aided design systems, incorporating a database management system, may provide part of the answer. For instance, handling constructional data such as that of cranage is not inherently different from handling material component data. Indeed, the commonly accepted requirements of a computer-aided design system – namely, overlay, clash and consistency checking etc. – could all be applied to this type of data once incorporated in the system's library. A prerequisite of this kind of approach is the formalisation of the construction planner's thinking in terms of physical spaces etc. with regard to their respective locations, logical sequence and timescales for all the so-called constructional data. Fig. 10.10 shows how crane

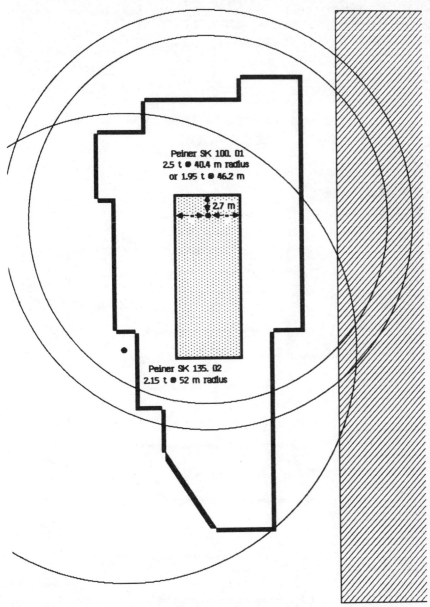

Peiner SK 100. 01
25 t ● 40.4 m radius
or 1.95 t ● 46.2 m

2.7 m

Peiner SK 135. 02
2.15 t ● 52 m radius

10.10 *The testing of crane positions using a simple 2D tool*

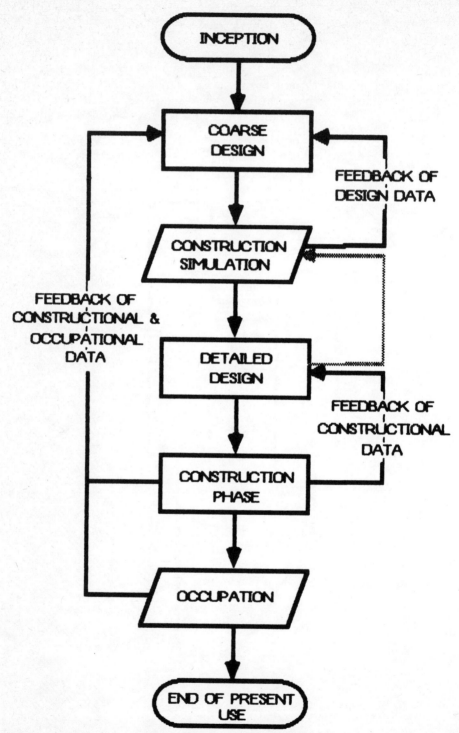

10.11 *Testing design before proceeding to construction*

positions can be rapidly tested by superimposing them on outline plans with the help of a simple 2D drawing tool; this example has been taken from a live project.

Simulating the construction process for successive stages of coarse design before progressing on to more detailed design should reduce complexity and the occurrence of interference. Naturally, this begs the question of how much design would need to be completed before simulation was a realistic proposition. A further task, therefore, must be to determine the level of, and stages at which, design can be tested. In this context, design is not seen as a totally sequential or linear operation, but one which relies on the iteration of detailing from coarse design to simulated construction and back again to design (see Fig. 10.11). In this way, modifications can be made to the design before it is finally committed to operations on site.

The above approach is a synthesis of design permitting more reliably built forms to emerge: it places a significant onus on the decision-making processes within operational planning. Buildings produced in this way should afford greater certainty in construction planning and cost control, whilst at the same time freeing architects from some of their less productive duties and allowing them to concentrate on designing better buildings.

Links between design and construction

An expansion of computer-aided design systems to take account of constructional data such as time, resources etc. is certainly not a new idea but one which may now be more practicable. The Department of Construction Management at the University of Reading is conducting a project supported by the Science and Engineering Research Council into the use of computer-aided design systems as tools of management.[7] Part of the programme of work is concerned with establishing a link between design and constructional data in the generation of design options. It is expected that a computer-supported technique will be developed whereby construction managers may examine the client's requirements relative to budgets and programmes, prior to detailed design being commenced. This is likely to involve a link-up with certain project management techniques such as critical path analysis, resource analysis, cash flow forecasting etc. to provide a more immediate feedback of the viability of the design at outline proposal stage.

IMPACT UPON THE CONSTRUCTION INDUSTRY

Professional roles

Biggs[8] expressed the view that the new technology was, in many ways, being used to perpetuate professional barriers and, as we have seen already in this chapter, the natural forces opposing integration have arisen out of the quite separate and distinct disciplines which have long existed in the construction industry. Certain organisations might well be blamed for their resistance towards integration and, in particular, some computer companies may feel they have too much to lose if they open-up their systems.

Computer-aided design has been shown to be much more than a design aid – it is considered to have the potential to provide a good deal of management information as well. Furthermore, the increased usage of computer-aided design systems is likely to accelerate the erosion of professional barriers, particularly since both technology and cost have now moved within the reach of even the most modest of organisations. Now, the individual members of the design and construction team can be more effective in bringing their own skills to bear on the common problem of producing economical buildings that will last, be on time and within budget.

Drawings and bills of quantities produced faster will do nothing to improve the overall efficiency of the industry. Furthermore, it is likely that buildings produced on this basis will still fail to be completed on time and within budget. In any event, faster bills of quantities will hardly improve the contractor's understanding of what is required of him. Therefore, the greatest possible waste of the new technology would occur if it were used simply to replace the existing manual methods. The result will be that existing practices will be by-passed where they can no longer justify themselves. What is really required is the direct link from design to construction management which will then provide the client with a more certain solution to his needs.

Utilising the more sophisticated computer-aided design systems (i.e. those with a 3D capability linked to a relational database) will pave the way to the more effective use of this technology, as well as fulfilling the more generally accepted role of draughting. In fact, systems of this type will support the extraction of data in a form more consistent with the needs of all its users (see Fig. 10.12).

Distribution of workload

Contractors in particular should investigate the potential of computer-aided design now. Once they become accustomed to working with these systems they will begin to command a greater say in the way buildings are designed as well as constructed. Some architects are concerned about the competition from within their own ranks by the increasing use of computer-aided design systems. When contractors become sufficiently aware of the wider applications for computer-aided design, some of the work which would normally go to architects will go directly to them.

Computer-aided design will provide opportunities for management in addition to fulfilling its more obvious role in design. However, little real benefit will accrue to the industry as a whole if the professions within it do not free themselves from their parochial attitudes. Acceptance of computer-aided design by *all* sectors of the industry will be a beginning, but its widespread use will be essential before the element of uncertainty in the present process is reduced to a more acceptable

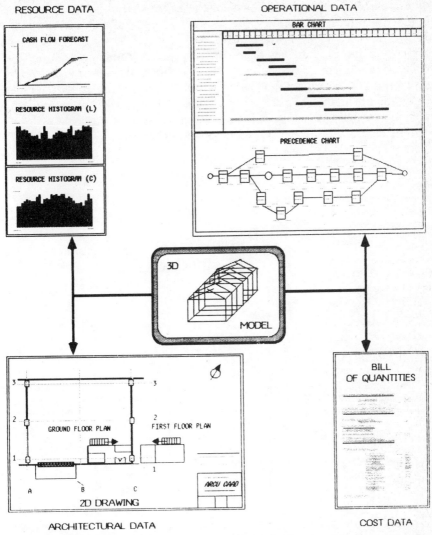

RESOURCE DATA

OPERATIONAL DATA

CASH FLOW FORECAST

RESOURCE HISTOGRAM (L)

RESOURCE HISTOGRAM (C)

BAR CHART

PRECEDENCE CHART

3D

MODEL

GROUND FLOOR PLAN

FIRST FLOOR PLAN

ARCU CAAD

2D DRAWING

ARCHITECTURAL DATA

BILL
OF QUANTITIES

COST DATA

10.12 *Computer-aided design satisfying the needs of many users*

level. It is the latter which clients in particular find frustrating and often costly.

FUTURE DEVELOPMENTS

Networked systems

The shape of things to come may be visualised in the form of single user dedicated workstations, as Fig. 10.13 illustrates. They will be provided with a bit-mapped display offering multi-window features, a multi-tasking virtual memory operating system (such as UNIX) and local mass storage. Connection to similar machines will be accomplished by a local area network, possibly of the Ethernet type. File storage will be either distributed around the network or concentrated at a *file-server* node. Plotting/printing will be handled in a similar way to the present arrangements, in that it will be concentrated at separate nodes.

The major benefits that these systems will bring about is the opportunity for the entire design/construction team to work together on the common problem – the evolving building design. Acceptance of these systems is likely to be much swifter than with previous generations of computer graphics systems. This will be because many users will find

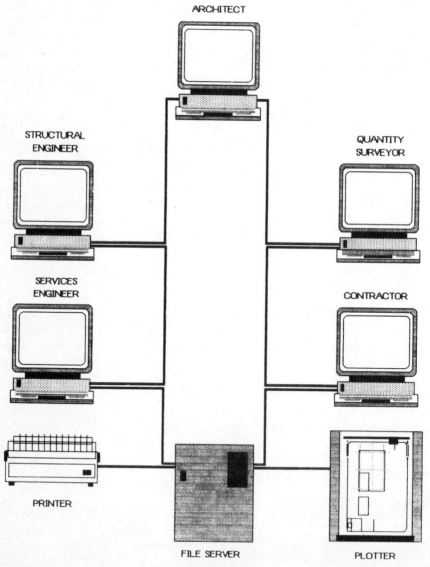

10.13 *A local area network of single user workstations (not drawn to scale)*

both the technological sophistication and machine operation more in keeping with their existing microcomputer systems; cost will also be an important factor.

Man/machine interface

A good deal of work has been undertaken over the years in attempts at improving the ease with which man may work more successfully with the computer. Indeed, Alvey[5] places great importance on this area of the technology which was felt, in its present form, to be a barrier to the more widespread use of information technology. So far in this chapter we have seen how attempts have been made to improve simple communications with the system. Tablets, mouse devices etc. have all reduced the amount of keyed-in input, but there is still much to be done. In fact, the current state of the art in user interfacing is many years behind other sectors of information technology. Without a doubt a more rapid means of communication across the man/machine interface is necessary if the full potential of the technology is to be realised. Chapter 11 outlines some of the current developments in this area and suggests how improvements might be made, especially by a more positive effort on the part of the construction industry itself.

Knowledge-based systems

The now fashionable term *expert systems* has created as much interest with non-computer users as it has with computer enthusiasts. There may be many reasons for this, not least of all the realisation by the lay person of the benefits of having a machine that can think ahead and make decisions of its own. Unfortunately, it is not as simple as it may seem, since the massive investment required to produce any knowledge-base is often conveniently overlooked. A realistic view of the development of knowledge-based systems would suggest a five to ten year time lapse before anything of commercial value is likely to become available. As for *intelligent* knowledge-based systems, the prospect of having a fully operational system in the foreseeable future is too speculative to be discussed here.

Expert systems may well be in their infancy, but some useful work has already been done to identify the ways in which they may help designers. Landsdown[9] has developed some elementary expert systems to provide specialised architectural consulting: for example, in making planning applications and in dealing with timber defects problems. A possible further opportunity might be the application of inference *engines* or systems to design databases to provide a form of criticism of the design as it evolves. This concept could then be expanded to take account of the construction implications as well and thus provide a more complete feedback system.

There are many obstacles to be overcome if the construction industry is to develop worthwhile expert systems. Firstly, it must be disciplined enough to question the validity of its own decision-making, and secondly, there must be common agreement on the structuring of the knowledge-bases. Bijl[10] suggests that design is not a knowledge-based discipline but evolves from the experience of many individual practitioners. By this it is implied that the use of knowledge by designers cannot, on its own, be constituted as a formal model for presentation to other designers. This presents serious problems for the designers of generalised computer-aided architectural design systems.

CONCLUSIONS

The prospects for the future look promising, but that may be all it amounts to for many organisations. No doubt more significant progress will be made as the new generation single user networked workstations become established. These are likely to force more people and organisations to work together to resolve common problems.

It is suggested that, as more contractors become involved in design and build contracts, the demand for computer graphics systems will increase. Eventually, the market for these systems will be dominated by construction organisations rather than design-oriented consultancies: as a result, this may well create new pressures on the distribution of the industry's workload.

The combined efforts of C.I.B., F.A.C.E. and C.I.C.A. should provide the necessary stimulus for tackling many of the problems which are unlikely to be solved commercially. The future prospects are encouraging, especially since there are many people and organisations with a wealth of expertise to offer the rest of the construction industry. It now remains for those commercial organisations, be they involved in architectural design, engineering, construction or whatever, to force the obvious benefits from this emerging technology; then more clients will begin to recognise and enjoy the full measure of professionalism which the construction industry has to offer.

REFERENCES

1 The Construction Industry Computing Association, *The automation of draughting work*, Cambridge, 1981

2 The Construction Industry Computing Association, *Computers in engineering and architecture in Japan*, Report of a FACE industrial mission, Cambridge, 1983

3 The Construction Industry Computing Association, *Computer aided designing*, Cambridge, 1984

4 MIT's early *Whirlwind* computer of the 1950s already supported simple line drawings. *Sketchpad* was developed in the early 1960s as a prototype computer-aided architectural design system. It was the forerunner of today's systems.

5 *A programme for advanced information technology* (The Report of the Alvey Committee), HMSO, 1982

6 HOWARD, R., *Integrated CAD – The problems and the possibilities*, Integrated computer aided design CIB Working Commission, W78 Colloquium, Watford, 1984

7 ATKIN, B. L., 'A computer supported information interchange for construction projects', Science and Engineering Research Council supported project, Department of Construction Management, University of Reading, 1984–86

8. BIGGS, W. D., *Breaking barriers*, Building supplement, *Building*, September 9, 1983, p. 14
9. LANDSDOWN, J., *Expert systems: their impact on the construction industry*, Report to the Royal Institute of British Architects Conference Fund, 1982
10. BIJL, A., *Integrated CAAD systems*, Final Report of DoE funded research project, EdCAAD, Edinburgh, 1979

ACKNOWLEDGEMENTS

DEC, VAX and PDP 11 are registered trademarks of Digital Equipment Corporation.
PRIME is a registered trademark of Prime Computer, Inc.
SCRIBE is a registered trademark of Ecotech Design Ltd.
RUCAPS is a registered trademark of GMW Computers Ltd.
BDS and GDS are registered trademarks of Applied Research of Cambridge Ltd.
INTERGRAPH is a registered trademark of Intergraph Corporation.
MEDUSA is a registered trademark of Cambridge Interactive Systems Ltd.
DESIGNER and CDS are registered trademarks of Computervision Corporation.
CADAM is a registered trademark of CADAM, Inc.
UNIX is a registered trademark of Bell Laboratories Inc.

11 A Construction Industry Computer Workstation – Towards an Integrated Management Information System
G. N. Fisher & B. L. Atkin

INTRODUCTION

Over the last decade the U.K. construction industry has experienced many changes in response to major recessions within the U.K. economy. Such changes have caused many firms within the industry to evolve new organisational and management practices. The Ashridge study[1] concluded that the practices and general characteristics of many firms were inappropriate to their needs. It is suggested that the use of computers can aid the flexibility and collaboration that new conditions in the marketplace demand.

Traditionally, the industry has been expected to accept computer limitations, and many firms have had to use non-standard computer systems which had originally been designed for other purposes. This has resulted in the limited development of computer systems for construction and generated a view that the industry is using computers to perpetuate professional barriers.[2]

This chapter attempts to bridge the existing gap between the theoretical appreciation of current concepts in information technology and their practical implementation into construction management procedures. It identifies the interface problems within the industry and establishes the concept of modelling through proposed integrated software. Certain data classification concepts are briefly reviewed, and specific operational activities are identified against existing communication systems. This introduces the concept of the integrated workstation, and actual specifications are produced at various levels of sophistication which could meet the needs of construction managers within the industry. Before proceeding, we must make reference to a publication by the Construction Industry Computing Association (C.I.C.A.) entitled 'The specification of a building industry computer workstation'[3]; this document provides an important background to the writing of this chapter, since it deals with the wider issues of the workstation concept, including those of marketing and finance. The term *workstation* has been defined by C.I.C.A. as 'the computer equipment dedicated to one user at one time'.

REVIEW OF ESTABLISHED PROCEDURES

Background

Some disciplines within the construction industry have been quick to exploit the potential of the newer forms of information technology, while others have made very little progress. In particular, a number of organisations have computerised some of the more tedious and repetitive tasks, but these represent only a small proportion of the total design/construction process.

Construction industry users of information technology now face an important decision. As the computing industry constantly finds

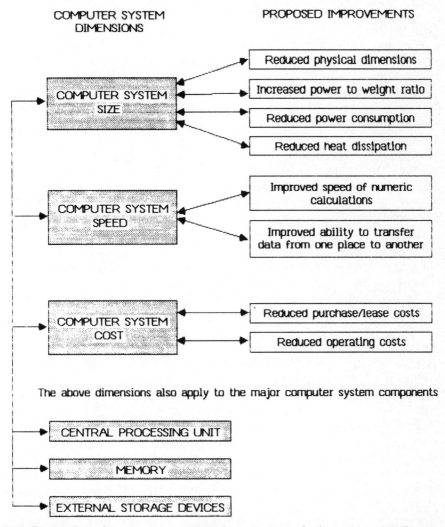

11.1 *Dimensions for computer system improvement (source: Yourdon Report – unpublished)*

solutions to problems at lower costs, it remains for those in construction to anticipate changes within their respective infrastructures and to specify needs more clearly. This dynamic approach highlights the need for more adaptable software and hardware, and demands that those in construction appreciate such change. The magnitude of change in computing during its relatively short lifetime has been impressive: Fig. 11.1 illustrates the main areas of likely progress over the next two to three decades. These dimensions of improvement, namely size, speed and cost, will ensure that information technology becomes even more firmly entrenched in daily routine.

In an unpublished report by Yourdon, Inc.[3a], it was claimed that computer technology had improved by three orders of magnitude over the last 30 years. Yourdon believes that three more orders of improvement are likely over the next 20 to 30 years. Fisher and Rigg[4] reviewed the impact of information technology on the construction industry: they identified certain key factors from existing facilities and systems, and attempted to show the direction that such technologies might take within the construction environment. Such factors undoubtedly represent fundamental business catalysts, which partly explains why there has been a shift away from manufacturing and a current trend towards a service-orientated information-based economy.

Historically, there have always been problems in passing information between people and those organisations which are responsible for the various stages of the design/construction process. With buildings increasing in complexity, and rapidly changing technologies, the adoption of standard procedures to aid communication becomes crucial. Many studies on construction information systems and classification have been made but no clear solutions have yet emerged. This is a point for concern, as the amount of construction literature continues to expand exponentially in most areas, especially in government publications and British Standards, which appear to be doubling in number every five years. The major areas of development concerned with construction information appear to have been directed towards improving the quality of general information for the industry and the structuring of project information where the control of content is crucial.

The changing quality of general information can be considered against those developments made in the areas of commodity coding, trade literature, central commodity files and specific feedback systems. Each of these has developed at different rates over the years and some have been heavily restricted in their application within construction. In fact, no major progress has been made in construction commodity coding since a report was published in 1971.[5] Although some research on coding has been made by the British Standards Institute, this has simply emphasised the conflict which exists in the actual use of standard commodity codes and their complexity when used in practice. The ultimate aim of commodity coding is to create unique descriptive references for those construction products and materials which the industry uses. If this is to be achieved, a juxtaposition of different commodity codes, via their data definition languages, needs to be made. This could identify the kind of composite structure which as a whole describes the product information that the industry needs. However, this is a daunting task and such a project would probably require government backing over a number of years.

It is only recently that manufacturers within construction have realised how important it is to specify their products in a systematic and comprehensive way. This has been caused through the underlying impact of British Standard 4940 which is entitled 'The presentation of technical information about products and services in the construction industry'. This simply sets out the requirements for a small number of experts involved in the design of trade literature. Much of the content and pattern of B.S. 4940 has now been accepted by the C.I.B. in their efforts to present trade literature at an international level.

Working practices

In common with any discipline, construction management will begin to move rapidly into the use of microcomputer-based systems when it sees clear benefits. Indeed, the concept of a workstation is viewed as complementary to the role of the construction manager: the workstation providing the necessary support facilities to allow the manager to arrive at better decisions.

Actual working environments will have a bearing on the degree of flexibility required of the workstation. The working environment and its domain is distinguished by its being that part of the system which is visible to the user (Fig. 11.2). In almost all cases the form of the workstation will reflect the needs of the individual, the organisation and the projects which they handle. Accordingly, the physical representation of the workstation may vary considerably from one organisation to another, with shifts in professional interests dictating the majority of the variations that occur. In this connection, it should be expected that, in the case of an architectural design office, there will be a greater emphasis upon the handling of the graphical attributes of a project rather than either pure number or text processing: these functions must,

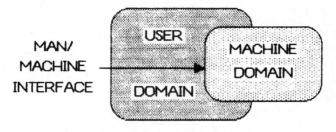

MAN/
MACHINE
INTERFACE

USER
DOMAIN

MACHINE
DOMAIN

11.2 *Working environment and its domain*

of course, be incorporated. Moreover, the need to display, modify and refresh images will necessitate both high resolution (raster-scan) display and high speed processing. Undoubtedly, the most significant development towards an integrated system would be the combination of graphics with powerful database management systems. Chapter 10 argues that too many so-called computer-aided design systems fall far short of the basic need of *hanging* component, cost and other related data on to the graphical form. An ability for the entire design/construction team to be able jointly to evaluate an evolving building form is seen as the logical direction in the development of the workstation. By examining a coherent model of a building, the entire design/construction team is able to explore options previously denied by constraints of time, cost and sheer physical impracticality.

Geographical and locational difficulties would appear to have been virtually ignored by computer system designers, who assume that all hardware will be placed in a healthy environment. Since much of the construction industry's work is site based – this also applies to other manufacturing-orientated industries – the need must undoubtedly arise for the development of a rugged technology workstation. Indeed, such a workstation has been developed by the U.K. based CAP Group Ltd.[6] using well-proven technology integrated into a single operational unit which can be located anywhere where man can go in the world – providing there is some form of power supply close at hand! (A fuller description of this workstation is provided later in this chapter.) Technological convergence will bring many presently independent facilities into one desk-top unit by the combination of established technology such as telephones, televisions and the newer computer-related technologies of facsimile, teletex, teletext and viewdata.

Finally, there is another more general but often overlooked trend that will affect the environment in which all this will take place: that is, the whole concept and implications of rapid satellite-based world communications, and the effect these will have on an increasingly information-demanding society.

MODELLING AND COMPUTER SOFTWARE

Modelling rationale

One of the areas in which information technology will greatly affect how a manager does his job is that of modelling. Aaker[7] defines a model as 'a representation or abstraction of a real world system; that is to say the formal (or simplified) representation of the notions that we have about a phenomenon or those aspects of a real situation that are thought to be important to the model builder (or user). After suitable testing, the model builder is free to change the model if factors that have been omitted are found out to be important . . .'. Rigby[8] identifies four different types of model of which three are of direct interest to this work:

Iconic – a scaled down representation of the end product, which could be an automobile, an aircraft or a *building*.

Analog – although this type of model may not physically look like the system or entity it represents, it will nevertheless behave in a similar way.

Symbolic – this type of model uses mathematical or other symbols to represent relationships that are known to exist or have been identified in certain situations.

There are an increasing number of modelling programs for most types of computers. They range from H.M. Treasury's model of the U.K. economy (a symbolic model) to general purpose financial models. How these models might manifest themselves with respect to a computer-based approach can be best appreciated by referring to the software itself.

Current software such as the now familiar *spreadsheet* are part iconic and part symbolic models, hence their much-used alternative name, *financial modellers*. As an extension to this concept, the sort of image now becoming visible on computer VDU's can be used to represent buildings as 3D models, having the effect of blurring the edges between iconic, analog and symbolic models.

Advances in both general computing and computer-aided design have opened up the idea of a manager using microcomputers to communicate directly with models; that is to say, using the models interactively. This process can aid designers and managers in the understanding of the problems confronting them. It can enable them to look at very many more possible design solutions than would be feasible if the same problems were tackled manually. One widely held misconception about models is that they are based on very large amounts of data. Most successful models use information that relies on knowledge from decision makers themselves.

Problems with compatibility

The problems of matching software to a hardware base have existed as long as computing itself. Attempts by a number of organisations to introduce standards and, in some cases, foist them upon the rest of industry has led to a jungle for those not sufficiently well versed in computing. Often marketing strategies and the media, at large, are to blame for promoting so called *de facto* industry standards, only to see them submerge beneath the increasing number of newer systems. Compatibility is sometimes viewed as a quantifiable commodity, with many degrees existing between the states of slight and total. In reality, compatibility either exists or does not exist – there is nothing in between.

The current state of the art in terms of operating systems would suggest four major product divisions:

1 UNIX and look-alike systems
2 CP/M and variants

3 MS DOS/PC DOS

4 Other manufacturers, e.g. IBM (except PC), APPLE, Commodore.
UNIX has often been referred to as the *de facto* portable operating
system: portable in the sense of machine independence. The major
advantage of UNIX is its ability to support multi-user, multi-tasking
activities, which has favoured the development of independent and
portable applications packages. Such a technological advantage would
seem to favour a broadly based workstation concept.

CP/M, in its original form, was written for the emerging generation
of 8 bit microcomputers, and has now progressed upwards to the stage
where, in some areas, it offers competition for UNIX. MS DOS is
becoming particularly well established on quasi-16 bit machines such
as the Victor/Sirius 1 and the IBM PC (called PC DOS), and is seen
as the direct competitor of CP/M. Other manufacturers, such as Apple,
have tended to maintain their independence of the portable operating
system cult, due primarily to the instant success of their Apple II 8 bit
microcomputer with its following in the form of an extensive support
industry. Indeed, if the software exists in abundance for a particular
computer system, then the choice of operating system is to some extent
irrelevant.

Undoubtedly, there are native operating systems with more to offer
the specialist user than UNIX. However, its main asset is its ability to
transfer across a wide range of machines. It is considered to offer a
sound, universal development environment which must ensure that
software development costs are kept to a minimum, and it also has the
attraction of being capable of downloading to target microcomputers.

Programming languages are sometimes incorrectly regarded as the
most important factor when considering the choice of a computer
system, and yet in reality they are of little consequence to the majority
of commercial users. Whilst some may prefer either the mental challenge
of their own devised problem-solving routines or the ability to adapt
and develop software, the sheer economics of producing one's own
solution renders it an often pointless task. The low cost of an increasing

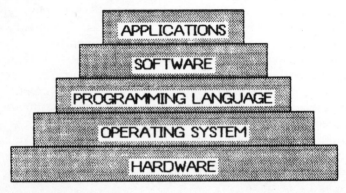

11.3 *A hierarchy of subsystems*

number of robust and widely applicable software packages is a boon for the computer user.

Fig. 11.3 illustrates the hierarchical relationship between the component subsystems of a complete computer system.

Software and its integration

Before considering how software might be integrated to produce a single, coherent body of data, a brief definition of the concept of integration would be helpful. Integration is the term applied to *the grouping and organisation of data into a single, coherent body for input into a computer system. Once within the computer such data can be reorganised and processed into an output form consistent with the individual needs of a number of different users.*

The need for integrated software is as commonly accepted in computer circles as user-friendliness is amongst users. To date, the limitations imposed by the technology have thwarted most attempts at developing low cost integrated software solutions. The emergence of the 16/32 bit microprocessors, typically the Motorola MC68000 series, has seen a marked increase in the number of systems offering integrated software packages and, by implication, has accelerated the move away from singular, fragmented applications. More sophisticated operating systems which combine multi-window and multi-processing displays allow the user to move more easily between applications than was previously possible. Interestingly, a number of integrated software packages have been developed for 8 and quasi-16 bit microprocessor-based systems although, in the majority of cases, true multi-processing is more apparent than real.

The concept of integrated software is no longer a futuristic hope made impractical by the limitations of current technology: it is here now. It is expected that many of the routine demands of the construction industry can soon be computerised by the integration of both graphical and textual data. Systems capable of this degree of computer power are not recent developments but, as mentioned previously, are more likely to represent the shape of the future rather than the sequential, fragmented approach of the present.[9]

It is suggested that a clear distinction must be drawn between those computer applications which merely automate existing manual processes, and those which seek to solve the real problems facing the construction industry. In the case of the former, the speeding up of existing archaic processes will simply not provide any worthwhile solutions. If the procedure for building design/construction used in the U.K. were about to be invented, it is extremely unlikely that it would follow the same form as that which has evolved.

Operational activities and data

It should not be difficult to imagine the classification, form and extent of data that would need to be an integral part of the workstation for it to function adequately. A means of identification, abstraction and

163

calculation of data, in any category of work, would be necessary if the user is to be permitted to explore the more usual range of construction-related applications:

Financial modelling (cash flow forecasts, profit and loss monitoring, valuations and payments etc.)

Resource planning/control (labour, materials and plant; supervision; time and cost), and

Information management (material and component specifications, codes and standards, prices and stock control).

Once the software is widely accepted, the benefits that the new technology could have are considerable. For example, site records, such as goods-in, daily reports, plant sheets, variation orders, safety records, time allocation sheets, copies of orders and bonus/productivity information could all be held in one single, readily accessible database.

As already suggested in this chapter, the greatest influence on the shape of computer applications within the industry is likely to come from the direction of computer-aided design – not simply as an all-purpose draughting and billing aid, but as a powerful modelling tool that will provide information for management as well. Until recently, a typical system was outside the reach of most organisations, not simply because of cost and size, but also in terms of its demand on the manpower resource needed to drive it. Now, with the emergence of the powerful and relatively compact 16/32 bit processors, such as the aforementioned MC68000 series, the cost and accessibility of the total system is within the reach of many more organisations. The downward trend of cost and size of hardware, together with the downloading of software from the mainframe and mini installations, further emphasises these points. Contrasted with the increasing sophistication and capability of the super microcomputers, there seems to be an interesting convergence of technology wherein both categories of systems will meet somewhere in the middle. The question is, 'Which species of system will prevail: the enhanced super microcomputers or the scaled-down mainframes/minis?'

An increasing number of portable data capture devices (PDCD's) are already on the market, and some of these are under test by several U.K. builders. They are being used as electronic dimension books, such that a day's site re-measurement can be recorded and then transmitted onwards without having to duplicate work. This is achieved by the simple task of plugging the PDCD into a site-based computer/terminal or via a telephone (modem) link to the Head Office computer; the measurement information is then transferred very rapidly to the corporate database.

Problems with fragmented databases

Yourdon[3a] found that most corporate computer systems that have been developed over the past 20 years have had their own local databases.

Thus, from the viewpoint of the whole organisation, there are many fragmented chunks of data in different computer systems. Yourdon summarised the major problems normally encountered with dispersed or fragmented databases:

Redundancy – the same information exists in multiple copies in different places making updating difficult.

Inconsistency – the same information has different names in different places and multiple copies are not always updated in the same way at the same time.

Security – it is harder to protect confidential information if there are copies of it everywhere.

Incompatibility – difficulty in communicating with fourth generation programming languages.

IMPACT OF NEW INFORMATION TECHNOLOGY

Communications technology

The technological advancement experienced during the last decade has decreased the ratios of business employees to computer terminals. It is estimated that by 1986 the ratio of employees to terminals will have dropped from 48:1 to 10:1 across the board (U.S. figures). Coupled with this will be a marked increase in the processing capabilities of hardware. Today's typical personal computer is capable of between 0.5 and 1.0 million of instructions per second (mips); normal mainframes rate between 3 and 25 mips. By 1990 the Japanese intend to have reached 100 (bflops).

Two areas that will significantly affect how a manager of the not too distant future does his job and the effectiveness with which he operates are those of communications and peripherals. In terms of communications and the new information technology, there are currently four methods of communication that offer considerable potential for the manager:

1 The existing telephone network. Firstly, because it exists and most people have a personal terminal (telephone). Secondly, because of improvements in equipment (such as electronic exchanges) and in optical fibre transmission lines.

2 Improved radio transmission services; for example, cellular radio.

3 Short and medium ranged laser transmission (several laser based private telephone services are currently available).

4 Satellite communications using equipment in geo-stationary orbit.

Despite the exponential growth of computer power and with it the ability of systems to perform independently without reference to any other source, there is, none the less, much to be gained by linking and sharing resources which would otherwise be outside the normal capabilities of the individual system. In any situation where the need arises to share expensive resources (for example, peripheral equipment

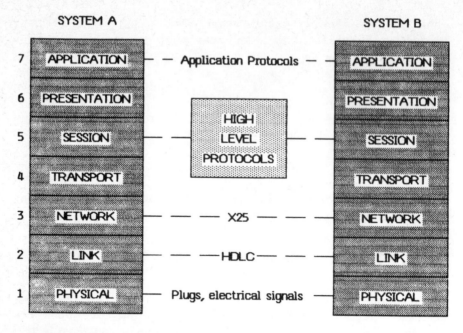

11.4 *The ISO 7-layer reference model*

– laser printers, mass storage etc.), some provision must be made to ensure that it occurs according to a predetermined plan. Therefore, clearly defined rules or *protocols* must be adhered to, otherwise disastrous results are inevitable. For the main part, protocols (or standards) prescribe an acceptable pattern of communication between work-stations. The International Standards Organization (ISO) has been instrumental in laying down guidelines for the increasingly popular local area network (LAN). Fig. 11.4 illustrates the seven layers of the ISO reference model wherein each layer represents a module in the hierarchy relative to the functionality of an LAN. By definition, a local area network has to be just that: local, perhaps contained within a building or even a single room; and a network, implying some form of connection or physical linkage within the designated area.

Much of the original work in the field of LAN's was undertaken by Xerox Corporation in the U.S.A., leading to the development of Ethernet and similar systems by others. In the same way that there exists a number of operating systems, so too there is the problem of many individual LAN standards, each competing for market domi-nation. By far the most serious effect of this multiplicity of standards is the inevitable dissipation of resources within the computer industry and the inherent time delay in reaching a common conclusion. Such a conclusion would bring both manufacturers and users closer to the true sense of compatibility. However, there is a marginal advantage in the multiplicity of standards, since it forces the less reliable and undersupported products from the marketplace.

Network topologies

The design and planning of individual LAN's is dependent upon the technology employed. Four generally accepted topologies are:

1 *Star*
2 *Ring*
3 *Bus*
4 *Connected graph*

Fig. 11.5 illustrates the major differences between these topologies. Of these, perhaps star, ring and bus are the most commonplace. In many quarters, the ring topology is considered to be far superior to the others, and much development is under way in the U.K. along these lines (for example, the Cambridge ring).

Whilst each topology may have its own *traffic protocols*, the same set of operational aims exist, notably those of minimum delay response time, collision avoidance and data integrity. The least expensive options will, as experience has shown, be less able to deal effectively with tendencies towards data loss and data merge. Ideally for the user there should be no degradation of the service when others are using it. It is known that some systems fail to operate effectively under conditions of heavy demand, with a resultant failure of the entire system and consequential loss of data. Furthermore, it appears that possibly the

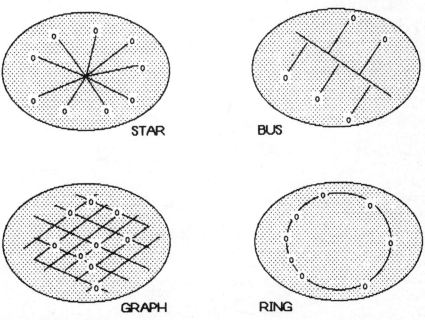

11.5 *Local area network topologies*

greatest practical problem facing systems designers is the avoidance of disruption and failure when individual *satellites* (or workstations) are taken out of, or introduced into, the network. With faster transmission rates over hard-wired links, and an increased tendency towards local processing, the incidence of failure should be progressively reduced. However, for the time being at least, data corruption will continue very much as before.

What then are the new communications systems and those likely to become available soon? Essentially, there are two kinds of communications systems, namely voice-based and data-based. Voice-based systems such as telephone and radio telephone have been with us for some time, and current developments into the application of these technologies to computers is producing results. Specifically, voice recognition and speech synthesis are regarded as a natural development in the man/machine interface, which is one of the areas identified by Alvey[10] as being of particular significance to the advancement of information technology. Of more immediate interest to this chapter are data-based communications such as:

1 *Facsimile*
2 *Telex and teletex*
3 *Videotex*

Facsimile systems

A facsimile device (FAX) is a means of transmitting a photocopy quality copy of a document by telephone or radio telephone on a subscriber to subscriber basis, provided equipment is compatible. Once a telephone or radio link has been established, then the sender switches his FAX machine to 'transmit' and the recipient switches his FAX machine to

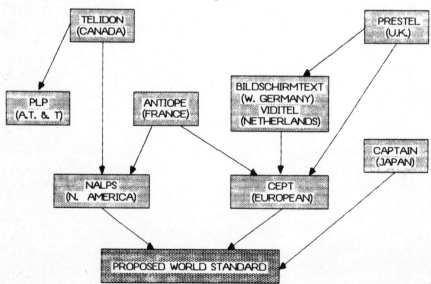

11.6 *Videotex systems and standards*

'receive'. The sender inserts his document into his machine and a photocopy is printed by the receiving machine, in just a few minutes for a full A4 document. The convergence of technology will mean that we shall soon see equipment that is not only a facsimile terminal but is also capable of being used as a photocopier.

Telex and teletex systems

The telex system is more than 60 years old and, in its present form, has reached its technical limit. It is not capable of supporting up-to-date high speed communications equipment and is unlikely to last much longer.

Although based on telex, teletex is a more advanced system and has many forms, both simple and complex, depending largely on equipment configuration and terminal sophistication. For example, the system can support any or all of the following:

1 Much increased speed of transmission – up to 2,400 cps
2 Message storage facility
3 Automatic error detection and correction
4 Word processing facility
5 Facilities to tell terminals when to send messages

Videotex

This is the generic term for a range of new information systems. Videotex systems can be split into two broad types:

1 *Teletext* (not to be confused with teletex)
2 *Viewdata*

Teletext is a broadcast system with information in the form of pages, and it is transmitted as part of a normal broadcast by, for example, the B.B.C. in the U.K. It can be received on a suitably modified television but is limited to information flowing in one direction only (broadcasted).

Viewdata is more advanced than teletext, in so much as the data, once received, can be stored and edited locally on a typical microcomputer. Essentially, the local microcomputer talks to a remote database via a modem on a standard telephone line. Unlike teletext, this system only broadcasts data to a user when requested and for a charge depending upon the data accessed and time spent using the telephone service. The database for the viewdata system is held on a computer which can be accessed by the user's microcomputer automatically dialling the computer's number. Information contained on British Telecom's public viewdata service, PRESTEL, ranges from plant hire charges to property details. It is also possible to access private viewdata systems supported by non-compatible hardware through a *Gateway*, provided the user holds the appropriate user name/password. Other viewdata systems exist worldwide, and it is possible in some cases to access a number of these directly from the U.K. Fig. 11.6 compares those systems currently in use.

One large firm of U.K. consultant engineers with projects around the world is known to be looking at ways of transporting information to

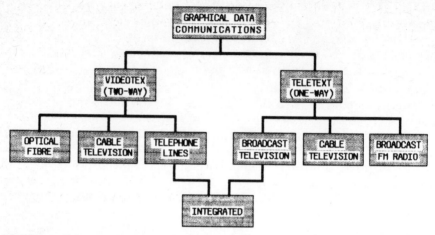

11.7 *Towards an integrated information system*

their projects, particularly those in under-developed countries. They have been considering the possibility of a satellite-based viewdata/video/facsimile scheme for direct communications that can by-pass conventional means.

It should not be long before an architect, a quantity surveyor, an estimator, a buyer or a site manager can ask his computer for a list of the nearest builders' merchants with a particular type of window in stock, as well as its price and availability. The computer (or before this service is completely available, the enquirer him/herself) will be able to search the viewdata pages which have been updated daily by each merchant. It may well be that builders' merchants and other material stockists will force the pace, as they are already prime candidates for computerised stock control. The development of an integrated information system that combines all the aforementioned technologies is probably not far away. Fig. 11.7 illustrates the likely pattern of convergence of these existing technologies.

LEVELS OF SPECIFICATION

Workstation concepts

The actual specification for a construction industry computer workstation may take many forms and must be considered at the various levels of sophistication which are possible. At the highest level, the fully integrated system is often referred to as an electronic office on your desk; at the lowest level, a simple 8 bit microcomputer is also a workstation.

Since the workstation may well be a link in the chain to other computers, the design of the man/machine interface is extremely important, especially since it acts as the point of exchange of information. It is suggested that an alternative and perhaps more suitable term for the workstation would be an *information interchange*. (A more complete account of the man/machine interface is provided later in this chapter.)

The Japanese manufacturer Toshiba has developed an integrated communication system (ICS) which has brought the concept of the multi-function workstation much nearer. The ICS consists of a telephone keypad dialling system, video screen and microcomputer based keyboard which produces a device capable of transmitting voice and data simultaneously. Storage and forwarding of electronic mail and collecting it is also possible: the device can be used to transmit graphics integrated with data. However, it is unlikely that these integrated systems will be commonplace within the immediate future, although the time will come when these too will be an accepted, integral part of the normal daily routine.

Another example of the multi-function workstation is one which can handle one or all of the communication and information handling systems so far outlined. Presently, it is as large as an office desk but dramatically cuts down paperwork, thus moving closer to the concept of the paperless office. In its most sophisticated form it could act as a:

1 Telephone (with message storage facility)
2 Photocopier
3 Word processor
4 Teletext link (possibly via satellite)
5 Viewdata system
6 Microcomputer
7 Intelligent terminal to a larger and remote computer
8 Electronic mail box

The work of C.I.C.A. with their Dutch and German collaborators[3] covered many facets of computing within a construction environment, although the actual development of a workstation was expressly excluded. Its main aim is to stimulate both suppliers and users of computers in Europe into developing much closer relationships and a clearer understanding of each other's needs. Their work does, in fact, consider a possible workstation design at three levels of specification. However, when taking account of more recent trends in the available technology and developments within construction management, it is clear that four levels of specification are now emerging:

Level 1: 8 bit and quasi-16 bit microcomputers supporting low cost standard software
Level 2: Enhanced quasi-16 bit and full 16 bit machines utilising integrated software
Level 3: 16/32 bit machines with fully integrated software and links into LAN's – distributed interactive processing
Level 4: Integrated communication systems – multi-function workstations

The following outline, based on a level 2 specification, takes account of current technology and is typical of a modular approach:

Monitor – a high resolution raster-scan CRT video display capable of supporting both graphics and text simultaneously; monochrome resolution at least 512 × 512 pixels; colour optional.

Tablet – a digitiser for graphics and menu inputs; variable active area; stylus or puck for locating/pinpointing.

Keyboard – a conventional QWERTY device with numeric keypad for rapid data input; user definable function keys optional.

Optical mouse – for use with bit-mapped screens when manipulating on-screen graphics, icons and text.

Processor – a device for local storage and processing of data; minimum 256 Kbytes RAM; 16 or quasi-16 bit microprocessor chip.

Mass storage – for storage of local data and larger sources of back-up data; 400 Kbytes minimum on floppy or microfloppy disk; 5 Mbyte hard disk minimum.

Printer/plotter – dot matrix (or A4 plotter) for local hard copy of displayed graphics and/or text.

Fig. 11.8 illustrates the synthetic nature of a total computer system. In addition, a number of other devices are necessary on the grounds of ergonomics and safety. Level 3 workstations provide an interesting

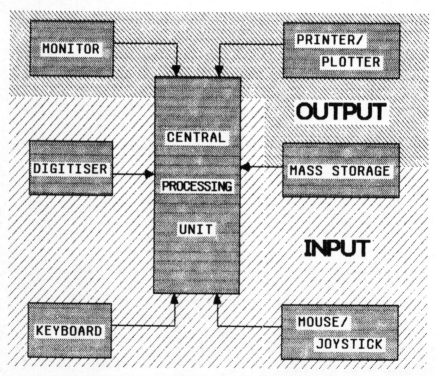

11.8 *Typical workstation components*

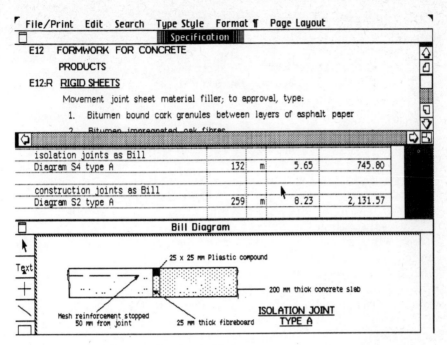

11.9 *Multi window facility for Apple Lisa*

opportunity for examining the concept of multi-window and multi-processing. By far the best examples are the Apple *Lisa* (Fig. 11.9) and Macintosh with their own working environment derived from the Smalltalk language system, developed by Xerox Corporation in the U.S.A. The *desk top manager* which organises both screen displays and processing enables the user to simulate the normal working environment more closely than has ever been possible before. What places these two machines above almost all others to date is their adherence to the concept of integration which permits the user to move more freely between applications than ever before. Also, these machines have been designed around the concepts of multi-windows and multi-processing rather than having them introduced later, perhaps by some third party. Other microcomputer systems can be modified to imitate the concepts developed by Apple but they are unlikely to be as successful since the technology was not designed first and foremost for these purposes. Accordingly, manufacturers adopting this approach cannot expect to make as much progress as Apple towards improving the level of the man/machine interface.

CASE STUDIES

Practical use of computer software
A management modelling tool, with construction industry applicability, has been field-tested by the authors in conjunction with a subsidiary of

a major international contractor and a leading firm of project managers. It was based on a popular 8 bit microcomputer and tested in three different ways:

1 To model different construction method ideas in order to assess the implications of each possible solution on time and resources at the tender and pre-contract stages.

2 To model the likely effects of factors such as variations, individual sub-contractor manning and progress, component delivery times, plant levels and availability, on sectional and overall completion times.

3 To investigate its uses as a decision-making aid to construction managers by suggesting to them how to react in a given situation.

The results of this study highlighted a number of interesting points of which the negative ones related exclusively to the limitations of the software rather than the concept itself:

1 The software demanded a much more disciplined approach to project planning than the contractor's staff were currently used to.

2 Despite the relatively low computer literacy in the construction industry, and contrary to popular belief, the contractor's planning staff were enthusiastic about the project generally and very keen to try out the system. However, some apprehension and fear was noticeable amongst older staff at both director and site manager levels.

3 At site level, due mainly to the short nature of the trial, no clear conclusions were reached regarding the fortnightly progress updating. The contractor's representative stated that 'progress reports had been undertaken on five contracts in progress and the computer analysis displayed reasonable conclusions. However, they generally required some manual adjustment in the light of factors which the network or precedence logic could not totally appreciate'.

4 The system was found to be particularly helpful at pre-tender planning stage where construction programmes were in outline only and subject to frequent change during the tender preparation period.

5 When used as a modelling tool, the contractor's planning and site management staff expressed considerable frustrations over limitations in the way the computer was able to present information. This was in part due to the limitations of the microcomputer, since 16 and 32 bit machines would have allowed the software authors greater scope in this area.

The contractor considered that, on the basis of the trial, great benefits could be derived from using this or a similar computer for producing standard charts of a repetitive nature such as the following:

1 Information schedules

2 Progress reports

3 Sub-contract schedules covering the process for placing orders

4 Drawing registers

5 Scaffolding schedules

6 Preliminaries analysis

More specifically, the professional project manager found that the system was of considerable use to him in two areas:

1 Making overall project strategy decisions, particularly at the feasibility and pre-construction stages, and also in identifying the precise time and resource implications of various design options. It was also useful for client discussions and for showing clients the implications in terms of time (and cost) of late variations to the project.

2 As a bargaining aid at site meetings with sub-contractors and before decisions on manning etc. were made. Here, the likely effects on sectional and overall completion could be quickly and accurately assessed.

The project manager was especially interested in the microcomputer's ability to be operated from within a robust travelling case which allowed the computer's capability to be transferred from one site to another, usually in the boot of a car!

PRESENT AND FUTURE TRENDS

Individual workstations and transportability

For the time being, it is not envisaged that each employee in an organisation will be located at a fully operational workstation, since the main purpose of such a configuration is seen more as the focal point for the bulk processing and distribution of data (both graphical and textual) to a variety of users. Those individuals who already demand frequent use of calculators and even personal (micro-) computers will probably not require the full sophistication and capability of the workstation. Moreover, they will most likely opt for their own semi-intelligent terminal offering a link to a more powerful but external source of computing power as and when required. In such circumstances, the data so processed and extracted may come from any number of separate sources; the *transparent* operating system will have eliminated the practical need for stating the location of the source. The virtual machine concept is well proven in the field, although some of the technology has still to be refined. The ability to link together all forms of computers and their peripherals within a local area is seen as a logical way of not only preserving the integrity of the installation and the data it holds but also of sustaining an effective means of achieving total information control.

Contractors may wonder how such machines could survive in their office or on a large site. Under test at the moment are rugged technology workstations[6] built to withstand conditions far worse than a construction site is ever likely to present. Modern computers are specifically designed to require the minimum of maintenance, indeed many are now approaching the reliability of the modern domestic television. The first of the rugged technology workstations on the market combines the facilities mentioned earlier into a single box about the size of a small filing cabinet. The equipment which this box can be expected to hold comprises:

1 Small microcomputer – say, 256 Kbyte RAM bubble memory and emergency power supply

2 Keyboard

3 High resolution screen

4 Dual floppy/micro floppy disk drives and Winchester hard disk storage in sealed removable cartridges

5 Dot matrix printer

6 Equipment for connecting to the electronic information systems

7 Radio telephone facilities for data transmission links, enabling the workstation to operate in remote and inhospitable locations

Thus with site or *Landrover* based generators, and dish aerials aimed at satellites on a geo-stationary orbit, it will be possible to have rugged technology workstations throughout the world giving instantaneous communications to their respective Head Offices.

The workstation is, therefore, evolution in action rather than a radical change, and the logical further integration of components and circuitry. It is to a conventional computer what a music centre is to a modular

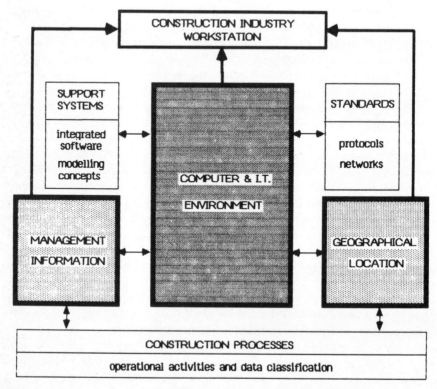

11.10 *The development of workstations for the construction industry*

hi-fi system. The shape of the construction industry workstation of the future will be borne out of the many interests which will have to be accommodated. Fig. 11.10 shows a synthesis of these interests.

Advances in technology

The use of lasers has already been mentioned, together with fibre optics. To add to these will be even newer forms of technology, each with its own contribution to make towards the ultimate system; for the construction industry, these will pave the way towards a fully integrated workstation. Already satellite and, with it, microwave technologies exist to speed up the transfer of large volumes of data across the world. With evidence of this kind it should not be hard to envisage the effects on the construction industry, say, ten years hence. Before then there will need to be a lot of serious thinking and a positive commitment if the industry is to reap the benefits of these promissory technologies.

A study by Bell in the U.S.A. identified twelve common information needs that could be further improved by the office automation technologies of electronic messaging (EM), teleconferencing (TC), wordprocessing (WP) and electronic filing (EF):

1 Access to greater amounts of remote information (EF)
2 Reduced interruptions (EM, TC)
3 Reduced delays in written communication (EM, WP)
4 Reduced unsuccessful phone call attempts (EM)
5 Support in composition of documentation (WP)
6 Decreased irrelevant information (EM, TC)
7 Increased flexibility of contracts (EM, TC)
8 Reduced unnecessary contacts (EM, TC)
9 Reduced media misunderstandings (EM, TC, TC)
10 Support in contacting communication participants (EM, TC)
11 Reduced travel (EM, TC)
12 Reduced time for written communication records (EM, TC, WP)

Alvey[10] confirmed much that was thought wrong with the uncoordinated U.K. approach towards information technology. The report of the Committee concluded that much could be done to exploit existing information technology before moving on to the more advanced technology. It further considered that it was particularly important to improve the capability of existing users of information technology. The background to this report was the Japanese Fifth Generation Computer Programme, which is aimed at improving the ease with which the technology can be used and the development of knowledge processing technologies as opposed to data processing ones. Indeed, four major technical areas have been identified by Alvey within the proposed Advanced Information Technology Programme and, in fact, work has now commenced under the control of the Alvey Directorate:

1 *Software engineering* (SE)
2 *Intelligent knowledge-based systems* (IKBS) – the so-called expert systems

3 *Man/machine interface* (MMI)
4 *Very large-scale integration* (VLSI)

EEC efforts to complement individual member states' work has produced ESPRIT (European Strategic Programme for Research in Information Technology) which is likely to suffer from budgetary problems rather than anything else. Together with Alvey's recommendations, the U.K. is at least part of the way along the road to advanced information technology of the type that the Japanese are said to be developing.

Man/machine interface

The construction industry has always placed great importance upon the need for communications in a medium which can be readily comprehended by the majority of its workforce. The increased use of computer graphics in the construction environment is to be welcomed, but their degree of penetration and the often limited use to which they are put must cause concern. Graphics inevitably demand greater investment in technology and human resources to achieve acceptable standards. However, once these are achieved, graphics will significantly improve the interaction of man and machine, leading to a more efficient use of both resources (see Chapter 10).

Despite the ever-increasing power of hardware and the greater sophistication of software, little has been done to improve the ease with which computers can achieve levels of user-friendliness acceptable to the majority of users. This situation is not peculiar to the construction industry: it affects virtually every other industry and also the professions. The Japanese Fifth Generation Project sees the major opportunities for advancement within information technology as coming from the closer interaction of man and machine within the realms of knowledge processing.

In recognising the importance of computer-based technologies in helping to improve the overall efficiency of the construction industry, it seems wholly appropriate to seek out ways of improving the application of computers as tools to aid the management of the construction process. Before any sensible progress can be made in this area, it would be necessary to undertake the following tasks:

1 Identification of the weaknesses in man/machine interface of computer systems currently in use within the construction industry
2 Determination of the most effective ways of representing construction data in a form suitable for providing management information

Further tasks to deal with more specific matters would be:

1 Development of a specification for an improved means of data exchange between a range of computer systems when used in a construction environment
2 Establishment of a method of classification and description for representing the various facets of construction work, such as components, resources and operations, possibly by the use of graphics symbols

3 Establishment of a methodology for the development of computer systems in a construction environment by the provision of a common approach to software design and systems implementation.

The relative absence of computer systems on construction sites is considered to be a barrier to the more efficient management of the construction process. A number of factors hint at the reasons for the absence; not least of these is the dearth of reliable and robust low-cost computer systems with an acceptable level of user-friendliness. On occasion, computer systems have been provided for the needs of site management, but these have often been used instead for surveying and associated duties. Two of the most common reasons given by site management for their apparent lack of use of microcomputers are a difficulty in understanding the operation of the system and a fear of spending too long on keying in data at the expense of *real* work.

A number of the more powerful microcomputer systems are being adapted to make use of the interaction between optical pointing mouse devices and on-screen symbols (icons). The main claims of the mouse/icon approach are that it reduces the amount of keyboard action and permits users to move rapidly between various sets of data held within the system. Any solution which genuinely reduces the quantity of keyed input must be worth a closer examination, although it is recognised that keyed-in numeric data will continue to be necessary. Digitisers and their associated graphics tablets are already an established form of data input, particularly in computer-aided design where their use is a virtual necessity.

Other methods of improving the interaction between man and machine exist, some of them relying upon sound. However, developments in voice recognition and speech synthesis are unlikely to advance significantly over the next few years. Besides, the physiological effects of talking to a machine all day have hardly been considered, neither has the likely impact of the additional noise, generated by man and machine, upon the working environment, and the eyestrain caused by VDU glare.

The major progress in the development of the man/machine interface over the next few years is likely to involve the concepts of graphics symbols and multi-process operating systems: the latter will permit a simulation of the user's own workstation with on-screen graphics imitating the natural processes of having to refer to a number of different documents at any one time (for example, drawings/diagrams with specifications and bills of quantities – see Fig. 11.9). The use of multi-window displays is central to these concepts.

It is suggested that a specification should be developed which will demonstrate how graphics can be used to improve and extend the interaction of man and machine within the construction environment. The specification could then be adopted by software engineers and systems integrators as a basis for developing solutions to construction management problems. If such a specification was adopted, it could well provide the most secure basis for a range of portable software products. Furthermore, it would avoid the duplication of resources and time that would occur if a number of conflicting specifications and methods were developed separately.

CONCLUSIONS

The business community – and this includes the construction industry – is, essentially, moving into a new era. As the information revolution moves forward, so the media language and speeds will change. Those who do not adapt will be unable to communicate with others in a commercially acceptable way and will thus be at a severe disadvantage. Each organisation is part of the business world and must communicate effectively with other parts. Organisations will, therefore, have to introduce the new technology whether they want to or not, simply because clients, Government or other industries will do so regardless. Just as the industrial revolution replaced human muscle power with mechanical power, so the computer revolution will eventually replace brain power with artificial intelligence, for certain applications.

Newer developments within the computer industry would confirm the trend towards the single-user *decision support or management information system* that can be built to individual users' needs. Coupled with this will be rapid growth in the area of expert systems, not to replace professional skills but rather to provide them with a sharper decision-making edge.

Major shifts in the computer industry have been associated with the demands for distributed interactive processing rather than centralised batch processing, and the change in emphasis from hardware to software. However, a number of problems remain:

1 High costs of workstations relative to their cost effectiveness
2 Incompatibility of many systems which will not interface with other computers, even those in the same organisation
3 Problems with ergonomics which have been virtually ignored
4 Feeling of professional people that their work is being reduced to a clerical level

The workstation is here now but the question remains – will the construction industry demand a workstation designed to suit its own specific needs, or will it adopt someone else's?

REFERENCES

1 Ashridge Management College. *Flexibility and efficiency in the construction industry*, Berkhamsted, 1975
2 BIGGS, W. D., 'Breaking barriers Computers '83', Building supplement, *Building*, September 9, 1983, p 14
3 The Construction Industry Computing Association, *The specification of a building industry computer workstation*, Cambridge 1982

3a Unpublished report presented by Ed. Yourdon of Yourdon, Inc. at a conference in London, October 1983

4 FISHER, N. & RIGG, R., 'The impact of I.T.', *Building Technology and Management*, Chartered Institute of Building, Ascot, April 1982, p 20

5 National Consultative Council Working Party on Data Co-ordination, *An information system for the construction industry*, HMSO, 1971

6 FISHER, G. N. & WILLIAMS, A., 'A mobile electronic office for the remote mega construction project', *Proceedings of C.I.B. W-65*, Vol. 4. Fourth International Symposium on Organisation and Management of Construction, University of Waterloo, Ontario, July 1984
  Also:
  'Seaview' – multi-function workstation and mobile office', CAP Group Ltd., CAP House, 20–26 Lambs Conduit Street, London, WC1N 3LF

7 AAKER, D. A. & WEINBERG, C. B., 'Interactive marketing models', *Journal of Marketing*, Vol. 39, October 1975, pp 16–23

8 RIGBY, P. H., *The conceptual foundations of business research*, Wiley, New York, 1976.

9 ATKIN, B. L., 'Time to move on. Computers '83', Building supplement, *Building*, September 9, 1983, pp 4–5

10 The Report of the Alvey Committee, *A programme for advanced information technology*, HMSO, 1982

ACKNOWLEDGEMENTS

The authors gratefully acknowledge the contribution of R. D. Thomas, BSc, during the preparation of some of the work for this chapter.
UNIX is a registered trademark of Bell Laboratories Inc.
CP/M is a registered trademark of Digital Research Inc.
MS DOS is a registered trademark of Microsoft Corporation.
IBM & PC DOS are registered trademarks of International Business Machines.
Apple II, Apple *Lisa* and Macintosh are registered trademarks of Apple Computer Inc.
Ethernet is a registered trademark of Xerox Corporation.
PRESTEL & GATEWAY are registered trademarks of British Telecommunications.

12 An Estimating System for a Medium Sized Speculative Building Firm Using Fourth Generation Software
N. Ewin and R. Oxley

INTRODUCTION

The building industry has been slow to adopt new computer technology. This slowness is usually blamed on the industry's inherent conservatism. Other problems exist, however, within both the building and computing industries, which are also responsible for the delay.

The current state of software

The decreasing cost, and increasing power of computer hardware has made the application of computers possible in many new areas.

The cost of software production has not fallen and, in any new system, the software will cost more to develop than the hardware to purchase. As Richard Fairly states: 'Typically 80 per cent of the cost of developing a computer system is in software development. This figure is expected to exceed 90 per cent in the next five to ten years'.[1] The high cost of software is delaying the application of computer technology in many areas. There are a number of approaches which may reduce this cost.

Applications packages

Where a market exists, i.e. a number of prospective users require a computer solution to a particular problem, software houses will produce, and attempt to sell, applications packages to solve that problem. The price of the package is usually determined according to market prices; the software house hopes to sell enough copies of the package to cover development costs and leave a profit. The price of the package is therefore much lower than the cost of having a similar bespoke system written.

The major drawbacks with the package solution are that where only a few prospective users exist, suitable packages are probably not available, and, although a number of organisations may carry out the same function, each will have its own variations on the method.

Packages impose standard procedures and sequences for carrying out functions. These may conflict with the previous and natural procedures and sequences, causing inefficiency and making it harder for the users to understand and use.

The successful implementation of a computer system is dependent upon the goodwill and co-operation of the people who will use it. If the system is totally alien to the users, this will be harder to achieve.

Applications packages can be given a degree of flexibility by modular and parameter driven programming techniques. By a and amending modules and parameters, a package can be tailor suit a particular user.

User programming

There is an increasing awareness of computers amongst the general public. Most people leaving education have some idea of how to use and program computers, typically using BASIC, the most popular microcomputer programming language. This interest and knowledge can be exploited in simple applications by providing the user with a microcomputer, and saying 'You know exactly what you want, write it yourself'. Specialist advice must obviously be available as and when it is required. New *high level* languages are becoming available which make this approach easier.

Fourth generation systems

Fourth generation is a term used by software suppliers to describe a wide range of products. Most of these products do not aim to replace programmers but to increase their productivity. Typical claims range between tenfold and fiftyfold increases. Software can, therefore, be produced quickly and cheaply. It is difficult to define what a fourth generation language is, but it should include a database, some form of applications program generation, and an integrated methodology encompassing systems analysis, design and implementation.

Most of the well-known fourth generation systems, such as Burroughs LINC and Mathematicas RAMIS II systems, have been designed for mainframe and minicomputers. Unfortunately there are few, if any, such packages available for the popular microcomputers that have sufficient power to be useful general purpose tools.

Computers in the building industry

The building industry is becoming increasingly aware of the benefits that can be gained from computerisation. The first applications were usually in accounts departments for the following reasons:

1 A large number of financial accounting packages already existed, which could be applied to building companies.

2 The accounting personnel were usually those most aware of computer technology.

3 Many of the procedures followed during the preparation of accounts are readily computerised.

Computers are now being applied in other areas of the building industry, notably project planning, estimating and, in some of the larger organisations, computer-aided design.

Application of computers to estimating

There are a large number of packaged estimating systems available. In the April 1984 edition of *Construction Computing* there were 38 systems listed. These range greatly in cost and complexity. At the bottom of the range, for around £500, there are packages which will run on the Apple II computer, and provide the estimator with a calculator which will also record and print out his calculations. At the other extreme, there are comprehensive multi-user systems which run on minicomputers with vast data stores on fixed and exchangeable disks, costing £50–60,000.

Most of the packages are designed with the general contractor in mind (the largest market). Builders who do not fall into this category, such as speculative house builders, have a restricted choice, and may require bespoke systems.

Estimating for general contractors and speculative house builders

The differences between estimating for a general contractor and for a speculative house builder can be attributed to two factors:

1 General contractors seldom build a particular design more than once: speculative house builders build a few designs repeatedly.

2 The objective of the estimate for a general contractor is to allow the company's management to produce a competitive tender for a particular contract, and, ideally, to provide cost control information if the tender is successful.[2] A speculative house builder does not produce tenders for contracts. His estimator provides information to aid management decision making and control. To this end, the estimator has a number of functions which typically include:

(i) To estimate the cost of building a new house type, which can be compared with the estimated selling price and other similar designs to show whether the design is cost effective.

(ii) To estimate the cost of developing a new site, which can be compared with the estimated site revenue to indicate the site potential.

(iii) To produce periodic site budgets, which form the basis for cash flow forecasts to maintain the planned level of site construction.

(iv) To provide information to enable accurate cost control during the site construction.

Estimating packages designed for general contractors are usually unsuitable for speculative house builders as they do not provide sufficient levels of analysis for both sites and house types, and do not provide sufficient information to generate all the required outputs.

Aims of the proposed system

The aims of the proposed system are twofold: firstly, to produce a specification for an estimating system which will be suitable for a medium sized speculative house builder, and secondly, to demonstrate that such a system can be implemented using fourth generation software tools and techniques such as those developed during the research project undertaken in the Department of Building, at Sheffield Polytechnic.

SYSTEM SPECIFICATION

The following specification outlines the system requirements, and forms the basis of the eventual system.

Estimates are produced by pricing bills of quantities, which are *taken off* site and house type drawings. There are two classes of estimate produced by the estimator in a speculative house project: estimates of site cost and estimates of house type cost.

Site estimates, e.g. site appraisals and site budgets, must be calculated at two levels: site and plot. Management require information at a high level, i.e. at site level, for most purposes. However, houses are sold individually, and so it is important to know the estimated costs of the individual plots. Once a complete bill of quantities has been drawn up for a site, it is broken down by plot. Those costs not directly attributed to any plot are apportioned between all the plots.

Bill of quantities

A complete bill of quantities for a site is produced by combining a bill of quantities for site costs with individual bills of quantities for the house types to be built on each plot.

Direct house costs

When a new house type has been designed, a bill of quantities is produced. This bill is then applicable to every house of that type built. The bill is, of course, amended as the design is updated.

The structure of the bill of quantities is hierarchical, and is composed of *operations* and *items*. An item is a unit of value, e.g. a physical quantity of a material, a unit of an operative's time, a subcontracted operation, or a unit of plant hire. An operation is the combination of items required to build a certain element. Operations are hierarchical, and are assigned levels. A high level operation may be composed of both items and lower level (simpler) operations.

To produce a bill of quantities for a new house type, the construction of the house is considered to be a single high level operation. This operation may then be broken down into a number of lower level operations and items; those operations can be further broken down to yet lower level operations and items, and so on, until eventually all operations are specified in terms of items. Obviously there must be some limit on the number of operation levels allowed, and systems investigation has indicated that three levels are sufficient.

As all operations can be described in terms of items, by giving each item a unit value or price, the bill of quantities is priced.

To give a very simple example: suppose the construction of a particular house type included the digging of a trench, 5m (16ft 5in) long, 1m (3ft 3in) deep, and 0.5m (1ft 8in) wide as a second level operation. Suppose there is also a primary operation to dig 1m (3ft 3in) of trench that is 1m (3ft 3in) deep, by 0.5m (1ft 8in) wide. This primary operation states that it requires one labourer for one hour, and a pick and shovel for an hour to achieve this. If these items are priced, e.g. pick = £0.10 per hour; shovel = £0.10 per hour, and labourer = £4.50 per hour, the cost of the primary operation can be obtained – namely £4.70 – and the cost of the secondary operation, the 5m (16ft 5in) trench, is five times the primary rate: £23.50.

Site costs

There are two categories of site costs: those which are directly related to the house types, and those which are related to site construction and maintenance.

Site costs in the first category are included in the house types bill of quantities. In practice, they are, for various reasons, difficult to allocate to individual houses. A site total is calculated and then apportioned to each plot.

The second category of site costs covers those which are directly related, and unique to a particular site. These include the cost of roads, sewers, and any special works. A bill of quantities is produced for these site costs in exactly the same way as for house types, i.e. using a hierarchy of operations and items. Some materials such as sand which is delivered to a site rather than to individual plots, are totalled and included in the priced site bill, even though they are specified in the house type bills of material.

Site costs are apportioned by multiplying the total site cost by an apportionment factor. This factor is based upon a feature of the house type rather than the actual plot, so all houses of the same type have the same amount of apportioned cost. Typically the factor is derived from the plot frontage for a house type.

Bill of quantities maintenance

Due to the volume of data, the input and maintenance of bill of quantity information must be simple and efficient. Priced bills of quantities should be updated automatically as item prices are changed.

Cost codes

The estimating system is to form part of an integrated information system; it must, therefore, complement the costing system which is yet to be developed. This will enable direct comparisons between estimated and actual cost information. To achieve this, the estimating system must incorporate the code structures used for cost recording.

Operations are grouped under cost code categories, e.g. foundations, superstructures, oncosts etc. A cost code consists of up to nine digits: the first three form the site code, the second three the plot number and the last three the cost code category. Site cost codes do not include the plot number (i.e. they are six digits long). All estimate analyses are expressed in terms of cost code categories.

Site appraisal analysis

Before purchasing a new site, a site appraisal is produced. The purpose of the appraisal is to help management to decide whether or not to proceed with the purchase, and, if they do proceed, the maximum price they should pay.

The estimator is given a plan of the proposed site, which is divided into plots, and each plot allocated a house of a specified type. To produce the site appraisal, the estimator must draw up a bill of quantities for the site, and then price it. The bills for the individual plots are available immediately from the house type bills of quantities. Site costs must be calculated separately. This may be done by producing a bill of quantities for site costs building down from high level operations to item level, or, if there is not sufficient time, the estimator can use his experience and judgement to price high level operations, omitting much of the detail.

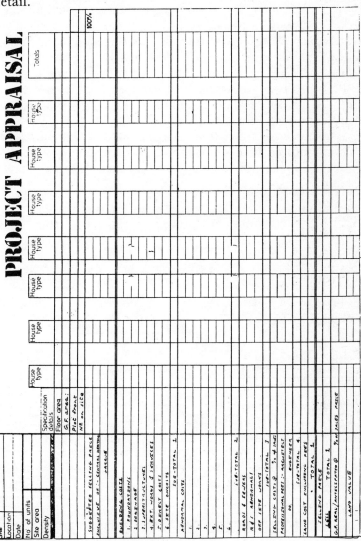

12.1 *A manual pro-forma for project appraisal*

Once the bills of quantities have been combined, the information may be printed out in an agreed format as the project appraisal (see Fig. 12.1 for manually-produced appraisal format). The appraisal must also include estimates of the selling prices of the houses, thus allowing a comparison between estimates for cost and revenue, indicating the potential profitability (or otherwise) of the site.

Site budget analysis

The frequency with which site budgets are required depends upon the individual company. Some produce budgets annually, or more frequently; others produce budgets to cover phases of construction. The purposes of site budgets are to provide a basis for cash flow forecasts, and to provide a comparison between estimated costs and actual costs over a given period or phase.

Site budgets are produced in a similar way to site appraisals: a bill of materials is drawn up which represents the units to be constructed within the budgeted period or phase, and the site costs incurred to build and sell them. This bill is also a combination of house type and site cost bills of quantities. The site budget analysis is expressed not only in terms of cost category but also in terms of item type, i.e. labour, materials, subcontract etc. (see Fig. 12.2 for manual equivalent). This analysis is required because of the different payment periods for these categories. Estimates of sale value are not included in the budget.

House type cost analysis

Once a bill of quantities has been drawn up, and priced at item level, it should be a straightforward process to calculate and produce a cost

SUMMARY OF BUDGET COST

SITE:- NO. OF UNITS:-		PROG:- ISSUE:-							PRICE DATE:- PREP DATE:-		
SECTION											TOTAL COST
FOUNDATIONS											
DRAINAGE											
SUPERSTRUCTURE											
GARAGE											
EXTERNAL WORKS											
DIRECT COSTS											
SITE ON COSTS											
TOTAL											
ROADS & SEWERS											
SPECIAL WORKS											
DEVELOPMENT COST											
MATERIALS											
SUBCONTRACT											
WAGES											
PLANT & EQUIP.											
HAULAGE											
SITE EXPENSES											
SUPERVISION											
TOTAL											
ROADS & SEWERS											
SPECIAL WORKS											
DEVELOPMENT COST											

12.2 *Summary of budget costs*

analysis for the house type. This analysis should summarise the bill of quantities, yet retain sufficient detail to indicate sections where building costs are abnormally high when compared with other house types. The analysis should also include the value of items that are usually charged to the site and then apportioned.

FUTURE ENHANCEMENTS AND SYSTEM INTEGRATION

The estimating system described above is the first part of an integrated computer system for a speculative house builder. Consideration must, therefore, be given to the data flows between the estimating function and other functions. Some of these functions, and how they may be integrated with the estimating system, are summarised below.

Cost analysis and control

One of the prime aims of the estimating system is to provide information for comparison with actual costs. Thus, the cost analysis and control systems are closely related to the estimating system. The surveyors collect cost information from the site as the costs are incurred, e.g. from goods received notes as materials are delivered, and from work measurement. The information is recorded using the coding system described on p. 182. Actual and estimated costs can then be compared using the common cost codes, on a plot-by-plot basis.

Purchasing

Material item prices are maintained from information passed to the estimating department from the buying department. As there are many thousands of material items, it will take a constant effort to keep the database up to date. If the purchasing function is computerised, then, while entering order details, the item prices used by the estimating function can be updated automatically.

Project planning

The estimating system can provide the project planner with a great deal of information concerning resource requirements, without modification. If a project planning system is implemented, a resource schedule can be produced from the project plan via the bill of quantities data. This may then be used by the project planner to confirm his plan, and then by the actual resource management functions.

FOURTH GENERATION SOFTWARE TOOLS

The system to date represents the first stage in the development of a fourth generation programming package, to allow the user, a computer specialist, to generate comprehensive business systems quickly with the minimum of actual programming. The complete system will encompass database generation, screen generation, report generation, a degree of process generation, and a menu system. The package is self-generating, i.e. it has been written using the same tools and techniques that it provides.

This system enables the user to generate databases and screens quickly and easily from the results of systems analysis.

Data dictionary

Although standard MICRO FOCUS COBOL indexed sequential files are used, they are organised in such a way as to give the appearance of being a database. Standard database terminology is used to describe the database:

File = Entity Type, e.g. a file of suppliers

Record = Entity (an occurrence within an entity type), e.g. a particular supplier

Field = Attribute, e.g. the supplier's name

The data dictionary is central to the development of systems. Its purpose is to record system details during system design and development, e.g. database descriptions, screen descriptions and report descriptions etc. A number of entity types are used to record this data dictionary information.

Once a system has been designed and the details stored in the data dictionary, it is generated. This generation essentially consists of the insertion of the data dictionary information into MICRO FOCUS COBOL programs representing the various screens, reports, and entity types that constitute the system. The data dictionary information is therefore bound at generation rather than during execution. The early binding obviously makes the system less flexible to maintain, but does not incur the performance overheads of run time binding – an important consideration for systems based on microcomputers. The information contained in the data dictionary is used to produce the system documentation, and is the basis for system maintenance.

The data dictionary has been implemented for entity type and screen format descriptions.

Database control

A database consists of a collection of entity types. Each entity type has many occurrences (entities), and is composed of a collection of attributes. The data dictionary contains the descriptions of the attributes. There are two dictionary entity types used for this purpose: the first contains attribute descriptions, i.e. number of characters, type, short name, and its physical position within the entity type (there is one entry in this dictionary for every attribute in each entity type); the second dictionary entity type contains attribute validation criteria. If the field is numeric, then the criteria will be minimum and maximum values; if the field is alphabetic or alphanumeric, the criteria are in the form of a list of up to ten four-character alternatives for that attribute value.

Only attributes with validation criteria have entries in this dictionary entity type.

All entities must be in third normal form,[3] i.e. there must be no repeating groups of attributes (e.g. arrays), no partial dependency on key fields, and no transitive dependencies. The resulting data structures are simple and tabular in form. Data normalisation is necessary to produce efficient database storage, and to implement the screen and report generators included in the package.

Attribute descriptions are entered via a single screen. This screen also allows the amendment, deletion and interrogation of attribute details. Once all the attribute details for an entity type have been defined, a database handler program is generated, encompassing all the information held in the two dictionary files.

All database access, whether at entity or attribute level, is made through the database handler programs. Conceptually, an entity can be seen as an object, and the database handler its object space, i.e. where the object (entity) is manipulated. Data access is, therefore, strictly controlled, and any data input is automatically checked against the validation criteria for that attribute. The database handler program may be edited by the user to include further controls on data access.

All entity types are held as MICRO FOCUS COBOL indexed sequential files. Entities can, therefore, be accessed both randomly and sequentially (through the file access programs).

Screens

Three data dictionary entity types are used to describe screen formats. For every screen there is a screen header entity; this contains general screen information such as screen title, the files it uses, and screen type.

Screen specifications are input into the data dictionary and amended through a screen painter. This allows the user to design the screen format interactively. The screen painter accepts two kinds of field: text fields, i.e. data that is permanently displayed on the screen, and data fields, i.e. those fields that are actually entered by the user and displayed by the system.

There is an entity type for each of these field types. The text field entities contain the text value and the screen co-ordinates at which it is displayed; the data field entities contain the screen co-ordinates, the identification of the corresponding data attribute, whether it is an input or output field, and whether it is optional or mandatory.

There are two basic screen types: simple screens, which are single entity projections, i.e. contain data from a single entity, and complex screens, which are projections of two entity types with a one-to-many relationship, i.e. one entity type is parent to the other. The parent entity is projected in the top part of the screen, and the instances of the child entity type in the bottom part, line by line. If there are not sufficient lines available, the bottom part of the screen may be scrolled.

The standard screen logic allows the user to create, amend, delete, or enquire from a single screen definition. Thus each screen has four functions.

The screen program is generated from the information held in the data dictionary. This includes not only the entity types describing the screen format, but also those describing the data attributes used in the screen. The generated COBOL program may be compiled and run, or amended to meet any specific requirements of the application. The program is designed to make amendments of this kind simple, and without the user needing a detailed knowledge of the whole program. Guidelines to aid this process will be provided both in the generated program source code and in documentation.

Methodology

The eventual systems analysis, design and implementation methodology is still under development, and has not been formalised. However, some guidelines have been established.

The traditional view that exhaustive systems analysis and design is rewarded by much easier implementation, and a higher success rate, is challenged by fourth generation systems. Such systems offer a new approach – prototyping. After an initial, reasonably thorough investigation, a prototype system can be quickly and easily produced using the fourth generation tools. This prototype can then be shown to the user for comment. If the prototype does not satisfy the user, he can specify exactly what is wrong in terms of screen formats, report formats, etc. rather than abstract ideas on paper. The prototype can then be easily amended to the user's satisfaction, and developed into the eventual system. The prototype may be considered as part of the system specification.

Systems analysis and design

The database system forms the core of the fourth generation package; the system functions are built around it. The emphasis must, therefore, be to get the data requirements correct. To this end, the systems analysis and design methodology recommended is that of Gane and Sarson.[4] The first steps of this methodology concentrate on building a global data model of the system. It shows the inputs to and outputs from the system, outlines the processes involved between, and the data stores required.

Database design

The system data requirements are described in the global data model. These requirements are normalised, and a revised data model produced consisting of entity types in third normal form. The attribute details are formed, e.g. attribute type, number of characters, and validation criteria, and recorded in the data dictionary.

Screen design

The global data model should illustrate all system inputs, and specify the data input. This information forms the basis of the screen specifications. Once the database description has been stored in the data dictionary, screen formats can be input and amended interactively using the screen painter.

Report design

System outputs are also described in the global data model; this includes reports. The fourth generation package will eventually include a report painter and generator; until then, however, the programs must be produced manually.

System generation

Once the complete system specification has been entered into the data dictionary, the system can be generated from the data dictionary producing a suite of applications programs. These programs may then be amended to suit the particular needs of the specification. Once these amendments have been made, the programs may be compiled and tested.

System testing should be aimed particularly at those parts of the system which have been manually produced.

Maintenance

The database handler mechanism gives a high degree of data independence. Data structures can be amended without affecting applications programs, and amendments to applications programs do not affect the database handlers.

The data dictionary provides extensive and accurate systems documentation, and also a base for maintenance. Amendments are made to the data dictionary, and then the relevant parts of the system regenerated, rather than the actual applications programs being amended.

SYSTEM IMPLEMENTATION

The following section is a summary of the application of the tools and techniques described on pp. 185–9, to produce the estimating system specified on pp. 181–5.

Global data model

From the initial systems investigation, conducted via interviews with key personnel, and the study of procedures and documentation, a high level global data model was drawn up (see Fig. 12.3).

Database design

The contents of each data store can be established by examining the data paths which flow into it. These can be compared with the data paths leaving the data store for a useful control. If there is data leaving the data store which is not included on any input data path, then clearly the input data paths are not complete, or the output data paths are coming from the wrong source. If data input to the data store is not

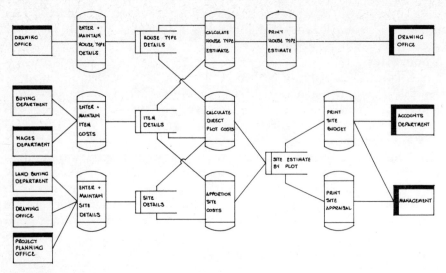

12.3 *Global data model of the estimating function within a speculative house builder*

included in any of the output data paths, then either there is data redundancy in the data store, or the output paths are not complete.

Once the contents of each data store have been established, a list of attributes is drawn up, and an initial data structure produced. It is quite likely that this data structure is large and unwieldy, and must be simplified by normalisation before it is suitable for database implementation.

ENTITY NAME : SITE ESTIMATE BY PLOT.

ATTRBTE	SHORT NAME	KEY	TYPE	MIN LENGTH	MAX LENGTH	INTEGER PLACES	DECIMAL PLACES	SIGNED
1	SITE CODE	Y	9			3		N
2	PLOT NUMBER	Y	9			3		N
3	COST BREAK	Y	9			1		N
4	COST CODE	Y	9			3		N
6	MATERIAL CST	N	9			7	2	N
7	LABOUR COST	N	9			7	2	N
8	SUB-CON COST	N	9			7	2	N
9	PLNT HLG CST	N	9			7	2	N
10	ON COSTS	N	9			7	2	N
11	SELLING COST	N	9			7	2	N
12	SUPERVIS CST	N	9			7	2	N
13	ESTIMATE CST	N	9			7	2	N

12.4 *A typical entity type specification*

Normalisation is a method by which complex data structures can be simplified into tabular structures (called relations) which allow easier data base design, and greater freedom of data access. Although normalisation is based on complex mathematical theory, it can be achieved by following a series of mechanical transformations on the initial data structures. Descriptions of these transformations can be found in most database text books, e.g. *Fundamentals of Data Base Systems* by S. M. Deen.

The resulting attributes are then individually analysed, and decisions concerning the physical properties of the attribute made, e.g. attribute type and length, and validation criteria. The attribute descriptions are then entered into the data dictionary (see Fig. 12.4 for entity type specifications). Code structures must also be decided upon; e.g. for operation and item codes a six character code has been selected. The first three characters are descriptive, e.g. BRI for brickwork, or bricks; the last three characters are a sequence, thus BRI001 may define a particular brick item, or brick work operation. Note that operations are not defined by code alone, but by operation level and code.

Screens

All data input processes are implemented as *screens*. These processes are easily identifiable from the global data model. An input process may be implemented as more than one screen, and there are four occasions on which this is necessary:

1 There are too many data attributes to be included in a single screen.
2 The attribute values arrive at different times, and/or from different sources.
3 The entity types within the data store are logically distinct, and so cannot be meaningfully included in the same screen.
4 There is more than one one-to-many relationship within a single data store.

```
                    SITE OPERATION MAINTENANCE      ACTION : INPUT KEY
-----------------------------------------------------------------------

    LEVEL : 9  CODE : XXXXX   DESCRIPTION : XXXXXXXXXXXXXXXXXXXXXXXXXXXXXX
                                           XXXXXXXXXXXXXXXXXXXXXXXXXXXXXX

           UNIT : XXXXXXXXXX   COST SECTION CODE : 999

ITEM/LEVEL  CODE   DESCRIPTION                        QUANTITY   WASTAGE %
     9     XXXXXX  XXXXXXXXXXXXXXXXXXXXXXXXXXXXXX     99999.9999     99.99
     9     XXXXXX  XXXXXXXXXXXXXXXXXXXXXXXXXXXXXX     99999.9999     99.99
     9     XXXXXX  XXXXXXXXXXXXXXXXXXXXXXXXXXXXXX     99999.9999     99.99
     9     XXXXXX  XXXXXXXXXXXXXXXXXXXXXXXXXXXXXX     99999.9999     99.99
     9     XXXXXX  XXXXXXXXXXXXXXXXXXXXXXXXXXXXXX     99999.9999     99.99
     9     XXXXXX  XXXXXXXXXXXXXXXXXXXXXXXXXXXXXX     99999.9999     99.99
     9     XXXXXX  XXXXXXXXXXXXXXXXXXXXXXXXXXXXXX     99999.9999     99.99
     9     XXXXXX  XXXXXXXXXXXXXXXXXXXXXXXXXXXXXX     99999.9999     99.99
     9     XXXXXX  XXXXXXXXXXXXXXXXXXXXXXXXXXXXXX     99999.9999     99.99
     9     XXXXXX  XXXXXXXXXXXXXXXXXXXXXXXXXXXXXX     99999.9999     99.99

-----------------------------------------------------------------------
```

12.5 *A typical rough screen format*
(key: × = alphanumeric value
9 = numeric value)

For each screen a list of attributes is drawn up, and these must relate to attributes already entered into the data dictionary. A rough screen format can then be designed, and entered interactively into the system data dictionary via the screen painter (see Fig. 12.5).

Screen programs sometimes need amending to meet particular requirements. Once the screen format has been stored in the data dictionary, these amendments should be listed and numbered. The listing is included as part of the screen documentation. Once the screen program has been generated, the MICRO FOCUS COBOL code to implement these amendments is inserted into the program. A copy of this extra code should also be included in the documentation.

Reports

As yet, the system does not include fourth generation tools to produce reports. However, a strategy has been developed to help the programmer. The strategy consists of three steps:

1 The report format is drawn up, shown to the users, and amended as required (see Fig. 12.6).

2 The attribute details exhibited in the report are located in the data store entity types, and their data dictionary reference noted, thus checking that the required data does exist.

3 The report program is written in MICRO FOCUS COBOL. This can be achieved by using a skeleton program, and inserting the attribute details and sources, and any special control requirements.

DATE : 99/99/99   PAGE : 999

SITE APPRAISAL FOR XXXXXXXXXXXX

PLOT NUMBER : 999   HOUSE TYPE : XXXXXXXXXXXX

COST CENTRE	MATERIALS	SUB CON	LABOUR	PLNT & HLG	ON COSTS	SELLING	SUPERVISN	ESTIMATE	TOTAL
FOUNDATIONS	999999.99	999999.99	999999.99	999999.99	999999.99	999999.99	999999.99	999999.99	999999.99
DRAINAGE	999999.99	999999.99	999999.99	999999.99	999999.99	999999.99	999999.99	999999.99	999999.99
SUPER STRUCTURE	999999.99	999999.99	999999.99	999999.99	999999.99	999999.99	999999.99	999999.99	999999.99
EXTERNAL WORKS	999999.99	999999.99	999999.99	999999.99	999999.99	999999.99	999999.99	999999.99	999999.99
DIRECT COSTS	999999.99	999999.99	999999.99	999999.99	999999.99	999999.99	999999.99	999999.99	999999.99
SITE ON COSTS	999999.99	999999.99	999999.99	999999.99	999999.99	999999.99	999999.99	999999.99	999999.99
ROADS AND SEWERS	999999.99	999999.99	999999.99	999999.99	999999.99	999999.99	999999.99	999999.99	999999.99
SPECIAL WORKS	999999.99	999999.99	999999.99	999999.99	999999.99	999999.99	999999.99	999999.99	999999.99
TOTAL COST	999999.99	999999.99	999999.99	999999.99	999999.99	999999.99	999999.99	999999.99	999999.99
SALE VALUE									999999.99
GROSS PROFIT									999999.99

12.6 *Estimating system report formats*

```
           SYSTEM MENU                 ACTION :
 _____

         OPTION                        CODE

         SITE DETAIL MAINTENANCE.......   SIT
         HOUSE TYPE DETAIL MAINTENANCE.   HOU
         ITEM MAINTENANCE..............   ITE
         ESTIMATE......................   EST
         SYSTEM MAINTENANCE............   SYS


         ENTER OPTION, OR 'X' TO EXIT :  <   >
 _____
```

12.7 *A typical menu specification*

Processes

The specification and generation of process logic is very much more complex than for entity types, or screen and report formats. As yet, tools have not been developed for process generation, and the user must implement processes by writing COBOL programs. The database, and database handlers, are of course available to the programmer.

The three processes required in the system – house type estimating, direct plot cost calculation, and site cost apportionment – essentially carry out the same operation, breaking down hierarchical bills of quantities into tabular formats. From the user's point of view, the two site estimate processes have been combined.

Menus

The various applications programs are combined into a complete system via menu programs. A menu consists of a table of options available to the user. Each option may represent a process, a screen, a report or another menu. If there is a large number of options, then a hierarchy of menus can be used; the highest level menu, the *system* menu, can be *booted* into straight from the operating system, and thus the user never needs to issue any CP/M commands, or see the CP/M prompt A>. The estimating system uses a hierarchy of four menus (see Fig. 12.7).

OPERATION OF THE SYSTEM

The system is very simple to use. Procedures and standards are the same throughout the system, so once one element of the system has been mastered, the user can easily come to terms with the complete system.

All screens follow the same logic: the screen format is displayed on the VDU, and the user is invited to enter the first field. The first fields entered are *key fields*; there may be a number of such fields, but it is seldom more than two. The key fields identify the screen occurrence to be entered or maintained. The current input field is always enclosed by brackets > <. Once the key fields have been entered, then the relative screen occurrence is searched for; if none is found then the screen logic assumes the user wishes to enter information, and goes into *create* mode. If a corresponding screen occurrence is located, then the *enquire* mode is entered, and the screen occurrence is displayed. Once the screen has been input, or displayed, the user is given the choice of exciting the screen, saving any input, amending the data displayed, or deleting the screen occurrence.

Bill of quantity maintenance (house type)

The bill of quantities is expressed in terms of *operations* and *items*. An item is an element of cost, e.g. a unit of material, an hour of labour, or a subcontracted operation. There are three levels of operations, and each operation is composed of lower level operations and items.

Item details are entered and maintained via the item maintenance screen, which is included as an option in the main system menu (see Fig. 12.7). Operation details are entered and maintained via the operation maintenance screen, which is an option of the house detail maintenance menu.

Bill of quantity maintenance (site)

The site bill of quantities is constructed and stored in exactly the same way as for house details. The item maintenance screen is the same one as is used for the house details above. The operation details are entered through the maintenance screen accessed via the site maintenance screen.

Estimates

Once the database contains the required bill of quantities, estimates can be produced and updated at will. House type estimates are prod-uced directly from the bill of quantities, in a suitable report format (see Fig. 12.6). This may be updated to include more, or less, detail as required.

Site estimates are calculated separately to the reporting as there may be a great deal of processing involved, taking a long while. Once calculated, the estimate may be expressed at a number of levels, e.g. plot, house type, and site, although only plot level has been included in this system (see Fig. 12.6). Site budgets and appraisals are both calculated in the same way, i.e. by the same process. There is a separate menu for the estimating options.

CONCLUSION

The estimating system was developed in stages over a period of time. In total it is estimated to have taken less than two man weeks from initial systems investigation through to system completion. Using conventional programming techniques, it would have taken two or three times as long.

The fourth generation tools described are primitive and still in their early stages of development. Given the more powerful tools that are becoming commercially available, even greater savings are possible.

Such tools help the builder in four ways:

1 Software should be cheaper, as less of its most expensive ingredient, labour, is required.

2 Cheaper bespoke software means that more specialist building areas can profitably benefit from the introduction of computer systems.

3 After seeing prototype system designs, the builder can adjust the system specifications to get the system he wants, without requiring extensive reprogramming.

4 Software packages should be flexible enough to be tailored to fit in with the individual builder, and not vice versa.

REFERENCES

1   FAIRLEY, R. E., 'Static analysis and dynamic testing of computer software' (tutorial)
2   *Code of estimating practice*, Institute of Building
3   DEEN, S. M., *Fundamentals of data base systems*
4   GANE and SARSON, *Structured systems and analysis: tools and techniques*

ACKNOWLEDGEMENTS

The authors wish to thank Dr. Poole of the Department of Computer Studies, Sheffield City Polytechnic, for his help in producing this chapter.

BIBLIOGRAPHY

1   *Infotech State of the Art Report: Micro Computer Software*, Volumes 1 & 2, Infotech International Ltd.
2   LOBELL, R. F., *Application Program Generators: a State of the Art Survey*
3   NAYLOR, C., *Choosing and Using Program Generators*
4   RICE, J. G., *Build Program Technique*, Wiley-Interscience, N.Y., 1981

III Behavioural Considerations

13 Information Systems and the Manager
Paul Barton

INTRODUCTION

One of the major factors affecting the successful implementation of an information system, particularly one involving the use of computers, is the interaction between the system and the individual manager.

At the onset, every manager will have a different perspective on the system. Some will feel threatened about losing their job, others may fear that they will lose status or that their work will become merely a matter of sitting in front of a terminal, leading to a loss of social contact with their colleagues.

A systems analyst can be counter-productive if, after discussing a manager's information requirements for half an hour, he gives the impression that a particular expertise which a manager has taken years to acquire is quite simple after all! This could typically apply in the case of estimating.

The systems can be used in a punitive way and cause more problems than they solve. For instance, if a contracts manager uses weekly reports on progress, prepared from information produced by site, to 'haul site managers over the coals' about their lack of progress, one cannot expect site managers to be fully committed to the system.

If computers are used, then there is the additional problem of the fear of the new technology. There are many construction personnel who have expressed the view, either directly or indirectly, that the use of computers is 'beyond them'.

The above are just a few examples of the many problems that can arise during the implementation of an information system.

The aim of this chapter is to examine in detail the interface between the manager and the information system, in order that the type of problems outlined above can be understood and their effect minimised.

THE MANAGER'S JOB

Firstly, it is important to understand the manager's job itself, a topic about which much has been written. Some writers have concentrated on the tasks managers perform, whilst others have concentrated on the skills they use.

For more than half a century, from Fayol's time, people have been listing the tasks which managers are supposed to perform. Typically, such lists included:

planning   – i.e. the manager sets objectives, forecasts, analyses problems and *makes decisions.*

organising   – i.e. he determines what needs to be done to achieve the objectives, classifies the work, splits it into manageable tasks and allocates these to groups and individuals.

motivating   – i.e. the manager inspires his staff to contribute their best, to be loyal, to pull their weight.

controlling   – i.e. the manager checks what has been done, comparing it with plan.

Implicit in these descriptions is the need for information. In fact, Fayol identified a further task of *communicating* which permeated all the other tasks.

More recently, writers have concentrated on the skills required by managers. The consensus appears to be that the most important skills are:

human or *social* skills   – dealing with people, motivating, leading

information handling skills   – obtaining and evaluating data

decision-making skills   – evaluating alternatives, reaching compromises, balancing long term needs

technical and *conceptual* skills   – the ability to understand the technical aspects of problems, use judgement and analyse situations systematically

The relative importance of these skills varies from one manager's job to another. Social skills are thought to be important to lower levels of management because of the number of contacts they have with non-managerial staff. Similarly, conceptual skills are considered important for the senior manager, who must make judgements about long term issues affecting the organisation. Middle managers handle a great deal of *information*, as they mediate between top management and the operational staff in the firm. They must be skilled in communicating information and ideas in the right form to the right people.

Fryer[1], applied these ideas to different types of manager in a construction firm (see Table 13.1). In his model, the site manager who regulates the technical core of the firm's activities is faced with short term problems which he can solve with computational decision-making techniques. The senior manager at head office decides broad policies for keeping the firm in business by ensuring that it remains attuned to environmental influences. His decisions have a long term perspective and are based mainly on judgement. Sandwiched in between these roles are the contracts manager and other middle managers mediating between head office and the sites.

Table 13.1 Differentiation in construction management roles (modified from Petit, 1967, p 349)

Type of manager	Task	Viewpoint	Technique	Time horizon	Decision making strategy
Site manager	Technical rationality	Engineering	Quantitative	Short term	Computational
Contracts manager	Co-ordination	Conflict resolution	Mediation	Medium term	Compromise
General manager (head office)	Uncertainty avoidance	Prediction	Opportunity searching; Strategy developing	Long term	Judgemental

Mintzberg[2] took a slightly different perspective, although many of his findings were broadly similar. He identified ten roles common to the work of all managers, contending that each manager stands between his organisational unit and its environment. Thus, as the senior manager looks to an environment consisting of competitors, suppliers etc., so the site manager guides his site and looks to other site managers and staff groups within the firm, and to suppliers and sub-contractors outside the firm.

The ten roles consist of:

1 three interpersonal roles – figurehead, leader, liaison
2 three *informational* roles – monitor, disseminator, spokesman
3 four decisional roles – entrepreneur, disturbance handler, resource allocator, negotiator

These are summarised in Table 13.2.

Significantly, his work makes several propositions relevant to these discussions, that can be summarised by the following extracts (quoted matter shown in italics):

1 The manager serves as the *'nerve centre' of his organisation's information system* (see Fig. 13.1 overleaf). His unique access to all subordinates and to special outside contacts (many of them nerve centres of their own organisations) enables the manager to develop a *powerful database of external and internal information*. In effect, the manager is his organisation's best store of *non-routine information*.

2 As monitor, the manager is *continually seeking and receiving information* from a variety of sources.

3 A good part of the manager's information is *current, tangible and non-documented*.

4 The manager uses his information to detect changes, to identify problems and opportunities, to build up a general understanding of his milieu for decision making, to determine organisational values and to inform outsiders and subordinates.

5 As disseminator, the manager sends external information into his organisation and internal information from one subordinate to another. This information may be of a *factual or value nature*.

6 The manager faces a 'dilemma of delegation'. Only he has the information necessary to make a great many important decisions. *But the information is in the wrong form – verbal and in memory rather than documented.* Hence dissemination of it is time-consuming and difficult. The manager

Table 13.2 Summary of ten management roles (from Mintzberg)

Role	Description
Interpersonal	
Figurehead	Symbolic head; obliged to perform a number of routine duties of a legal or social nature
Leader	Responsible for the motivation and activation of subordinates; responsible for staffing, training and associated duties
Liaison	Maintains self-developed network of outside contacts and informers who provide favours and information
Informational	
Monitor	Seeks and receives wide variety of special information (much of it current) to develop thorough understanding of organisation and environment; emerges as nerve centre of internal and external information of the organisation
Disseminator	Transmits information received from outsiders or from other subordinates to members of the organisation; some information factual, some involving interpretation and integration of diverse value positions of organisational influences
Spokesman	Transmits information to outsiders on organisation's plans, policies, actions, results etc.; serves as expert on organisation's industry
Decisional	
Entrepreneur	Searches organisation and its environment for opportunities and initiates 'improvement projects' to bring about change; supervises design of certain projects as well
Disturbance Handler	Responsible for corrective action when organisation faces important, unexpected disturbances
Resource Allocator	Responsible for the allocation of organisational resources of all kinds – in effect the making or approval of all significant organisational decisions
Negotiator	Responsible for representing the organisation at major negotiations

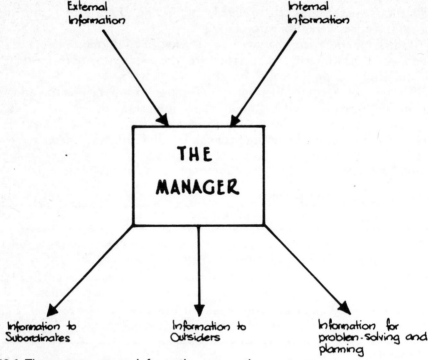

External
Information

Internal
Information

THE
MANAGER

Information to
Subordinates

Information to
Outsiders

Information for
problem-solving and
planning

13.1 *The manager as an information processing system*

must either overload himself with tasks or spend a great amount of time disseminating information, or delegate with the understanding that the job will be done with the use of less information than he has.

7 The manager must take full responsibility for his organisation's strategy-making system. He has the necessary authority and *information* to *integrate* all the *important decisions* made in his organisation.

Finally, Mintzberg contends that '. . . the ten roles suggest six basic purposes of the manager –

(i) to ensure the efficient production of the organisation's goods and services

(ii) to design and maintain the stability of organisational operations

(iii) to adapt the organisation, in a controlled way, to its changing environment

(iv) to ensure that the organisation serves the ends of those persons who control it.

(v) to serve as the *key information link* between the organisation and its environment

(vi) to operate the organisation's status system.'

MANAGERIAL DECISION MAKING

Much of the work described to date has emphasised the importance of decision making in the life of a manager. Let us, then, view the decision-making process in more detail.

Principal phases

Decision making comprises three principal phases:

1 Searching the environment for conditions calling for a decision – *intelligence activity*

2 Inventing, developing and analysing possible courses of action – *design activity*

3 Selecting a particular course of action from those available – *choice activity*

Generally speaking, intelligence activity precedes design, and design activity precedes choice. The cycle of phases is, however, far more complex than this sequence suggests, each phase being a potential decision-making process itself. Nevertheless, however complex the cycle is, all the phases use *information*.

Decision types

Decisions can be polarised into two types – programmed and non-programmed – although, in reality, these are two extreme points on a continuum, with a large number of decision types in between.

Decisions are programmed to the extent that they are repetitive and routine, for which a definite procedure has been devised. Decisions are non-programmed to the extent that they are novel, unstructured and consequential. There is no cut and dried method for handling the problem because it hasn't arisen before, or because its precise nature and structure are elusive or complex, or because it is so important that it deserves a custom tailored treatment.

Decision-making techniques

Because of the above differences, different techniques have been developed for handling the programmed and non-programmed aspects of decision making. Table 13.3 (overleaf) shows the various traditional and modern techniques relevant to the different decision types.

THE IMPORTANCE OF INFORMATION SYSTEMS

All the views to date have expressed, either directly or indirectly, the importance of information to managers.

If one adopts the classical approach, it can be seen that information is necessary to carry out the various managerial tasks. Of the more recent writers, Mintzberg, in particular, emphasises the need for information in many of the ten roles. Even the interpersonal roles could be better enacted from a sound information base. 'Information is Power' is a statement whose truth has not been lost on many effective leaders and managers.

However, on closer examination, it should be noticed that much of the information is *soft*, i.e. subjective, opinionated, biased. Mintzberg states that 'a good part of the manager's information is current, tangible and non-documented'. It could be argued that even some of the more factual or *hard* information has some form of value judgement placed on it.

Table 13.3 Traditional and modern techniques of decision making

Types of decisions	Decision-making techniques	
	Traditional	Modern
Programmed: Routine, repetitive decisions Organization develops specific processes for handling them	1 Habit 2 Clerical routine: Standard operating procedures 3 Organisation structure: Common expectations A system of subgoals Well-defined informational channels	1 Operations Research: Mathematical analysis models Computer simulation 2 Electronic data processing
Nonprogrammed: One-shot, ill-structured, novel policy decisions Handled by general problem-solving processes	1 Judgement, intuition, and creativity 2 Rules of thumb 3 Selection and training of executives	Heuristic problem-solving techniques applied to: (a) training human decision makers (b) constructing heuristic computer programs

Systems analysis can help discover and classify the hard information, e.g. costs and time, but it is not so effective in identifying the other types of information so important to the manager, e.g. attitude of the architect, morale of site personnel. Even if such information could be identified, it would still be very difficult to capture and store it within the constraints of a formal information system.

The conclusions to be drawn are that formal management information systems, be they manual or computerised, only meet part of the manager's information needs and should be used in conjunction with informal information networks and the organisation's value system. The information system, if designed correctly, can provide the manager with certain types of information very efficiently, thus leaving him more time to collect the other types of data and to develop and use the skills required of the job.

THE IMPACT OF COMPUTERS

Nowadays information systems are closely associated with computers. Table 13.3 has already indicated the reliance on computers in modern decision-making techniques.

However, much of Mintzberg's work stresses the importance of informal, non-documented types of information. Such information is difficult to quantify and store using existing technology. Similarly, the principal phases of decision making (p. 205) still call for some form of human input. The intelligence activity demands that the manager has to recognise that problems exist. The design activity demands that appropriate criteria are created for analysing alternatives, whilst the choice activity requires judgement. These are facilities that current technology cannot provide.

The only real impact made by computers, to date, has been to make current manual systems more effective, thus saving managerial effort in using the system. GIGO (Garbage In/Garbage Out) still applies. Unfortunately, because computers are accurate and quick there is still an air of authority associated with computer printouts that can make managers place too much reliance on the information they contain.

Computer systems themselves should be acceptable to the manager. Donald Sanders and Stanley Birken, in their book *Computers and Management in a Changing Society*, suggest the following criteria for 'humanising' management information systems:

1 Procedures for dealing with users
Transactions with the system should be courteous, the system should be quick to react and relieve the user of unnecessary chores. It should include provisions for corrections and ensure that management is held responsible for mismanagement.

2 Procedures for dealing with exceptions
A system should recognise that it deals with different classes of individuals, and that special conditions might occur that require special action. It should allow for alternatives in input and processing and give individuals a choice on how to deal with them.

3 Action of the system with respect to information
Provisions should be made to permit individuals to inspect information about themselves. There should be provisions for correcting errors and evaluating the information stored in the system. Individuals should be able to add information they consider to be important. The information in the system and its use should be known to all.

4 Guidelines for system design having a bearing on ethics
Systems should not trick or deceive; they should assist users and not manipulate them. A system should not eliminate opportunities for employment without a careful examination of consequences to other available jobs.

Not only should the systems follow these criteria; they should also be easy to use. *User-friendliness* and the *manager/machine interface* are two often-used pieces of computer jargon, and much effort has been directed towards them. Simplifying data input and output, the use of menus, split screens and help messages during the use of software, and the integrated approach of the Apple Lisa are examples of how this objective is being achieved. The result is that a manager can, under the right circumstances, feel that he is in control of the computer, rather than that the computer is in control of him. Consequently he is more likely to take advantages of some of the benefits that the computer can offer.

We do, however, hear of intelligent computers and expert systems. Computers are now being used to diagnose a patient's medical problems. Other chapters in this book are an indication that such systems are possible and are being considered in construction management. What, then, is left for future managers in the construction industry? Is the whole job of management going to be replaced by a computer?

In the short term, the answer is no. In the long term, we cannot be so definite. However, there is one consoling factor in the process of being 'taken over' by computers, which was neatly summarised by F. W. Lukey (Computer Age 1980).

'Machines, even intelligent machines, can only take their value judgement from us. I worry about what I am doing, where I am going and the reason for going there anyway. The computer does not. There is no question but that we can build artefacts which can outperform us in every conceivable, specified way. Yet, we do the specifying – it is we who give meanings to the categories and tasks built into these machines.

There is, thus, a human perspective built into any intelligent machine. These machines must reflect the categorisations and hence the value judgements we make.'

CONCLUSIONS

At the start of this chapter, typical problems associated with the use of information systems by managers were identified. These include fear of redundancy, loss of status, reduction of job satisfaction, and fear of the new technology. Such problems are amongst the most difficult to resolve when implementing information systems.

As a result of the subsequent discussion, however, it is possible to put these issues into perspective.

The most important point to realise is that the use of information in problem solving and decision making is only part of the manager's job. There are other roles he has to perform, other skills he has to acquire.

Secondly, the information needs of the manager consist of both quantitative and qualitative information. The latter is difficult to identify and quantify, yet constitutes a significant part of the total requirements. Formal information systems cannot provide all these needs.

Whilst computer systems are easy to use, they can only make formal information systems more effective within the constraints of current technology and the data available. Some of the constraints may be removed in the future but there will always be the need for some form of human input.

Consequently it is difficult to envisage the entire manager's job being 'taken over' by a 'system'.

REFERENCES

1 FRYER, B. G., 'The development of managers in the construction industry', MSc thesis, The University of Salford 1977
2 MINTZBERG, H., *The Nature of Managerial Work*, Harper and Row, 1973

BIBLIOGRAPHY

FRYER, B. G., *The Practice of Construction Management*, Granada 1984

14 The Construction Company and its Systems
P. Harding

Introducing a computer into a company often causes problems of an organisational nature. This is because the computer system and the organisational system are different in kind. Matching them is possible but has to be managed. Part of the problem stems from calling them both 'systems'. A system may be defined as 'a whole having parts in a definable arrangement. The parts which are included are those in which the relationship is definable by the analyst or observer as having a relevant dependency. By including or excluding parts a boundary is identified, those parts not being included forming the relevant environment of the system' (P. Harding 1979).

Using this definition, it may be seen that a computer can be viewed as a system, as can an organisation. So, too, can the information which links the two. But what kinds of systems are they?

A computer has been engineered to perform predictable activities. If the right connections are made in its electrical circuitry then it is possible to guarantee a particular outcome. It can be thought of as a *hard* system, having a high level of predictability and a real existence in physical terms.

On the other hand, organisations are probabilistic. They are managed to a certain degree so that fairly well-defined inputs lead to probable (and hopefully desired) outcomes. The connections in the process are between people, are non-physical and sometimes difficult to comprehend. We can say, for example, that communication is taking place, but the detailed elements in the process, particularly loaded feelings, are difficult and sometimes impossible to describe. Because of this dependence on non-physical structure, the organisation can be considered to be a *soft* system.

The concept of hard and soft systems is helpful when contemplating the use of a computer in a construction company. Starting with the idea that two systems of different kinds have to be matched can help managers to avoid some of the common pitfalls involved.

This chapter considers some of the organisational aspects involved in introducing computers and formal information systems into a construction company, and identifies issues which have to be dealt with to ensure a measure of working compatability.

ORGANISATIONS AS SYSTEMS

To say that a construction company is a system is a starting point, but what sort of system is it?

Is it: a management system
a production system
an economic system
a people system
a communication system
an information system
a control system
a political system
a technological system
a professional system
a market system
an authority system?

Of course it is all these and more. And all at the same time. It is possible to list these as separate systems because one can take a particular stance and analyse the organisation from that point of view. A consultant often does that. The problem which managers face every day is that they are rarely able to take a stance in relation to one of these separately. They have to deal with situations in which all of these are operating in a dynamic way. These different systems interact with one another to produce a complex continuum. The outcome at each point in time is a continually changing and developing situation. But because the managers themselves are a part of the system, they too are developing and changing. They are adapting to the almost imperceptible changes which evolve day by day, and becoming educated by participating in the process. Herein lies the problem of introducing computer systems into a company. It is not a development resulting from day-to-day operation; it is an imposed event which interferes with gradual adaptation and which therefore has to be managed in a different way. The adaptation demanded of all people in the organisation will be substantially greater than normal. The changes required are perceptible and their anticipation can raise uncertainties in people's minds which gradual adaptation may not do. The changes present a challenge to the capacity of people to adapt. A recognition of this is fundamental to introducing computer systems into a company.

One of the causes of failure when introducing new techniques into a company is that the active participants (whether managers or consultants) may have only a hazy perception of the real nature of their company. Too often techniques which have been developed for other technologies or for different size companies are transferred without adequate consideration. Each company is unique and has to have techniques and systems tailored to meet its particular needs. This is not to say that there is not a measure of similarity between construction companies at a general level. There is, and it is a useful starting point to consider this before undertaking a detailed study of a company. This will help the manager to see his own company in relative terms.

THE SYSTEM OF CONSTRUCTION ORGANISATION

A construction company exists to meet the objectives set for it by its directors (those who own the capital interest in the company or those engaged by the capital owners to direct the affairs of the company). Objectives are, therefore, first and foremost business objectives. The need to create an acceptable return on the capital employed in the company is a prime aim of the stockholders and therefore of the managing director. To achieve this prime aim it is necessary to identify other, supporting objectives. In order to meet the profit levels required, it may be necessary to engage in certain trading arrangements, to achieve a certain market share, to engage a certain type of employee, to ensure the growth and continuity of the company and to project a certain image to clients. This immediately shows the value of the systems approach. It is clear that, whilst the company will have an identity of its own, be identifiable as a unit in its own right, it is, nevertheless, dependent upon other organisations outside its boundaries. Also its own unity is a complex one: the company is made up of many parts, each one dependent upon the others.

Because the construction company is operating in a dynamic market, it can be considered as an open system. It trades for resources from its environment, and then re-trades the resulting outcome with other organisations. The outcome may be a physical product, as in the case of a housebuilder, or it may be a service, as in the case of a management contractor. A general contractor produces both a service and a product, the latter being the result of the former.

The directors of a construction company will need to state clear objectives. But their achievement will depend upon the conditions which prevail in the company's environment from time to time. All the organisations with which the company trades or interacts in some way are also attempting to meet their own objectives. This creates a condition of perpetual change. To cope with this it is necessary to build an organisation which is adaptive and responsive to external conditions.

The deliberate change induced by the introduction of a computerised information system would be in addition to such changes and would need managing in a different way. The organisation has to be prepared for both trading adaptations and critical events.

ORGANISATIONAL ADAPTATION

Being able to maintain the integrity of the company in conditions of change is the greatest challenge which faces its managers. The key to this is twofold: firstly, to understand the nature of the environment within which the company operates, and secondly, to define appropriate policies which will ensure the internal stability of the company in relation to its environment. For this it is necessary to have up-to-date information and to be able to process it rapidly and efficiently.

Change within the company will be induced from two main sources: firstly, arising from the company's own objectives and policies, particularly growth and the introduction of new technology, and secondly, from demands in the market and the company's total environment.

CHANGE THROUGH GROWTH

There are very few companies which begin on a large scale. Characteristically in construction the large company is also a mature one, having grown from small beginnings over many years. Usually growth is through a combination of evolution and revolution. At certain points in the life of a company, the evolutionary growth produces tension within the organisation which can only be released constructively by a complete change.

Larry Griener[2] has suggested that growth can be categorised into five phases (Fig. 14.1). Each of these phases brings its own characteristics of condition and response. The tension which develops in the enterprise through its own evolutionary response he calls a crisis point. This is the point at which it becomes apparent to all involved that something needs to be done to preserve the integrity of the enterprise. For the managers, particularly the managing director, this is a crisis. To do nothing would lead to decline and possibly disintegration of the

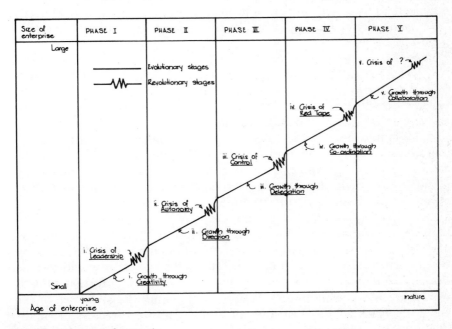

14.1 *The phases of growth*

company. To make small, comfortable changes may stave off the crisis for a while but possibly move the company into a more unmanageable situation.

Making radical changes presents managers with a major task in addition to their day-to-day management of operations. The latter ought to be a full-time job. To carry out a re-organisation as well needs a commitment and level of organising ability well above the normal level expected from employees. This crisis tests the quality of management throughout the enterprise, but particularly at the top. Many innovations fail because of the lack of attention paid to managing their introduction. The blame is usually attached to the innovation.

Stephenson and Oxley (Chapter 3) have made the point that it is essential for an analyst to have a clear idea of the background of the company before designing an information system. The stage a company has reached in its development is an important element in this picture.

The phases of change
Phase I
In the early stages of a company's existence, the founders bring to the scene an enthusiasm and originality which drives the enterprise forward. They will have found a service or product which has an element of uniqueness about it sufficient for them to establish the company in the market. By their continuous creative efforts they gain advantage over competitors and possibly forge a new market marginally different from others. The company grows to the limit of the ability of the founder's independent creation. A crisis of leadership is met. To go forward needs an organisational change. Usually this means separating leadership from operation.
Phase II
New roles are adopted, the founders relinquishing some of their day-to-day duties to others. A functional structure is adopted. They now become directors of others' actions, which they are able to do because the enterprise is small enough for them to be in face-to-face contact with all employees. By careful selection of employees, and attention to the needs of their now traditional clients, the company may again achieve growth. Age and size are, of course, increasing. A characteristic of this phase in its mature stage is that the directors find that their autonomy is challenged: their employees have developed a feeling of ownership of the company, and the company itself takes on an existence separate from that of the founders. They are no longer 'the company' and face a real crisis. To retain autonomy would mean that the company should consolidate, stand still. The risk would be that it would lose its competitiveness and then decline. To move forward to further growth would mean adopting another role and changing the structure of the company. This is the most difficult crisis of all for directors of small/medium size companies, particularly in the construction industry. It

marks the point where the company, if it were to change, would be substantially different from its previous state.

Phase III

The crisis can be overcome and growth continued through delegation. A management team is formed with clear functional duties and responsibility assigned for different areas of the company's activities. The managing director is now in charge of a group of managers who have a high level of autonomy in the performance of their sphere of operation. As each of these managers develops their own area, growth is achieved and the company again becomes progressive and expansive. Three developments now take place. One is that the market has become differentiated, i.e. different services are being offered to different sectors of the market. Secondly, specification amongst the staff has become greater, and each specialised section develops its own work and pursues policies its members see as beneficial to the company. Thirdly, distances have increased as the company expands geographically. Communication, therefore, becomes more difficult and more time-consuming. The directors now experience a feeling of loss of control. Managers may feel that they are working within a leaderless enterprise because of lack of direction from above. Lower level managers may feel isolated and that they are having to take responsibility for a wider range of activities. The tendency is to become more bureaucratic: to carry out one's duties so as to protect oneself and one's immediate task rather than develop opportunities. The crisis is one of control. The adaptation demanded by the market environment is neither perceived nor responded to. A period of stagnation induced through lack of information and appropriate forms of control ensues. The enterprise is becoming disorganised.

Phase IV

To move forward from this stage in a company's development, the wholeness of the enterprise has to be re-established: the various parts of the enterprise have to be co-ordinated, and the contribution of each part has again to be linked with those of all other parts.

This usually involves a substantial investment in re-appraisal of the company and its opportunities. The market has to be analysed in detail and potential areas of growth and/or security identified. The technique of management by objectives is often adopted because it gives a co-ordinated package which ensures that all areas of the company's organisation are reviewed and renewed. The strategy that is adopted tends to use the existence of the company in the market as a positive force, i.e. the company uses its power to create the right market conditions for itself. To do so it must have sophisticated information about its total market and develop an organisational unit to deal with it. This is typically a team of corporate managers whose task it is to ensure that the relationship between the company and its environment is properly regulated. This provides a level of security within which the company's operations can grow.

The growth comes through defining different services and creating an organisation to suit each one. A management system has to be imposed over all these divisions which ensures that the whole enterprise is co-ordinated. The operational manager's role is much more related to information processing as a result. Not only has he to get things done but he has to ensure that others know what he proposes, that he is delegating tasks to them, and that these tasks are then done. This ensures that all operations are synchronised and compatible. To regulate all this, a management information system may be introduced to provide managers with the appropriate information at the right time. To do this, objectives have to be clearly defined, policies promulgated and procedures highly detailed. Inevitably staff have to have a level of organisational ability different from their functional task. Skill in using information technology and mature social skills are essential if the enterprise is to operate in a co-ordinated way. A company culture has to be developed.

Phase V

Through shared objectives and participation in decision making, the employees in a mature sophisticated enterprise can continue to meet the growth goals set by the directors. Growth itself may be seen in a different light: not simply physical size, but culturally creative. The enterprise may now be so important a part of the environment that threats to it are also threats to the environment itself. The only way to achieve continued progress is to adopt a management approach which is collaborative both internally and externally. Within an overall strategic plan it may be necessary to use less-permanent structural forms, less-permanent relationships with trading partners. Internally this may mean task-teams are set up only for the duration of a specific task. Externally it may mean temporary relationships such as project management. The total direction of the enterprise is by clear definition of what would be an acceptable measure of success at a given time. This would be reformulated as each new set of conditions approached. Control of the total enterprise is obtained through setting targets and rigorously analysing results obtained through ratios of performance.

For operational managers, rapid processing of relevant information is much more important than following procedures. Adaptability becomes the order of the day. Management liaisons are made at a lower level because task accomplishment is more important than meeting outdated aims. The demands made upon staff are clearly different from before, and high levels of both intellectual ability and experience are demanded.

RESPONDING TO THE CHALLENGE OF CHANGING ENVIRONMENTS

The environments in which a company at Phase I and a company at Phase V are operating are the same in general terms. But in organisational terms they are different. The elements in the environment of the first company are infinitely less and different in kind to those to which the second company has to respond. Similar elements may be there for both of them, but they are not equally relevant. For example, legislation may be extant for the control of large cranes. It exists for both companies but may only be relevant to the larger company. Only the latter needs an organisational response to deal with it. There are, therefore, types of environment as well as types of company. What defines the environment is, firstly, its relevance to a particular company. Once defined, it is unique to that company, however similar it might be to others. Its second definition is the strength of dependency of the company on that environment and the elements in it.

Environments vary both in complexity (the number of factors to be taken into consideration and their type) and dynamics (the rate of change taking place). For each result and mix at a given point in time there is an appropriate organisational response, and a body of data related to the enterprise and its environment which will feed into the company's information system. It is obviously not possible here to characterise all the possible environments which could be encountered by a construction company. For examples of the range, the classification adopted by Emery and Trist (1965)[3] will be used. They outlined four types of environment.

Environment
The placid, randomised environment

This is one in which the objectives of the enterprise are not directly connected with forces in the environment which support or are in opposition to it. These latter forces arise occasionally and are randomly distributed, i.e. there is little complexity and it is placid, not dynamic. The enterprise does not depend upon them for its survival and has only to deal with them when they arise. An example of this would be a small builder working in a localised area in which there is always more work than builders to complete it. Competitors exist but they do not interfere with the objectives of the small builder. If a problem arises (a client doesn't pay on time or a supplier ceases trading) he deals with it discreetly at that moment. There are other clients and suppliers who will support him and he need not rely on those who disappoint him. There is little point, then, in entering into sophisticated training programmes or devising strategic plans to take care of such events. They may not arise again and other problems which do arise may be different in nature. He learns to cope with issues such as these on the basis of trial and error, and, over a period of time, experience is gained which gives a set of approaches to classes of randomly recurring problems. His response then is purely tactical. (This class of environment is similar to 'perfect competition' in economics.)

The placid, clustered environment

In this environment there is a certain amount of connection between objectives and opposing forces. The latter are not randomly distributed but have some degree of predictability. This leads to the necessity to have information about the environment so that potential relationships can be understood before they arise and steps taken to prepare for them, i.e. strategic plans are developed, resources are concentrated and a particular competence is developed to ensure that objectives are met.

This type of environment is placid and not dynamic but, if the enterprise were to pursue only tactical goals, however desirable they may appear at the time, it could lead to dangerous results. Avoiding an immediately difficult issue by taking tactical action may divert the enterprise away from potentially rewarding areas. There has, therefore, to be subordination to a main plan, and tactics are only used within this overall strategy. Planning can be successful because there is little dynamics in the environmental relationships. If we consider the small to medium size builder market we can see that in most geographic regions there are many builders. There is probably over-capacity, but they can survive because each one offers a service which is slightly different to that of the others, i.e. there is imperfect competition. By careful planning, a well-developed organisation structure and effective control, an enterprise can plot out a service which will obviate competition and also deal with forces in the environment which, if not taken into consideration, could destroy it, e.g. planning legislation, tax laws, trading arrangements etc.

There is a tendency for enterprises in this type of environment to grow in size, particularly by adding service and regulatory roles, to become hierarchical and more centralised. This process very often leads them towards the next type of environment.

The disturbed reactive environment

This is one in which there is more than one enterprise of the same kind. Each enterprise does not simply have to take account of the others when they meet at random, but also has to consider that what it knows can also be known by others. The part of the environment to which it wishes to move itself in the long run is also the part to which the others seek to move. This is typical of large construction companies. In this market, if one of them develops a new major strategy, it will affect the survival of the others. They are so dependent on the actions of the others that there is little point in one of them attempting to maximise its share of the market, because the reaction of the others could be so severe that it might threaten the survival of the enterprise.

The policy of the enterprise in this type of environment depends on how it *thinks* its competitors will react to its moves, and the outcome of the policy depends on how they *do* in fact react. So that, in addition to strategy and tactics, it is necessary to have an intermediate level of response, i.e. *operations*. This consists of a campaign involving a planned series of tactical initiatives, calculated reaction from others and counter-actions. Actions have to be taken which will draw off the other organisations.

Take, for example, the decision of an enterprise to set up a manage-ment contracting division. Its competitors would most likely follow with a similar service. How would this change the market, and what should the next decision be? The process might be to launch the service with a modest amount of marketing, develop expertise in the first few pilot projects and wait for the competitors to launch their service. Just at the point where they are ready to establish themselves, a highly-developed marketing campaign can be mounted, backed up by a (now) well-developed service. Marginal advantage could thus be gained until the next initiative is required.

It is clear that the enterprise needs a sophisticated information processing system and also to have sufficient decentralisation which will enable it to respond quickly and efficiently. We should bear in mind that opposing and competitive forces are not only other construction enterprises; they may take many other forms such as government action, pressure groups, or investors looking for a take-over.

The instability of this type of environment may perhaps only be overcome if there is a certain coming to terms between competitors (e.g. a cartel).

Turbulent fields

The environment in which some enterprises operate is so complex and dynamic that the whole field of operation is turbulent. This character-istic is not wholly or directly a function of the enterprise's own actions nor of its dependencies, but is the nature of the whole environment of which the enterprise is one part. The whole system now has to be seen as the total relevant environment, not simply one enterprise. The trends which lead to the development of these environmental forces are:

1 In an attempt to overcome the effects of environment (p. 214), the linked sets of enterprises and very large enterprises tend to grow and develop strong dependencies on one another. This induces changes, not only in their own interactions, but also throughout the environment. An exponential ripple effect arises out of the workings of the environ-ment itself (autochthonous process, e.g. an effect similar to that of soldiers marching in step over a suspension bridge – the relationship between the marching soldiers generates effects in the 'ground' under their feet which may magnify beyond their power to control).

2 The major components of the environment other than the enterprises themselves tend to develop richer interdependencies: economics may be used more widely in the control of public order; legislation may be used in the economic field; pressure groups may develop political organis-ations to gain a voice in public affairs.

	Environment 1	Environment 2	Environment 3	Environment 4
	Phase I	Phase II	Phase III	Phase IV	Phase V

	Phase I	Phase II	Phase III	Phase IV	Phase V
Organisation structure Grouping pattern	} informal	} functional	Divisionalized Geographic Line and staff (functional)	Divisionalized product / service Line and staff (highly defined)	} Matrix
Characteristic	Paternal	Centralized bureaucratic authority	Decentralized bureaucratic authority	Decentralized bureaucratic authority	Co-active responsibility
Style	Individualistic and entrepreneurial	Directive	Delegative	Regulative	Participative provisional
Decision-making	Tactical combined internal-external regulation	Strategic and tactical (reactive) combined internal-external regulation	Strategic and tactical (proactive) internal-external regulation separated		Strategic and tactical. Directive correlation. Temporary combinations of internal-external regulation.

14.2 *Organisation related to environmental conditions*

3 In an attempt to gain marginal advantage over competitors, enterprises may invest in more innovations, which themselves create a change gradient in the environment.

The result of these trends for an enterprise is a gross increase in relevant uncertainty. Effects are amplified and become unpredictable. There is little relationship between one decision, its resulting effects and the next decision to be made. The future appears to be disjointed and discontinuous.

Radical responses have to be developed for enterprises to operate in these conditions. To obtain stability in an unstable environment it is necessary to combine all the forces available and to lift them to a higher order than the level of any one enterprise. Inter-system relationships have to be developed which provide control over a wide sphere of interactions. Macro policies representative of all the elements in the environment have to be developed. We see in practice the combination of what appear to be competitive enterprises which put aside their competitiveness for a higher social value, e.g. survival and continuity for the benefit of all. Federations, consortia, unions all meet this need.

There are very few examples of turbulent environments in practice in construction, and the effect of the responses mentioned above stabilises those which do arise back to the placid, clustered environment conditions. However, if the structure of an enterprise is inappropriate to the demands placed upon it, or if the quality of management, particularly in large enterprises, declines, then turbulence will almost certainly be induced, which may lead to dissolution of the system at this level.

The result could be that an even more powerful force (e.g. Government) would be brought to bear to re-establish a stable environment.

It is clear that managing an enterprise in disturbed and turbulent environment conditions is different from doing so in the other two.

If these two approaches (Griener and Emery and Trist) are drawn together (Fig. 14.2) it can be seen that adaptation through organisational development is a prime requirement for the management of an enterprise. Internal stability can only be attained through regulating the relationship of the enterprise to its environment. This can be achieved through gaining relevant information and processing it effectively. It is essential to have a well-developed system of information processing in any size of company. As the company grows and encounters different environmental conditions, the amount of data and the speed of reaction required lead to the introduction of company-wide management information systems. Almost invariably this will involve computerisation.

INTRODUCING A COMPUTERISED INFORMATION SYSTEM

There is a tendency to think that a computer can solve management problems. Computers are new, and have a glamour associated with sophisticated technologies. Because many people do not know how they work or how to use them, they have an aura of the 'desirable unknown' about them.

A computer, however, is only as good as the information system with which it is associated. It comes at the end of the system, not its beginning. It is essential to get the information system right before attempting to use a computer. More importantly, it is essential that a management information system is not introduced into a poorly-developed organisation with bad management. An MIS will not cure bad management, but bad management can nullify a good MIS.

It must be borne in mind that a management information system is designed to enable staff to meet the objectives of the company. It follows, then, that the objectives have to have been clearly stated.

Many studies over the last three decades have shown that the most successful companies are those in which the directors have stated well-defined objectives and developed policies whereby they can be achieved. Without clear company objectives the MIS will be aimless. An essential pre-requisite for the design of an information system is a statement of company objectives. This can be supported by policies (how the objectives are to be reached) and procedures (detailed activities required to be carried out in each function of the company's operations).

By involvement in the process of establishing objectives, policies and procedures, staff are able to adapt to the proposed new system. Asking them to look critically at their current work processes helps them to cope with the transition to a different situation. The effectiveness of the new system will rely upon the commitment of the staff. There should be complete involvement in the whole process of analysis and implementation to assist staff to learn new techniques and allow gradual adaptation to take place.

CONTROL INFORMATION

Most information systems are designed to enable staff to carry out the basic functions of the company. Within each function information is processed which ensures that short term aims are realised. In addition to this functional information it is necessary for managers and directors to have information on the performance of the company as a whole. A feedback system is required, by means of which sections, departments and divisions are monitored in relation to objectives. This has organisational implications. Control information spans across functional disciplines. For example, materials will be dealt with by estimators, buyers, planners, site managers and surveyors. Therefore, one aspect of the policy of a company should be to state what aspects of its operations need control, i.e. what information needs to be fed back to the managers and directors. This requirement should be supported in the job descriptions of staff, who may otherwise tend to concentrate on functional activities and find the reporting process an interference. By involving staff at an early stage in the analysis, and by providing clear objectives and policies, a company may overcome such resistance.

REFERENCES

1 HARDING, P., *Building Trades Journal*, 1979
2 GRIENER, L., 'Evolution and revolution as organisations grow', *Harvard Business Review*, July/Aug 1972
3 EMERY, F. F. & TRIST, 'The causal texture of organizational environment', *Human Relations*, Vol. 18, 1965

Index